getting away with

MURDER

getting away with MURDER

DUNCAN McNAB

VINTAGE BOOKS
Australia

Getting Away with Murder – important

The title of this book is a reflection of a culture which existed in Australia at the time of the events of this book and is a combination of many combining social factors such as changing viewpoints, devastating disease and extreme intolerance amongst some of those trusted with authority to uphold the law. It is not a statement about any person or persons named or referred to in this book and the reader should not regard these words as inferring any specific person referred to is guilty of murder or any other crime.

Due to suppression orders in place around the further inquest relating to the death of Scott Johnson, some names have been withheld from use in this book.

Every effort has been made to identify individual photographers and copyright holders where appropriate, but for some photographs this has not been possible. The publishers would be pleased to hear from any copyright holders who have not been acknowledged.

A Vintage book
Published by Penguin Random House Australia Pty Ltd
Level 3, 100 Pacific Highway, North Sydney NSW 2060
www.penguin.com.au

Penguin
Random House
Australia

First published by Vintage in 2017

Addresses for the Penguin Random House group of companies can be found at global.penguinrandomhouse.com/offices.

National Library of Australia
Cataloguing-in-Publication entry

McNab, Duncan, author
Getting away with murder/Duncan McNab

ISBN 978 0 14378 078 6 (paperback)

Cold cases (Criminal investigation) – New South Wales – Sydney
Hate crime investigation – New South Wales – Sydney
Police misconduct – New South Wales – Sydney
Murder – New South Wales – Sydney

363.2509944

Cover images © Luke Causby and Fairfax Syndication
Cover design by Blue Cork
Internal design by Midland Typesetters, Australia
Typeset in 12/17 pt Minion by Midland Typesetters, Australia
Printed in Australia by Griffin Press, an accredited ISO AS/NZS 14001:2004 Environmental Management System printer

Penguin Random House Australia uses papers that are natural, renewable and recyclable products and made from wood grown in sustainable forests. The logging and manufacturing processes are expected to conform to the environmental regulations of the country of origin.

CONTENTS

CHAPTER 1

THE MORE THINGS CHANGE . . .

Just before midnight in the summer of 1981, an anonymous male made a call to the emergency line 000 from a public telephone box. He'd found an unconscious man in the men's toilet at the Collaroy Surf Club, but he didn't wait around for the emergency services to arrive.

First on the scene was an ambulance crew from nearby Narrabeen, who found a man in his late fifties face-down in the drain hole at the centre of the stainless-steel trough that lined one wall of the toilet. He was amid the beads that unsuccessfully tried to mask the smell of urine and provided target practice for generations of boys. The usual grate that covered the drain hole was missing, and the man's face was torn by the rough welds where the trough met the drainpipe. What was immediately apparent was that the man had been viciously assaulted. There was damage to the back of his head and neck caused by repeated blows, and probably broken fingers. His breathing was ragged. The ambulance officers called for police assistance and acted quickly and carefully to extricate the man and take him to the emergency unit at Mona Vale District Hospital, just under six kilometres away.

The uniformed police working the night shift at nearby Collaroy Police Station headed straight to the hospital. An examination of the man showed head injuries so severe that there was a risk of him dying or suffering extensive brain damage, so the doctors decided the safest course was to transfer him to the specialist care offered by Royal North Shore Hospital at St Leonards. While the medical staff were stabilising their patient and alerting their colleagues at North Shore, the police took brief details from the ambulance officers. The police searched the man's clothing and found his pockets empty: no wallet or car keys. He wasn't wearing the chunky identification bracelets that were chic at the time, or rings or pendants with any inscriptions, and he hadn't regained consciousness at any time. The man's identification was unknown, which was not unusual in cases that looked like an assault and robbery. The police knew from experience that it was a mystery likely to be resolved in daylight, long after they'd finished their shift at 7am and headed home to try to sleep through another hot, humid day.

The uniform coppers then went into the surf-club toilet, now a crime scene, and en route contacted the night-shift detectives who prowled the region from the Harbour Bridge to the south, Rydalmere to the west and Hornsby to the north. Their role was to triage serious crimes. It was either do the basics and leave it for the morning-shift detectives to follow up or, if the crime needed a full investigation to start immediately, get the local detective sergeant in charge out of bed, which he would in turn do to his staff. When the detectives joined the uniformed police at the toilet, they decided that little could be accomplished at night, and with the condition of the man still uncertain and no witnesses around, there was no rush. They made sure the scene was locked up and secure, took the registration details of the couple of cars in the car park, and left the uniformed coppers to track down the owners in the hope one would be the injured man, and alert 'Scientific' – the two detectives stationed at Chatswood who looked after all the forensic work on the north side of the harbour – who would be needed when they came on duty in the morning.

At 8.30am I started my day's duty at the Mona Vale detectives' office. I was twenty-four years old and nearly two years into my training to be a detective. I'd begun my police career at Manly, working there in uniform for eighteen months before being accepted into criminal-investigation training. After a few months working in the detectives' office on 'A' list – then the first step of training – I was sent to the famous – or infamous, depending on your viewpoint – No 21 Division at the Criminal Investigation Branch (CIB), which was the next obligatory step in an aspiring detective's career. At 21, we cruised Kings Cross and other crime hot spots looking for felons on the run or plotting deals, raced to be the first at crime scenes and learned how to drink – both on and off duty. Dinner on a quiet afternoon shift was spent with the police truck parked outside Bill and Toni's in the 'little Italy' of Stanley Street in East Sydney, with the windows wound down and the radio turned up so we could hear the calls from our table on the balcony above. On the menu was a plate of spaghetti Bolognese or the minestrone along with bread and iceberg lettuce, followed by schnitzel with cheese. We skipped the free cordial unless the night was stinking hot, and instead watered ourselves from a flagon of red bought at the Lord Roberts pub on the corner.

The less desirable duties at 21 included trying to catch SP bookmakers in hotels – a role at which I was lousy because I looked too much like a schoolboy on an excursion to the wrong place – raiding casinos, arresting drunks to get them off the street and let them sober up in the cells, and 'peanutting', which was the dying art of loitering around public toilets or parks in the hope of being propositioned by another man, and then arresting the poor sod.

Working in a backwater like Mona Vale had been surprisingly instructive. For my first few months I'd been paired with George Hunter, the former rugby league star and a man who seldom strayed from either the office or his table at the Manly Warringah Leagues Club. George ended his career a few years later when he was arrested and sent to prison for his role in a large marijuana deal. I'd worked on two murder investigations in the eighteen months I was stationed out there; on both occasions I was one of the first through the door to arrest the killers but sidelined for the interviews. It was the days of the unsigned record of interview in which the culprit allegedly confessed to some useful points in the investigation of the crime, but declined to sign the interview. Sometimes this actually happened, but in many cases the record of interview was a neatly concocted script written by the detectives then presented to the court as a persuasive document. It is one of the reasons the introduction of tape-recording interviews became an imperative.

That summer morning, I was working with a senior detective who was a kind, honest man, a regular attendee at mass on Sundays. Not someone who forced his religion on you, but you knew his views. The morning routine was to begin with coffee, often fairly drab instant in the days before plungers and espresso machines, and read through the previous night's circulations – telex was king and you waded through concise information littered with spelling mistakes, telling of crimes around the state, cars and descriptions of crooks to watch for. With that done, it was either working on briefs, out to court, or in our case to Collaroy to meet the forensic investigators and inspect the scene of the assault. It was a grisly moment.

Fortunately the uniformed police from the Collaroy night shift had locked the toilet and so we had a crime scene in good condition. DNA evidence was a decade in the future, and we relied on fibre, fingerprints – unlikely to be of much use in a public place such as a surf-club toilet – along with fluids, which had a similar problem to fingerprints in this place. A thorough investigation yielded only one piece of evidence that would help us in the investigation: it was the man's eyebrow, intact and stuck to a rough edge where the trough met the pipe. The brow had been torn off while the attackers stamped on his head.

Next came the legwork to identify the victim. A check of the car registration numbers from the night before and those in the car park that morning showed only one common number: a small, plain Japanese car in pristine condition that belonged to a man about the right age. We sent uniformed police from Chatswood to his address in a home unit building in Lane Cove, only a few minutes from Royal North Shore Hospital. While the unit was locked with no-one home, the police struck gold when they knocked on the neighbours' doors. It was a building of long-term residents who spoke to each other, and shared keys and next-of-kin contact details. Our probable victim was a middle-ranking Commonwealth public servant who lived quietly and alone, and his closest relative was a sister. The man hadn't reported for work that morning, and when we spoke to his sister she confirmed he was single and had never married. We didn't pry into his private life and she didn't offer any insights, but to my mind, given the time and venue of the attack, and his sister's information, there was a high chance her brother was gay. Back in those days the subject of sexual preference was not a common topic of conversation on the genteel Sydney north shore. She confirmed the man in the hospital bed was her brother. She took the news stoically, declined a lift from us and said she'd head to the hospital after she'd picked up a few toiletries and pyjamas.

Two days later, he had regained consciousness and was able to be interviewed. If you were hunting around the NSW Police of the time, you'd be unlikely to find two more easy-going and non-judgemental blokes, but unfortunately our demeanour didn't even begin to compensate for the deservedly lousy reputation police had among the gay community, and the terror felt by an older closeted gay man being 'outed' to his family and work colleagues. He was like many men of the times – discreet in his acts, and apprehensive that someone would find out about his sexuality; in most of Australia at the time, sexual acts between men were illegal and carried hefty penalties. Then there were the social and workplace penalties, such as being ostracised, the subject of a whisper campaign, your career stalling and your parents and siblings finding out. The term 'in the closet' nailed it.

We had both expected him to tell us all he could remember, which showed how naïve we were, and how misled police were about the power of the badge. He was polite but resolute. He'd just gone for a drive to get some fresh sea air, and decided to make a pit stop before heading home. He couldn't recall anything past that; he couldn't tell us how many assailants, what they looked like, accents or actions, and no, he didn't want to give a statement. As far as he was concerned, it was an incident to chalk up to experience and not urge the police to investigate. We'd hit a brick wall, and aside from the unlikely event that one of the assailants had a crisis of conscience and decided to tell all, we had no way ahead. We moved from the investigation of a serious crime to shuffling paperwork to bring the case to an unsatisfactory end. Back to Mona Vale to complete the report of the crime and the related intelligence forms that gave some background to other detectives about what was going on in the Collaroy surf-club toilet. Then it was time to slip across the road for a cleansing ale and a chat with our colleagues.

While it was common knowledge at the time that men frequented the toilets and deserted coastal bushland along Sydney's northern beaches from North Head to Palm Beach, I didn't know that the Collaroy Surf Club was known as one of the 'Stations of the Cross' to a generation of men who slipped across the bridge or down from the north shore for a spot of then illegal entertainment with kindred spirits.

The man's bashing was troubling enough, but what concerned me then, and still does thirty-five years later, was his fear of police and social consequences and how the hell we got ourselves into that pickle. What I didn't know then was that the situation was about to get a lot worse.

I resigned from the police in December 1986, but maintained a close interest in the police through work in criminal defence and the media. In the last years of the eighties I was aware of a growing number of hate attacks on gay men, particularly at the city's numerous beats. The frequency of violence was on the increase, but in that turbulent period when HIV was devastating the gay community and many were living hard and fast because there literally may not have been a tomorrow or to take respite from the harsh realities, the depth of the problem and the possible links between some of the attacks hadn't hit. Policing was similar, handling the attacks on a case by case basis, usually at a local level.

The murder of high profile gay man Ludwig Gertsch in 1990 was a wake-up call to us all, and finally prompted a cohesive look at attacks on gay men, and I reckon it was also a catalyst for police to finally end decades of institutionalised homophobia. It's also the case I remember most strongly from the time because of how poorly the initial investigation was carried out, and the view of the victim given by the man leading the investigation. It wasn't until there was a change of police that the investigation was finally handled properly, and by then it was too late. Those vital early days of a murder investigation had been squandered.

Fast forward two and a half decades to 13 April 2015, and ABC television's *Lateline* program. The lead story was an old story: the death of Scott Johnson, whose naked, battered body was found on 9 December 1988 at the bottom of a cliff at Blue Fish Point on the seaward side of North Head that marks the northern side of the entrance to Sydney Harbour. Scott's death was quickly called a suicide and alternate scenarios of either murder or misadventure were dismissed, along with the notion that North Head was a 'gay beat'. However, Scott's family have never accepted the police decision and have been agitating for police to review the finding they've stuck to for over twenty-five years.

On *Lateline,* Detective Chief Inspector Pamela Young of the NSW Police Cold Case Homicide Unit, who had conducted a two-year review of the case and prepared a 400-page brief for the Coroner, was selling the results. Young's view was that the original investigation had got it right. When host Emma Alberici asked her if the original investigation was flawed, Young responded: 'Not at all. It was to the standard of the day.' As a detective just two years out of the NSW Police when Scott died, I can assure the Detective Chief Inspector that there is a body of evidence that proves she was wrong. To one former colleague who'd been a senior homicide copper in the seventies and eighties, Young's assertion was, 'wrong, mate, just plain wrong'.

Young then turned her sights on Scott's family, and when asked about their allegation that up to thirty other men may have been the victims of unsolved gay-hate murders over a ten-year period from 1985 to 1995, she said, 'Well, again, they perhaps are using definitions of gay-hate crimes that suit their purpose,' but she did acknowledge that eight cases may have been. As for Steve Johnson, Scott's brother who had been doggedly pursuing police since 1988 for a competent investigation of the death, she said, 'I was disappointed that our relationship broke down. But I wonder if it might be that Mr Johnson always struck me as someone who was quite determined to have one outcome, that he used influence, including, I consider, influence on the Government, to make the death of Scott a priority in my office over other jobs that we had.'

It was the classic NSW Police response to criticism – go for the source of the noise. I had seen it practised regularly when I was at Internal Affairs in the mid eighties. But Young wasn't finished, and she described a meeting at the office of Mike Gallacher when he was Police Minister, saying, 'I saw a lot of what I would describe as kowtowing by the Minister and his staffers to Steve Johnson in particular. I was amazed and incredulous. I didn't understand. I was quite confused. I wasn't understanding what was happening.'

Young's comments struck a chord with me. A lot has changed for the better in the NSW Police since the bad old days of bigotry, racism, homophobia, verballing, perjury and so on, but one thing hasn't – criticise us and we fight back. Gallacher told me, 'The Johnson case and the deaths at Bondi presented an ideal opportunity for the police to heal the longstanding rifts [with] the gay community and particularly the older members.' Young's appearance on television came at a time when the police were in strife over incidents at the 2013 Mardi Gras. It was an opportunity squandered and prompted dark thoughts that some things have yet to change.

CHAPTER 2

BAD ATTITUDE

Colin John Delaney had careers as a butter maker, engine driver and tram conductor before he found his true calling and was sworn in as a constable in the NSW Police Force in 1919. On 14 October 1952, after a successful career both in uniform and as a detective – at one point in charge of the Vice Squad, some members of which profited handsomely by turning a blind eye to the brothels, notably of East Sydney, and took bribes from street workers, which the working girls, with black humour, called 'tax' – Delaney was sworn in as Commissioner. The Korean War was in full cry along with the Cold War in the northern hemisphere. At home, Prime Minister Robert Menzies was warning us of the dangers of the 'yellow peril' and 'communist hordes' and 'reds' lurking under our beds, usually in the guise of members of the Australian Communist Party he was trying to outlaw. Menzies was a Liberal and passionate about freedom of speech, provided you were speaking a language of which he approved. By attacking the Communist Party that held sway in the union movement, Menzies hoped to get a stranglehold on the nation's industrial-relations scene. It didn't work.

Delaney was interested in reds under beds, but he was obsessed with what went on in the beds of the state he was sworn to protect and serve. He was an example of the recruitment policy of police at the time and one that stretched for another two generations of officers. If you complied with the basic height requirement (there were no short officers); your weight, at least at the time of recruitment, was in proportion to your height; you could pass a medical examination focused on coughing while the police medical officer applied his cold hand to your testicles; and you passed simple spelling, dictation and maths tests – where the pass mark of fifty per cent was a struggle for some – then you were in. The police attracted working-class men – women were few and relegated to lecturing in schools, guarding pedestrian crossings and interviewing the female victims of sexual assaults – some from trades but many whose post-school expectations involved hard labour, poor pay and lousy working conditions. The force was bleached white, with literally a handful of men from non-European backgrounds, and most with antecedents from the British Isles. Smith, Brown, Jones and O'Somethingorother or McEtc were common. I can't recall one person of South East Asian background, and only a few Indigenous men, recruited primarily to give them a job while they pursued a second career in rugby league.

Fortunately a chunk of police, and in particular those in the Detective or Prosecuting Branch, were bright men who simply wouldn't have the opportunity to progress socially had they not joined the coppers. The police offered decent pay and the chance for capable men to rise above the station they were born into, and get their hands on a career that offered power, influence and, in bent old New South Wales, lots of cash that you didn't tell the tax man about.

Under Delaney's leadership, corruption thrived with no hindrance from the government or key social figures – the old police saying was, 'Everyone's in on the giggle.' According to police folklore, Delaney had inherited the ample 'dirt files' compiled by his predecessor William 'Bill' MacKay, who used his surveillance police to follow politicians, lawyers and powerbrokers, recording whom they were meeting with and where – with photos if possible. MacKay didn't mind if their affairs were straight or gay, they provided information he could use judiciously to get his way. My father, when a young copper working in the inner city around 1960, had an experience that summed up how New South Wales worked. He and his colleagues were tasked to raid the famous Thommo's two-up school, run by Joe Taylor. Thommo's had been around since before World War 1 as an illegal gambling den and moved occasionally, not because of any great threat from the police, but to make sure the police and politicians weren't embarrassed by having the place in the same spot for lengthy periods. In Sydney, appearances count.

Thommo's was raided occasionally by police, again as a show and usually by appointment. The night my father arrived, there had been poor communication. They were there to raid the place, and were somewhat confused as to why the 'cockatoo' – lookout – on the door smiled and let them in, where they found the room packed with men drinking and betting. The reason for the warm welcome wasn't because the raid was expected, but because they weren't the only police there that night. My father noticed both Commissioner Delaney and the Leader of the Opposition, Robert Askin, embroiled in the festivities, along with some prominent lawyers from the criminal bar and a couple of men he thought might be judges. Rather than risk a career pounding a beat somewhere west of Bourke, the men nodded respectfully to the Commissioner and left quietly.

While Delaney had a tolerant approach to Sydney's wild side, it didn't extend to gay men. What they did in their beds, discreet clubs and bars, or in the bushes of the plentiful beats, was abhorrent to him, and he wanted it stamped out – zero tolerance in today's policing terms. Garry Wotherspoon in the *Australian Dictionary of Biography* wrote: 'Because of his obsession, scarce police resources were diverted from areas where they might have been more usefully deployed.' From his earliest days as Commissioner, Delaney had the gay community in his sights.

In July 1953, Delaney and his force got a bloody nose in court thanks to the failed prosecution of Douglas Shenton Annand, a well-known artist and graphic designer. Annand had come to the public's attention with his design of a poster to mark the opening of the Sydney Harbour Bridge in 1932. He joined the armed services in World War 2 and worked as a camouflage artist in North Queensland. In December 1952 Annand had allegedly been loitering in a men's toilet in Chatswood Park on Sydney's genteel north shore where he allegedly 'solicited a man for an immoral purpose', presumably fellatio behind a locked cubicle door. The man was Sergeant SD Cameron from the Vice Squad.

In the lower court, Annand had defended the charge but was found guilty; however, instead of a conviction he'd been put on a good-behaviour bond and fined one pound for malicious damage to Cameron's sports coat, and five pounds each for assaulting both Cameron and his colleague, a Constable Conwell, and resisting arrest. Annand appealed the case, and in the Court of Quarter Sessions, Judge Nield described the sergeant's evidence as a 'wicked and dastardly lie' and ruled the charge 'baseless'. The judge took the unusual step of visiting the venue in question, prompting him to comment: 'This place, having regard to the almost complete absence of any light whatever – what may be regarded as stygian gloom – is certainly no place any person with any decent upbringing or associations would dream of resorting to for such a purpose as alleged here, unless he was the lowest type of pervert or under the influence of liquor.' He noted that: 'the most lynx-eyed sergeant in the force could not have seen what was alleged'.

Nield had been born into a working-class family in Kogarah, and after service in World War 1 made his way through law to eventually become a Supreme Court judge. At the age of seventy-three, he was awarded a Bachelor of Divinity.

Confronted with a robust finding against his police and lawsuits for wrongful arrest and assault heading his way, Delaney had little choice other than to suspend the sergeant from duty and then to sack him. However, it was an incident that stirred him. The NSW Police of the time didn't take criticism well. Not much has changed. The former sergeant was encouraged to take revenge by lodging an appeal with the Crown Employees Appeal Board. Justice Weir was on the Bench for the hearing along with two senior police officers, and opened the event to the public 'for the benefit of all parties'. Inspector Norman Allen, who was Delaney's acolyte and would follow him into the Commissioner's job, represented the NSW Police Force and called his boss to give evidence. Delaney described Cameron, an old colleague, as a 'good, conscientious, capable and honourable member of the Vice Squad', whom he'd had to dismiss because the judge's finding was one akin to perjury. Delaney also confirmed police had been investigating complaints made by the judge as far back as 1939, and in many instances found that evidence had been uncovered that 'there was possibly not the same amount of criticism warranted as had been levelled by His Honour'. Delaney was then led by Allen and Cameron's lawyer into a politely phrased trashing of Nield's reputation as a judge and agreed the judge was 'prone to be precipitate in criticism of police', which made the headline of the *Sydney Morning Herald* on 13 August 1953.

On 20 August 1953, Justice Weir ordered Cameron restored to his old job without 'loss of salary or rank', with the latter a reference to promotion by seniority that was the practice of the time. Weir said he'd heard 'an avalanche of unimpeachable evidence in favour of the sergeant', and one member of the Board, Sergeant Boston of the NSW Police, noted that if Judge Nield had been so concerned about the evidence, then he should have recommended Cameron be prosecuted for perjury. In his summing up, Weir plunged a knife into the back of his fellow jurist, saying, 'This Board is unanimous that the evidence leads to one irresistible conclusion. The evidence is overwhelming that it was possible for Cameron to have seen what he alleges he did in fact see, on the night of December 5.' Weir also pointed out that the alleged collusion between other police at the scene, to get their evidence straight, didn't happen.

Delaney's informal response to the incident was to ramp up his anti-gay agenda, and his timing was perfect. The immediate post-war years were a time when the deeply conservative held sway. The major religious organisations, in league with temperance advocates and the Country Women's Association (CWA), were busy forcing their views on the legislators. On 25 April 1948, the tabloid *Truth* newspaper, nicknamed *The Oxymoron* by some journalists at the broadsheets, celebrated Anzac Day by running an article on the growingly obvious number of gay men in the city, saying, 'The increasing rate of sex perverts in Sydney is causing grave concern not only to the public at large, but to the judges charged with the responsibility of administering justice,' and 'the authorities are apparently doing little to combat [it]'. Amid lurid tales of sexual assaults on women and gruesome murders, the article weaved in a thread about homosexual men, talking about more than thirty-five arrests for sex crimes at Wynyard Station and stating, 'Perverts in droves roam Hyde Park, the Domain, Belmore Park, Exhibition Park and even in the suburbs. They [police] continually arrest them and have them gaoled, but know that as soon as they are released, many of them will repeat their offence.' Inevitably, the *Truth* called for tougher new laws and stiffer penalties to deal with 'these mentally deranged menaces to society'.

At the long bar of the Australian Hotel, where judges often took a cold beer after a long day on the Bench, and the regulars talked about sport, nobody seemed overly concerned. At one end of the bar they mingled and chatted with their cronies, and at the other end, gay men met. My uncle, who drank with the sporting blokes and had spent six years at war, reckoned, 'Everyone could drink in peace at the long bar. Most of us had spent too long at war, so why come and start a blue?'

At the CWA's annual conference in 1949, the ladies joined the *Truth* and decided to campaign for 'heavier penalties for sex crimes'. Delaney, then a Superintendent, channelled the tabloid, describing homosexuality as 'the greatest social menace in Australia'. In 1951, the NSW Government had been so swayed by the chest thumping, it amended the Crimes Act 1900 to include the phrase 'with or without the consent of such persons', which neatly captured the consenting act between men. This joined the existing legislation against 'the abominable crime of buggery', which had been in the Act since Queen Victoria had been on the throne and, as a statutory crime, dated back to Britain in 1533 where it was 'the detestable and abominable vice of buggery committed with mankind or beast' with the latter a possible stimulus for the recent comments of some right-wing Australian politicians. The penalty was death, with the last recorded execution in 1835. Fortunately the prosecutions weren't vigorously pursued, much to the relief of members of the clergy and students and teachers of England's great public schools.

In a 2011 article for the Association of Commonwealth Criminal Lawyers, Michael Kirby described the laws as 'England's least lovely export' and noted that prosecutions thrived in New South Wales, 'possibly under the ceaseless urgings of the State Police Commissioner [Colin Delaney] for whom homosexual offences represented a grave crisis for the moral fibre of Australian society'. New South Wales added further laws to make prosecutions easier – and presumably to negate the problems of Sergeant Cameron and his dodgy arrest of Annand. Kirby's view of the tweaked laws was: 'Possibly in response to concern about the unreliability of police evidence in such offences, the State Parliament added a provision (s81B(2)) requiring that a person should not be convicted of such an offence "upon the testimony of one person only, unless such testimony is corroborated by some other material evidence implicating the accused in the commission of the offence. By 1955, in Australia, the infection of hatred had not yet died.'

Kirby wasn't quite right – the infection was spreading. In 1952, the public was gripped by a tale from Newcastle, then a working-class city where employment was usually either in maritime industries or the BHP steelworks that dominated life in the port city. The *Newcastle Sun* of 8 July 1952 wrote that police claimed they'd rounded up a 'society of perverts' and that Detective Sergeant Kempton told the Court of Quarter Sessions 'the society has a large membership and recruits reinforcements from Sydney'. Albert William Jones, an apprentice typewriter mechanic, then twenty years old, pleaded guilty to indecently assaulting one man, and committing the abominable crime of buggery mentioned earlier with two others. His defence counsel told the court he was a young, immature man well respected by his employer. Psychiatrist Dr Idris Morgan gave evidence that Jones had been looking after his mother since he was eight years old 'and was actually brought up as a girl. No attempt was made to counteract his female upbringing. At present, he was eighty per cent female and twenty per cent male.' The doctor's recommendation was he should be 'taken from his home and educated in manly activities. Membership of the Police Boys Club would be beneficial.'

His co-accused, twenty-three-year-old Army cook Kenneth Scotman, and twenty-five-year-old PMG (the forerunner of Telstra) mechanic Melville Davoren, also pleaded guilty. According to Detective Ladkin, Scotman had tried 'to get his brother away from a group of perverts. Instead, he succumbed.' In the same court on the same day, Detective Ladkin gave evidence in the cases of Michael Robbins, a twenty-three-year-old Army corporal, and Dudley Stevens, a twenty-seven-year-old storeman/packer. Both men had pleaded guilty to buggery charges, with Ladkin telling the court that Stevens had done a 'theatrical act' in

Sydney and had been invited to Newcastle to do a 'floor show at a function run by sex perverts and became associated with them'. Judge Russell Le Gay Brereton, then the youngest judge ever appointed to the Quarter Sessions (now District Court) Bench and either well read or a fan of Weimar era cabaret, said: 'This is beginning to read like Germany after the first war.' Ladkin replied, 'Yes, it is quite a shocking thing. The membership is quite large. They meet at Newcastle, Wallsend and other places. They go to Sydney and recruit reinforcements.'

The judge commented, 'It is obvious this pernicious practice must be eradicated, but how to go about it, is a problem.' Mr O'Neill, representing Davoren, helpfully suggested, 'By dispersal.' The men were given suspended prison sentences and good-behaviour bonds, which may have been an indicator that not everyone shared Delaney's hard-line approach. In June 1957 there was a repeat performance of judicial disdain in a high-profile case, when the famous Chilean-born concert pianist Claudio Arrau was arrested in Lang Park near Observatory Hill. Arrau had ambled into a lavatory and winked at a young man loitering inside. Unfortunately for the fifty-four-year-old Arrau, the young man with the come-hither look was a detective from the Vice Squad, who arrested him for 'offensive behaviour', though if you're hanging around in a dimly lit public toilet late in the evening waiting for a kindred spirit, or someone who thinks you're a kindred spirit, to arrive, then 'offensive' doesn't fit the bill. This practice was the art of 'peanutting' or being an agent provocateur, and was practised by police until the late 1970s. Arrau's arrest was reported in the daily papers, and the following evening when he walked on stage at the Sydney Town Hall to begin his recital, the audience gave him a standing ovation, thus making the point we weren't all barbarians. The magistrate had a similar view and fined Arrau five pounds for what he described as a 'completely trivial' case.

In the criminal law system of the time, local courts – then called Petty Sessions – dealt with the offences on the lower end of the scale, such as men caught loitering or more entangled in public toilets, with most pleading guilty in order to finalise the case and get out of court as quickly as possible, hoping it wouldn't be reported or that word of the incident wouldn't get back to their family or employers.

Delaney ignored the message being sent by the public and the courts, and instead ensured his police were ever more diligent in their approach.

CHAPTER 3

DETECTIVES AND DUNNIES

The need to have the evidence of the officer doing the entrapping supported by another witness in order for the prosecution to be successful meant having at least two constables loitering – or one loitering and the other close at hand to observe and then move in at the right moment. If the poor bloke who got caught decided to plead not guilty, then both officers could give evidence of their observations, and usually their story dovetailed, and quite often was fabricated. It was known popularly as a 'verbal', one of the dark arts of policing, and, like peanutting, it endured for decades. The practice was in its dying days when I joined the NSW Police.

In early 1980, during my days at 21 Division, I found myself, along with a few truly unlucky others, with an officer who had a particular quirk. The tall, well-built and good-looking man in his late forties was a passionate peanutter. He was nicknamed 'Town Hall Toilets' after his favourite hunting ground. As a bit of background, he had a few other quirks, including sunbathing nude on remote sand dunes where he could be glimpsed but not quite identified, and was an avid collector of Nazi SS memorabilia. In the days before selfie sticks, he managed the elaborate set-up with a camera on a tripod needed to capture himself dressed in the black Hugo Boss outfits.

He waited until around noon – the lunchtime rush, he reckoned – to drive to the Town Hall railway station, where we parked the truck illegally on the footpath and dutifully followed him into the underground world of troughs, piss beads, cubicles with 'glory holes' and the stink of overworked chlorine bleach locked in battle with urine. He knew the toilet's routine, and had dragged a generation of trainee detectives to the place. We loitered near the door trying to look inconspicuous while our sergeant positioned himself at the trough, waiting for a sideways glance that could spirit him and his quarry into a cubicle. We were lucky that in spite of his crotch rubbing and sneaky sideways glances, he didn't get lucky. 'Never, ever again,' I told him, and judging by the look on his face, it wasn't the first time he'd been told. However, by comparison to what I later found of police and beats, he was genteel.

Not only did Delaney change investigative techniques to up the conviction rate, there is anecdotal evidence from the days before crime statistics were part of a government's reporting that prosecutions against men for buggery and soliciting for an act of indecency increased dramatically. The *Sydney Morning Herald* of 11 June 1958 in an article headlined 'The Homosexual Menace comes to Sydney' quoted Delaney commenting that convictions had increased from 286 in 1954 to 475 in 1957. The *Truth* in Melbourne also reported increases in success from 91 in

1950 to 328 in 1955 in an article headlined 'The Boy is Damned' published on 21 July 1956.

An old Vice Squad detective who'd been stationed there in the fifties told me: 'Delaney had an obsession with poofs, and he'd occasionally pop in, usually on Friday or Saturday night as we were going on shift, to tell us to concentrate on the dunnies. We'd say, "Yes, sir," and he'd go away happy. We didn't give a damn what they got up to so long as they didn't do it in front of us, but he kept an eye on the synopsis [the summary of overnight arrests and incidents], so if we'd didn't lock up a few our boss would get a kick in the arse, and he'd share.'

The Argus of 6 February 1956 reported: 'The Vice Squad has launched a full-scale campaign to clean up homosexuality in Sydney. Almost one hundred police are making round-the-clock checks on the known haunts of perverts. Senior police are alarmed at the increasing number of homosexuals operating in the suburbs as well as in the city.' The police were 'determined never to let Sydney's homosexuals become organised into strong cults as has happened in some European cities. Police suspect homosexual cliques exist in some professional circles, especially those of a semi-artistic nature.'

Frank 'Bumper' Farrell, the former captain of Newtown Rugby League's first-grade team, was a senior detective at the Vice Squad. Bumper recognised that good media relations was part of rising in the ranks and he could be relied on for a bit of 'drum' (a tip) to police reporters over a cold beer, always paid for by the journalist. Not all of his media adventures were positive. As captain of Newtown League team he'd allegedly bitten the ear off an opposing player in a scrum, but produced his dentures from the dressing room to prove it couldn't have been a fatal bite to the ear. He'd also arrested Abe Saffron and a coterie of his friends for lewd behaviour he'd observed while peering through the window of a house in Whale Beach Road, Palm Beach. The problem with Bumper's sworn evidence became apparent when he was asked if he'd thought to bring a stepladder because the window he'd peered through was too high to see through without one.

Bumper prowled the streets of Darlinghurst and Kings Cross for most of his career. He knew the crooks and hangers-on who made the area their home and place of business, and as a street cop he built networks of informants that were the lifeblood of criminal investigation. The downside was, like many of his peers, he didn't say no to a 'quid' (bribe) from the brothels and liquor businesses that needed a blind eye from police to keep operating. But Bumper had a dark side, and like Delaney, was obsessed by homosexuals – and he wasn't subtle. If he had a whiff a man was gay, and Bumper was in the mood, then the poor devil would be grabbed by the scruff of the neck, frogmarched into a dark lane and given a 'serve' – a few punches usually to the abdomen, then a couple of kicks when the man was on the ground, followed by advice to 'Piss off and don't let me see you here again.'

Trevor Rupe, better known to Sydneysiders as the flamboyantly frocked and hatted 'Carmen', came to Sydney in the late 1950s. The strapping Maori boy worked as a waiter by day at the chic Chevron Hotel in Macleay Street, and at night performed as a drag queen, with guest spots at Les Girls, and more frequently in local brothels catering to specialised tastes and St Peter's Lane, a popular spot for drag queens and transsexuals to solicit passing business. Even in those conservative years the trade in servicing married men from the suburbs was brisk. Bumper Farrell particularly liked to give the drag queens a serve, and Carmen recalled,

'He was just a vicious mongrel.' Complaints about police violence to the coppers at Darlinghurst frequently resulted in the complainant being taken to a cell and beaten again.

Ita Buttrose said of Bumper, 'He had a huge reputation as the toughest cop ever, yet he was the most courteous man in that very policeman-like way . . . His courtesy and friendship made it easier for me to be a woman executive at News Limited, a place where you could smell the testosterone when you walked in the front door.' Like Alan Jones commenting in 2009, 'We need more Roger Rogersons' as he launched Rogerson's book *The Dark Side*, both commentators could have done a bit more research before offering their views. It was the high profile of men like Bumper and Delaney that resulted in the ingrained culture of thuggery against gay men mentored into the NSW Police for generations.

Delaney retired on 27 February 1962, with the NSW Police Force observing that he had enjoyed 'the respect, admiration, and affection of all sections of the New South Wales community' – with the likely exception of gay men and Judge Nield. His replacement was Norman Allen, a man who didn't share Delaney's obsession or career trajectory. Allen was a bureaucrat, nicknamed 'Norman the Foreman' or 'The Mushroom' (keep him in the dark and feed him bullshit) by operational police. Allen started his career with a brief stint in general duties in Redfern and transferred as quickly as possible from the mean streets of one of Sydney's toughest beats to the demure Prosecuting Branch where the days were nine to five and the only criminal you had to deal with was standing in the dock of a courtroom. He lasted six years and then transferred to headquarters where he became the assistant to three Commissioners, including Delaney. Allen, as my father – who occasionally drove him from his double-brick bungalow in Balgowlah to headquarters – said, was a 'prize prick who's never seen an angry man, but he could kiss arse for Australia'. To prove the mutterers wrong, and generate publicity for himself, Allen had a habit of appearing at crime scenes and nominally taking charge of investigations, an area in which he had no experience or demonstrable talent.

Two notable incidents were the Bogle–Chandler murders in the early hours of 1 January 1963 – a crime that remains a mystery – and the Wally Mellish siege at Glenfield in July 1968. Allen arrived at the siege where Mellish held his common-law wife Beryl Muddle and their baby at gunpoint as hostages. In a bizarre negotiation by Allen, he gave Mellish an Armalite rifle and 200 rounds of ammunition, acceded to Wally's demand to be married by calling in a vicar, who performed the service with Allen as best man. To complete the event, the police mobile canteen catered the wedding breakfast, though there wasn't a champagne toast. The siege took five days to resolve, fortunately without injury to anyone, but a dangerous situation turned into a farce, and one that grabbed the attention of the international media. When Wally finally gave up he was taken to nearby Ingleburn Army camp, because he wanted to join up and head to Vietnam 'to make up for the trouble I've caused'. It was a short trip, and the next stop was Morisset psychiatric hospital. The siege had been prompted by a visit from the police who were inquiring into a car-stripping racket they thought Wally had been part of.

Allen was 'in the chair' as Commissioner when two significant events impacted the relentless pursuit of gay men by police, and in the grand Sydney tradition, cash drove them both. Bob Askin, the Liberal member for Collaroy on the northern beaches, became Premier in 1965 and two years later, the first US Army troops arrived in Sydney for 'rest and recreation' leave from the Vietnam War.

The freewheeling Kings Cross, then home to the early days of striptease and nightclubs that were the birth of the nation's rock-and-roll industry, became the hub of gambling and vice for the nation. If the NSW Police were the 'best police force money could buy', Askin was likely to be the best Premier money could buy. NSW politics had always had a shady reputation, but under Askin corruption flourished, aided and abetted by a compliant Police Commissioner, and a Criminal Investigation Branch that was literally a law unto itself.

Askin wasn't interested in putting an end to the shenanigans that netted police, government and lawyers a hefty tax-free income. Money was plentiful from abortion, illegal casinos, the brothels focused around East Sydney, restaurants and hotels that sold booze well after closing time; and with the arrival of the Americans, business boomed. The by-product was that the Vice Squad and 21 Division, then the twin problems for the gay community, were distracted by profitable enterprises. The liberalisation of our society also took some of the heat away from the gay community.

With the vast influx of US servicemen, and problems with the management of the vice trade fighting with each other over turf, the sex trade began a migration from East Sydney to the hub of Kings Cross, with many working girls stepping away from managed brothels and freelancing on the streets or working seedy rooms at the back of bars and strip clubs. For the police, this was an opportunity to exert even more control. Street prostitutes were occasionally arrested – some reckoned there was a roster in place to save face and massage away any complaints that the police were shirking – and charged at either Darlinghurst or Central Police Station, and then bailed to appear the next morning, which allowed them to go back to work. They would dutifully front Central Court in Liverpool Street, represented by a solicitor such as Phil Roach, who died in 1982 and in his dotage would sometimes give a spiel he'd prepared for a different case, but the sausage machine of the lower courts didn't hiccup – fined $80, fourteen days to pay, next case.

With the police distracted, gay men slowly began to emerge from the dark and into the shadows with clubs such as the Purple Onion in Kensington, which pioneered the drag shows that would become a staple of the Sydney scene, and described by journalist Katharine Brisbane, writing in *Pol* magazine in 1969, as 'a place where anything is possible and nothing is what it seems'; and the Bottoms Up Bar at the Rex Hotel in Kings Cross, part of a hotel that also sported hardened criminals and coppers in one bar, a reasonably civilised restaurant, and accommodation upstairs available by the night or the hour.

On 19 September 1970, the *Australian* newspaper reported the formation of the Campaign Against Moral Persecution (CAMP) in Sydney by Christabel Poll and John Ware. Britain had decriminalised sexual relationships between consenting male adults in 1967, and now it was Australia's turn.

With an appropriate acronym in place, a political campaign for gay rights began, joining anti-Vietnam War and anti-conscription and women's rights. The first gay-rights protest was in October 1971 when around seventy people gathered outside the old Liberal Party headquarters in Ash Street in Sydney's CBD when Jim Cameron (father of Howard-era Liberal Ross Cameron), a fundamental Christian candidate, stood against then Attorney-General

Tom Hughes QC for pre-selection. Hughes is Lucy Turnbull's father and had outraged the right with his views on homosexual law reform when he gave a speech to the Australian Council of Social Service in May 1970 in which he said, 'It is one thing to disapprove on moral grounds of homosexual connection in a private place between consenting adults. It is another thing to permit such disapproval to drive one to the conclusion that conduct of that description should be classified as criminal.' Hughes won the pre-selection but left Parliament in 1972 and returned to the Bar.

The protests meant mainstream Australia now knew what gay men looked like, but progress toward acceptance, and civilised treatment by our police, would be painfully slow in arriving.

CHAPTER 4

A BONA-FIDE PROBLEM

Violence targeting gay men has been a sad fact of life for generations. In some instances the perpetrators are young men unsure of their own sexuality and rather than dealing with this, they direct their confusion at gay men. The other enduring thread is the attitude, actions and inactions of some parts of the NSW Police that meant gay men were reticent to complain about attacks on them, fearing they'd be treated badly by police, and 'outed' to their family and their employers. To report an attack was likely to be a lose, lose situation for the victim. Instead, the men kept quiet and tried to get on with their lives.

Edward (at his request I've changed his name) was one such man and told me his story nearly forty-five years later. He was a bright, good-looking, slightly built young man just twenty years old and sharing a large old apartment with harbour views in Macleay Street, Potts Point. It was his first move out of the family home and a world away from the suburbs where he'd grown up with a widowed mother and a brother with cerebral palsy. In Kings Cross, he could finally be himself and explore life as a gay man. It was 1972; Kings Cross was moments away and then the focus of Sydney's nightlife. The Cross offered music and cabaret venues, restaurants, late-night dining for the after-theatre crowd; and on the seedier side, there were strip clubs and brothels where you could purchase any service from a sympathetic ear to the more exotic such as dominatrix Gretel 'Madam Lash' Pinniger and transsexuals who plied their trade with unsuspecting drunk men from the suburbs or those whose tastes were a little different to what was on offer back home on the quarter-acre.

In contrast to the Cross of recent years, there was an order amid the hurly-burly of the only part of Sydney that came alive at sunset and closed down around dawn. Police and business owners made sure the exceptionally drunk either sobered up in the cells of Darlinghurst Police Station or were escorted out of sight by taxi or their mates. In the days before drink-driving crackdowns, driving home under the influence was only a problem if the driver ran into something. While pubs shut at 10pm, and small bars were decades into the future, getting a drink in the early hours of the day was easy thanks to a 'restaurant cabaret' licence that allowed the local venues to serve alcohol provided guests intended to dine. The fact that the establishment had a rudimentary kitchen at best, and the menu consisted of a superannuated sausage roll sitting in a warmer behind the bar, didn't matter – the letter of the law did and proprietors followed it, helped by a generous attitude toward some licensing police, and detectives from the Criminal Investigation Branch propping up the bar during their night shift and drinking free of charge.

For gay men, a few of the bars offered a place for them to meet safely, and for Edward, it was the Rex Hotel, and when that closed, the gloriously seedy Venus Room owned by Abe Saffron, which had started life as an upmarket venue and headed downhill fast. By the early 1970s it was popular with the very-late-night crowd and was a mix of detectives, criminals, sailors from the Royal Australian Navy and any visiting warships from other countries, strippers, trannies, sex workers and gay men. It was like having a drinking session in a demilitarised zone. You didn't have to check your guns at the door, and while peccadilloes and preferences might not have been accepted, they were tolerated.

The only problem was getting a drink on Sundays. Pubs were closed, and with alternative venues not getting underway until very late, and many gay men, like Edward, working a nine-to-five week, a late night was out of the question. Sunday could be a very dry argument. The solution was to become a 'bona-fide traveller', another quirk in the odd liquor licencing laws of Australia's history. If you drove thirty miles from your home (or the address on your driver's licence) to a pub and signed the 'bona-fide traveller's book' you could drink your fill in the bar, and then drive home. For gay men, it was a social Sunday afternoon at either Wisemans Ferry on the Hawkesbury River on the far north-western fringe of the city, or the Scarborough Hotel perched on a cliff above the ocean on the coast road south to Wollongong.

On a warm Sunday afternoon in 1972, Edward and his friends chose the ambience of Scarborough. Plans were always loose. Those who didn't drive would grab a lift down and sort a return trip over a few drinks with whoever was heading home at a suitable time. On the trip in either direction, you could make a brief stop at any of the numerous beats that were common knowledge to the inner-city gay community and local knowledge for men hiding their sexuality from wives, parents and colleagues but in need of quick, discreet encounters. Beats always held the risk of predators, bashers and police, but there was safety in numbers and the more frequent users knew the danger signs, and in the small close-knit gay community, word of problems travelled fast. The days were usually very social: a few drinks, a view and maybe a bit of fun if you were lucky.

Edward had a fine time and lingered longer than his friends from the city. He'd met and enjoyed the company of three blokes he hadn't seen before. They were a few years older than him, friendly and good-looking, and as closing time approached he was delighted and relieved when they offered him a ride back to Sydney or to a convenient train station. The drive home wound along the coast for a few kilometres, and at Stanwell Park, made famous by the aviation pioneer Lawrence Hargraves and more recently as a hang-gliding spot, it hooked left for the climb toward the Princes Highway. Edward was in the back seat, still enjoying the company of what he thought were a friendly group of blokes kindly giving him a lift, when the driver stopped the car on the side of road near the precipice rather than making the expected left turn. Then the evening took a dramatic turn for the worse.

The three set upon him, hitting him then dragging the struggling young man from the car and hauling him the short walk to the edge of the cliff. It was dark by then, traffic was scarce, and the only light came from the few street lamps and the glow from houses down the hill in Stanwell Park village. There were no safety fences at the cliff edge, and a drop of around forty metres to the rocks. Edward recalled, 'I knew they were close to the edge and they were still slapping me round. I was terrified. They said they were going to chuck me off.' Edward was so traumatised he can't recall whether he was dangled over the edge by the men or just poised to be thrown over. He said, 'What I do remember is I begged for my life, and had the wit to tell them about my widowed mother and my disabled brother. Something I said must have struck a chord with them, and they finally brought me back from the edge. Until that moment I thought I was dead.' The horror, however, had only begun.

Edward was overpowered and couldn't escape as they dragged him back to the car and bundled him into the back seat. He was shivering with fright and wondering whether they would drop him off somewhere – or if they had another plan. He was astounded when the man in the back seat told him he wanted Edward to give him a blowjob, and was then going to fuck him. The two in the front remained silent – had they played out this routine before, Edward later wondered. Amid his shock and distress, his self-preservation instinct kicked in and he thought that if enduring the brutal indignity of being forced to have sex with the man was what it took to survive, then so be it. As they drove deeper into the night, the man in the back seat kept slapping Edward hard with his open hand. Edward said, 'I can't recall how far we drove but at some point we left the main road and headed into the Royal National Park. It was obvious these guys knew where they were going. We stopped near a creek, and the three said they were going to have sex with me whether I wanted to or not. I didn't know what to do, I was so scared, but for some reason it never happened. I've got no idea why. First they're telling me they all wanted sex, then they changed tack and said they were going to kill me, weigh my body down with stones and dump me in the creek. I begged them to let me live.'

Edward went on: 'We were there in the car near the creek for a little while, then all of a sudden, we drove off again. No explanations. It was bizarre, but my luck must have finally changed. We drove in silence for quite a distance until we got to somewhere I think was in south-western Sydney where they stopped the car and pushed me out. To this day I don't know where I was.' They had taken his wallet, but Edward was fortunate to find a kind cab driver who drove the bedraggled young man home – a memorable act of simple humanity on a horrific night.

The next morning Edward considered his options and decided not to tell anyone what had happened. He said, 'I just couldn't tell my mother or friends and tried to put the whole incident out of my mind and get on with life. It got a little easier in the eighties with the law changes and liberation. We could finally openly lead our lives, and then the AIDS crisis hit and so many of our friends were sick and dying – it was a dreadful time. But what happened still nagged away at me. I worked out I'd been suffering from post-traumatic stress disorder for years, and finally sought professional treatment.'

When Edward's mother died in 1997 he began to think about telling his friends of the attack, and in 1999 he told a gay friend. After waiting nearly thirty years to share his story, the reaction of his friend was anti-climactic – he looked horrified and didn't say a word in response, and years later, still hasn't. Two years later, at the suggestion of his psychiatrist, Edward revisited the cliff-top scene of the attack, but he didn't get close to the edge. 'I just couldn't do it,' he said.

In spite of nearly forty-five years passing, and treatment for PTSD, that night is still with him and it left a lifetime fear of heights. He's a passionate traveller but is now careful in selection of accommodation after an incident in Italy where he and his travel companion had booked into a hotel perched on a precipitous hill; it gave their rooms a panoramic view but was a little too steep and a little too panoramic for Edward. His adverse reaction to his room was so strong they had to check out and find something closer to sea level. He said, 'When the owners saw the look on my face, I think they were relieved the mad man wouldn't be staying!' One thing, however, has changed, and Edward now talks freely of his experiences and the impact on his life. He had a great career in business and was openly gay as he rose through the management of a global corporation.

When I asked why he'd decided to keep quiet for so long, he was candid. 'I'd been around the Cross long enough to know that if I took my story to the police, there was a risk of being bashed by them too. I also had to think about the consequences of my mother finding out and the impact on my job. It was a very different world back then.' Some aspects of that world were very slow to change.

The attack on Edward was unlikely to have been a one-off, but like him, few of the victims contacted the police for similar reasons, and it's a fair bet the bashers knew they could carry on with impunity. In November 1994, criminologist Stephen Tomsen wrote in a *Quarterly Journal of the Australian Institute of Criminology* article titled 'Hatred, Murder and Male Honour – Gay Homicides and the Homosexual Panic Defence': 'An ongoing series of attacks and a related brutal killing inflicted on gay men in the Illawarra district of NSW in the mid-1980s would probably have invited intense official concern and media interest if another victim group were involved. But this violence even went unnoticed in the minds of most locals.'

CHAPTER 5

SOME THINGS CHANGE

At the time of writing this book, the question of same-sex marriage in Australia is still unresolved. We're slow to change and it's not the first time. Britain, then our social mentor, decriminalised homosexual acts between two men in 1967 when the Sexual Offences Act was passed; however, there were a few conditions. In the great British tradition, it had to be done in private and between only two people – threesomes or more remained illegal, and for those keen on the art of 'cottaging' – the British term for beats – legal trouble could come your way if you were 'in a lavatory to which the public have or are permitted to have access, whether on payment or otherwise'. The legislation also had specific reference to sailors and male prostitution, and the provisions of the Act didn't relate to Northern Ireland and Scotland. To paraphrase Winston Churchill: the buggers had to choose to stay in England or Wales.

Murder stimulated Australia's slow path to reform. On 10 May 1972, Adelaide law lecturer Dr George Duncan was attacked and thrown into the Torrens River, where he drowned. Duncan was born in London in 1930, and the family came to Australia seven years later. Duncan was a brilliant student at Melbourne's Church of England Grammar, and then went to Melbourne University and Cambridge. After academic postings in Britain, he returned to Australia in March 1972 to take up his post at the University of Adelaide. The *Australian Dictionary of Biography* described him thus: 'Tall and slim, with fair hair and blue eyes, he wore thick-framed glasses and possessed the demeanour of a dedicated, self-effacing scholar, but he was intensely shy and taciturn, and found it difficult to communicate with students and fellow academics.' Duncan was a regular churchgoer, described by his British university colleagues as a 'mystery', though the reason for that may have been solved when he joined the Gaytime Friendship Society headquartered in London and then the nation's largest organisation for gay men.

Duncan was living in Lincoln College when, late in the evening of 10 May, he took a stroll down to the southern bank of the Torrens, a location well known to Adelaide gay men and nicknamed 'Number One Beat'. About 11pm Duncan and another man, Roger James, had been near the river when they were set upon by a group of men, assaulted and thrown in the river. Duncan, who couldn't swim, quickly succumbed to the murky water and drowned, while James, who suffered a broken ankle in the attack, managed to crawl from the river and was picked up by Bevan Spencer von Einem and taken to the Royal Adelaide Hospital. (Von Einem was an accountant and would later become infamous as the murderer of fifteen-year-old Richard Kelvin in 1983. He kidnapped the teen, raped, tortured and held him captive for five weeks before the boy died from a beating and massive blood loss. Kelvin was the son of Adelaide television personality Rob Kelvin.)

Duncan's body was dragged from the river by police, but allegedly slipped back in so the recovery could be re-enacted for a television news crew that had belatedly arrived on the scene.

Within days, rumours were circulating that the culprits were members of the Vice Squad engaging in what was later described in the Coroner's inquest as a 'high-spirited frolic gone wrong' and no surprise to the Adelaide gay community, which had been harassed by the squad for years. One of their favourite spots to 'frolic' was the bank of the Torrens. The crime captured the city's attention and fuelled the debate on decriminalisation. Rather than go away, the story built snippet by snippet and by 20 May the front page of the *Advertiser* reported that police were being questioned about their possible involvement. On 13 June, the *Advertiser*'s editorial said the murder 'touched upon the broader issue of homosexuality and attitudes towards it in our society', and noted the problem with the investigation was the lack of witnesses prepared to come forward – men frightened into silence by the prevailing laws. On 26 July 1972, Murray Hill, a Liberal member of the state's Legislative Council, presented a private member's bill to Parliament to decriminalise homosexual acts. It was supported by the Labor Party, and later by some of the state's religious leaders who thought the matter was one best decided by God than criminalised by law. Their views weren't shared by letter writers to the *Advertiser*, however, with quotes from Leviticus about 'a man who lies with a man' and so on proving popular.

The spanner in the works for Hill's legislation came from his own party, which insisted on multiple amendments. Decriminalisation would take a little longer. The same applied to a competent investigation of Duncan's murder. Professor John Williams from the University of Adelaide's law school told the ABC in 2015: 'There was a perception in this school that the police were not taking this seriously and that this life shouldn't be just snuffed out without due processes being followed.' It was a view in Adelaide around the time as well, with the Dunstan Government pressured to launch a commission of inquiry into the incident. At the end of July, the Commissioner, Harold Salisbury, just appointed to the job and considered an odd choice for a Premier as progressive as Don Dunstan, ordered a fresh investigation.

Salisbury – a deeply conservative man, suspicious of change, and a fan of capital and corporal punishment – moved to divert the attacks on his police force by taking the unusual step of calling on detectives from London's Metropolitan Police to investigate to make sure 'absolute impartiality was being exercised in the case'. The results of their investigation weren't made public, but on 24 October 1972, the Crown Solicitor announced he had 'decided against proceeding with any prosecution'. The only plus was that three Vice Squad officers had refused to answer questions when directed to do so by their superiors, and so they were dismissed, albeit for a breach of discipline rather than for their alleged involvement in Duncan's death. Salisbury's tenure as Commissioner ended in 1978 when he was dismissed by Dunstan for allegedly misleading Parliament over the actions of the Special Branch, the part of the police force snooping around and building dossiers on anyone they considered to be subversive.

The Duncan case lay dormant until 1985 when Mick O'Shea, a former Vice Squad officer, came forward and alleged that Duncan's drowning hadn't been fully investigated and police were involved in a 'conspiracy of silence', and that outgoing Commissioner

McKinna had directed the initial investigation to be stopped. O'Shea went further, alleging it was standard practice for some police to harass gay men at beats.

O'Shea's evidence resulted in former Vice Squad officers Michael Clayton, Francis Cawley and Brian Hudson being charged with manslaughter on 5 February 1986. The case against Hudson was dismissed by a magistrate in the local court, but Cawley and Clayton faced trial and were acquitted in 1988.

In a 2010 interview with academic Dino Hodge, O'Shea talked about the policing at the time of the Duncan killing, saying, 'You could put a brief in about two or three blokes, loitering – fail to give satisfactory account – and if you dragged one aside and treated him the right way, like give him a biffing, he might admit to buggery.' O'Shea said police used the men's homosexuality to bully them into signing fabricated statements, because if they knew them, they were likely to plead guilty to get the matter over quickly, rather than brawl their way through a public hearing. He said of the afternoon shift, when the squad was its busiest: '[W]e had to have this afternoon-shift half-hour of funny-man stories in the Vice Squad office about the previous night's activities in luring homosexuals out of the toilets and around the River Torrens, there or otherwise in the parklands, and belt the fuck out of them or down the River just flicking them in – that was a huge game. It was a huge game.'

The only positive to come out of the entire Duncan saga was that sex between men was decriminalised in South Australia on 17 September 1975, on the third attempt to pass the appropriate legislation. The agenda for change had been driven by Don Dunstan, starting in his tenure as the state's Attorney-General in the 1960s and then as Premier.

The ACT followed suit on 4 November 1976 with a bill passed in Federal Parliament. Victoria came in third in November 1980; unlike most states and territories where consenting acts between men carried hefty prison penalties, until 1949 Victoria still had the death penalty on the books for those convicted of sodomy, but fortunately sanity prevailed and the penalty was never invoked. Though the attitudes of the public and politicians toward the gay community, both at law and socially, had changed, the attitudes of some of the NSW Police hadn't. Some senior police were still culturally attuned to the beliefs of Commissioner Colin Delaney. In the NSW Police, changes comes slowly and often unwillingly.

CHAPTER 6

EVERYONE LOVES A PARADE

Greg Glass, whose career on the Bench included a long term as NSW Coroner, said of New South Wales in the 1980s: 'These were not only extraordinary times, but for the citizens of this city, memorable and frightening times.' His comment came as part of the inquest into the disappearance and likely murder of Christopher Dale Flannery, also known as Mr Rent A Kill, a professional assassin, drug dealer, failed armed robber and rapist who'd decided to leave Melbourne and make the Emerald City his own. Glass's comments were deadly accurate.

While Queensland had graft and corruption bubbling away under the Government of Sir Joh Bjelke-Petersen, New South Wales made its activities seem parochial by comparison. In 1980, Professor Alfred McCoy from the University of New South Wales wrote in his book *Narcotics and Organised Crime in Australia*: 'During the eleven years from 1965 to 1976, with the Liberal–Country Party in power, the State endured a period of police and political corruption unparalleled in its modern history.' The professor was being kind.

Rodney Tiffen from the University of Sydney wrote in *American Behaviorist* in 2004 in an article called 'The Tip of An Iceberg or Moral Panic: Police Corruption Issues in Contemporary NSW': 'Allegations about police corruption in New South Wales are almost as old as European settlement of the continent.' The Askin Government ran from 1965 to 1975 and was one of complicity with corrupting influences, and the first years of Neville Wran's Labor Government from 1976 to 1981 was one of containment rather than progress. Stirred into the mix was Sydney's gay community. They had begun the slow and dangerous path, considering the attitude of parts of the community, the church, politicians, the police and most importantly the laws that could land them in prison if they were enforced, to public recognition. They were stirred following New York's Stonewall riot in the early hours of 28 June 1969, when customers of the Stonewall Inn in Greenwich Village decided to take a stand against harassment by police. Word spread rapidly and the crowd of protesters grew dramatically, but police reacted quickly and harshly and dispersed the protesters. However, it was only a brief respite, because by around 2am an estimated 1000 protesters gathered outside the Stonewall Inn chanting about gay power. The riot squad was called in, and after a fracas and arrest the protesters again dispersed. Over the next few days protests popped up around the city. The gay-rights movement in the United States was born. It had a place, a face, media and thus political attention, and it grew rapidly.

Stonewall came to Sydney nine years later. Sydney was reputed to have the third-largest gay population in the world, following New York and San Francisco, and a bit like estimated crowds at a Mardi Gras parade, there was a range of figures up to 500 000 reported in the *Parramatta Advertiser* of 18 February 1981. The same paper ran a story then most unusual: the views of an openly gay man living in Sydney's west. Mike Winter, then thirty-five, said he knew of many elderly gay people who 'live very much alone. In their day, it was advisable to be discreet. But in doing so, they have usually spun a web of secrecy around themselves so tightly, on retirement the loneliness becomes a prison and to them it is terrifying to move out into the open.' On his openness on his sexuality he said, 'I find if people know me as gay but also know me as a person, there is no trouble. I lived in Guildford and worked in Merrylands and had no trouble with people I knew, even at the local pub. Once they know you can play darts, shoot pool, have a beer and in some cases fight as well, you are not really looked upon as different.' Unfortunately closer to the city and in the gay mecca of Oxford Street, relationships between police and the locals weren't as rosy. The attitudes of some police, and particularly the middle and senior ranks, many of whom dated back to the days of Colin Delaney, weren't as accepting as the drinkers at Mike's Guildford pub.

One former detective, still keen to be anonymous, told me that some coppers, usually detectives, got some 'sport' at Bondi when they were 'full of the pen and ink [drink]'; pay nights, which were every second Wednesday, were favourites. In the time before ATMs and Internet banking, police were paid by cheque, and wise publicans offered a cashing service, guaranteeing plenty of cash going back across the bar. Some rather pissed young coppers led by the not so young would head to the south end of Bondi Beach, park the police cars, and then take a wander to the walkway where they'd terrorise men congregating at a beat with a view. My source said, 'There was a bit of light biff, but nothing too harsh. They'd scare the poor bastards, and then pat themselves on the back for a job well done.' On the upside some coppers, my source included, when they heard of the impending visit, would get there first and suggest the men scatter. He said, 'Those young blokes down on the water weren't causing any trouble. Our mob were gutless pissed pricks, but with the status quo those days all we could do was try to prevent any trouble. That's just the way it was.'

On a more positive note, another source who had done his early years of detective training at Bondi back in the early seventies, said, 'We all knew there were a few gay beats in the patrol and that gay men were getting a hard time with plenty of assaults and robberies, but with laws and community views the way they were, we weren't getting many reports of crimes.' He continued: 'Our bosses decided these blokes had to be stopped, and young blokes like myself, backed up by more senior police, spent many a long Friday and Saturday night out patrolling the beat areas. The toilets at the Bondi Pavilion were busy, as was the area around Marks Park and Mackenzies [Point]. The parks and bushes got busier when the council decided to lock up the toilets after dark. I don't recall we had much success arresting the offenders but I think we deterred them – word about our presence travelled fast.'

Antipathy between police and the gay community hit the front pages in 1978 in what became the first Mardi Gras parade. While there had been protests and lobbying of the incumbent government, there hadn't been a large-scale, in-your-face protest – that happened around 10pm on 24 June. The scene was Taylor Square, flanked by hotels, the crumbling (since spruced up) sandstone majesty of the court complex that adjoined Darlinghurst Gaol, and the eastern tip of the glittering Oxford Street gay strip. At

Taylor Square you could head left to the fleshpots and late-night drinking dens of Kings Cross, or head east or south back to the peace of suburban Sydney. It was a chilly but dry winter night, when a few hundred gay men, lesbians and their straight mates gathered. Some had dressed for the event in warm clothes while others had 'frocked up' in drag or eye-catching costumes, some notable for the braveness of their brevity, risking both a chill and a chilly reception from police.

Police had approved the gathering in accordance with the legal requirements of the time; however, as the evening progressed they revoked their assent, setting up the opportunity to end the march and arrest the participants who declined to obey what the coppers could claim were lawful directions. The purpose of the original gathering had been multi-faceted. It would commemorate the anniversary of Stonewall, celebrate a gathering of the political lobbying Gay Solidarity Group, protest against police harassment and discrimination of homosexuals in the workplace and in housing policies, and agitate for legislative change to the Crimes Act to decriminalise consensual sex between men. As an aside, lesbians had no such legal impediments – the law ignored them, and socially many relationships were viewed in Victorian terms as 'companionship'.

In those days, 'outed' gay people risked losing houses, jobs, friends and families. An added incentive for the protest was news of an impending visit by the UK Festival of Light campaigner Mary Whitehouse, who wasn't a fan of a range of things, from colourful language (such as the use of 'bum' on television), Benny Hill and his amply bosomed co-stars, through to the gay community. She'd launched a private prosecution against the UK's *Gay News* and editor Denis Lemon for blasphemous libel after the paper had published a poem and illustration with homoerotic overtones of the crucifixion of Christ and the reaction of a Roman centurion. Whitehouse won; Lemon was given a suspended prison sentence and he and the paper were fined.

As a truck with loudspeakers led the marching crowd down Oxford Street toward Hyde Park, police began to harass the truck's occupants. In those days, issues management and crowd psychology weren't part of the police curriculum, and it was a case of *Do as you're told or else*, a theory that had reached its use-by date. The noise of the crowd, and the kerfuffle caused by police, resulted in drinkers in the hotels and clubs that lined the street putting down their beers and gins, and joining the gathering. At Hyde Park, where telegrams of support from around the nation and the world were to be read out, police decided to confiscate the truck and arrest Lance Gowland, who was driving. The heavy hand of the coppers had the exact opposite effect of the one they had intended, and the crowd, now numbering around 1500, marched out of Hyde Park and up William Street towards Kings Cross. Police had called for reinforcements to close off Darlinghurst Road – the strip of Kings Cross known as the 'Golden Mile' to the producers of *Underbelly* or more accurately 'the Dirty Half Mile' to those of us who lived, worked and socialised nearby.

The police presence at the blocked road was beefed up with uniformed coppers from nearby stations, trainee detectives from No 21 Division for whom the Cross was a Saturday-night hunting ground, and detectives from local divisions and the CIB, hanging back and muttering about this being a 'uniform stoush'. When the protesters were corralled in Darlinghurst Road, heading to the gay beacon of Les Girls, where the 'female impersonators' would entertain straight couples from the suburbs, police engaged them:

the attack was heavy handed with batons, pushing, punching and kicking if the opportunity arose. Some police officers removed the identifying numbers from their tunics, an old trick to ensure their anonymity in a group of similarly sized, shaped, clean-shaven, uniformed men with the same haircut and from a narrow range of ethnic backgrounds.

The Australian reported the event thus: 'At about 10.30pm Australia's first Mardi Gras was in full swing, with about 1000 people singing and dancing down Sydney's Oxford Street, caught up in the excitement of a jubilant crowd. One hour later, the Mardi Gras had become a two-hour spree of screaming, bashing and arrests.'

Fifty-three protesters were arrested and hauled off to the cells at Darlinghurst, where some – and probably the most vocal – were assaulted. In the following days, there were large-scale protests at Darlinghurst Police Station and Central Court in Liverpool Street.

Even though the offences were minor, the *Sydney Morning Herald* published the names of those arrested. In 2016 the paper apologised, and marcher Steve Warren recalled, 'Some lost jobs, lost family contact, and some, over the years, committed suicide.'

The police did learn something from the furore; the following year around 3000 people participated, with no scuffles or arrests. Police hate being disobeyed, but even more, they hate bad publicity. However, they didn't shed their us-versus-them mentality easily and in 1983, with decriminalisation looming, they had their last fling when they repeatedly raided Club 80 at the lower end of Oxford Street in Paddington. In the great Sydney gay tradition, the entrance was discreetly up a dark laneway. To the horror of world-weary, seen-everything police officers, they were confronted by men watching gay porn on television and others engaged in assignations in cubicles. An unnamed police officer told journalists who had been alerted to the event: 'Downstairs there were three dungeon-like rooms and several cubicles made of hardboard. About 100 half-naked men cavorted about, engaged in various forms of homosexual activities.' Three men were charged with 'scandalous conduct' and 'performing an act of indecency with a male', and a fourth with 'causing serious alarm or affront', which wouldn't have happened if the police hadn't decided to raid the place. A sense of irony was something else lacking in the NSW Police at the time.

The colourful John Marsden, who would later become a member of the Police Board and be defamed by Channel Seven with allegations focusing on his sexuality, represented the men. At court on 11 February 1983 he assured the presiding magistrate he'd had discussions with the Police Minister and it was likely the charges would be withdrawn, as they later were.

The police responded with smaller-scale harassing raids on Club 80, prompting protests with the slogan 'Enough's enough'. To up the ante, Lex Watson and Robert French swore statutory declarations admitting the abominable crime of buggery and took them to the Vice Squad. If they had been arrested on the spot, two more men would have come forward with similar declarations each week. French said they weren't arrested and were 'sent away', only to be told later that the police had 'decided not to proceed'.

During the year, twenty-seven men were arrested during three raids at Club 80. Detective Inspector Ernie Shepard, who headed the Vice Squad, told the *Sydney Morning Herald* of 14 November 1983 the gay community wasn't being singled out, and charges were all 'laid in the normal course of police duty' following receipt of a complaint – though he didn't mention who the complainants were. Shepard said he was a family man who didn't drink, smoke or swear and observed, 'I go down on that sort of thing.' The NSW Ombudsman George Masterman QC received complaints from some of the men arrested and in November 1986 after lengthy review of the original police Internal Affairs investigation, and hearings of his own, Masterman found that police had acted 'improperly and illegally', and referred his findings back to the police to act on. They didn't. In October the following year Masterman criticised police for failing to act on his findings, and then retired. One of his staff involved in the case was Bruce Barbour, who would later become Ombudsman.

In November 1983, Terry Goulden from the Gay Counselling Service told a parliamentary committee that money may have motivated the raids, because the owners had declined to pay protection money to a police force whose corruption was accepted as a 'fact of life'. Giving a glimpse into the machinations of Oxford Street, he said, 'Though there is no cold, hard evidence and we have not proved anything, it is also believed there is criminal involvement in a number of fires that have occurred on Oxford Street. The point is that it is the criminal element that has provided the gay community with meeting places such as bars and discos. In a sense, the homosexual community has ridden on the back of crime for a while.'

The criminal element Goulden referred to was likely to be the pairing of Dawn O'Donnell and Roger-Claude Teyssedre, who were the dominant forces in gay entertainment of the time, owning drinking, dining and sex-on-premises venues. While neither had a criminal record, both had a shady reputation, and the usual joke was that you couldn't get drunk in one of their establishments because the drinks were so watered down as to render it impossible. Roger's suspicious death in 1990, and the saga that followed in which Dawn was a prominent figure, would be the catalyst for the NSW Police having a fresh look at gay-hate crimes.

Roger – his preferred pronunciation was not the hard Australian approach, but French in style with the final 'r' removed and a lilt on the 'e' – crafted his own story, recounting tales of his early life and successes to his cronies, who included a bevy of ex-lovers from his prolific and predatory sex life, and acolytes, many of whom had been promised a slice of the booty in Roger's will. He had grown up poor on the streets of Paris during the German occupation, and after the war sought adventure and prosperity, and Australia afforded both. He arrived in 1950 at the age of twenty, to a country that was deeply conservative and where being openly gay could result in anything from a police beating through to imprisonment for crimes described in Section 79 of the NSW Crimes Act 1900 as an 'unnatural offence'. Young, passably handsome and exotic looking, Roger rapidly slipped into Sydney's underground gay scene.

In his early years he worked as a flower arranger, then in men's fashion and hospitality, where his flamboyant demeanour and French accent wooed clientele, even though his cooking was rudimentary. The punters, with no experience to guide them, thought Roger was delivering a little slice of France. Unfortunately that wasn't always the case, and Roger was liberal with the truth if there was a dollar (or pound) to be made. Leo Schofield recalled dining at a Moroccan-themed restaurant where Roger, in his trademark caftan that covered a growing waistline, had got into strife with health inspectors. Schofield said, 'He had been charged once with selling horsemeat, and we used to jokingly ask him for two brumby-burgers.'

Dawn O'Donnell was born in 1928 in Paddington, once an elegant suburb but by then a working-class place home to criminals, sex workers, hospitality people and single men living in decaying once-grand houses that had been cut up into pokey little flats. Her mother was described as 'eccentric', which may have covered a variety of issues, and Dawn was brought up mainly by her grandmother. According to Dawn, she became a figure skater of international repute – though one of her old colleagues told me, 'Ah well, she borrowed my career, but she's a mate so she can have it!' – and married a Des Irwin, a local butcher. Dawn managed the shop and Des did the sausages and the slicing, but the marriage didn't last after Dawn found that her attraction wasn't to blokes but to women, and she became a regular at the Purple Onion.

Dawn was one of those business people who knew how to screw profit out of every square foot of space in her properties. She started her entrepreneurial career with a car park, and then invested in a row of rundown terrace houses in East Sydney, bought cheaply after their owner, Joe Borg, was blown up in 1968 by a bomb placed under the seat of his Holden ute parked outside his Bondi home. Joe was the biggest brothel keeper in the city, and the East Sydney houses were a hard-working cog in his empire. Dawn's first major gay venue was Capriccio's, which opened above the Oxford Street shops in 1969 and lasted until around 1981 when it fell victim to fire – not an uncommon occurrence in Sydney's gay venues of the time. Rumours that Dawn had instructed the drag queens to remove their costumes from the dressing rooms the night before spread faster than the actual fire.

According to their story, Roger and Dawn met while she was working with her husband, and he said, 'You've got the best pair of legs I've seen. You must be a lesbian.' Why a gay man like Roger was checking out chunkily built Dawn's legs as she served him a few lamb cutlets was not explained. The pair obviously saw opportunity in each other and Capriccio's was their first joint venture, followed by Patches and Ruby Reds nightclubs, and Jools, which had a restaurant and cabaret room downstairs adorned by statues of cherubs and carpet sticky from decades of spilled beer. Upstairs was a dark room where 'you could get a schooner and polish and be out in half an hour' according to one Sunday-evening regular. Jools also had a fire around the time profits were waning.

One of the secrets to their success was to find a large space, add some sly grog (these places weren't licensed to sell liquor unless patrons intended to eat there – which was unlikely), turn down the lights and charge admission. In a society where gay men needed discretion, not only from police but from family and work colleagues, places like these thrived. The revenues were so great, the pair poured their profits into hotels such as the Exchange on Oxford Street, and into residential and commercial real estate. However, while Roger and Dawn profiteered they did give the gay community safe venues in which to gather. Abe Saffron, once the King of the Cross, told me that few people in his long career had worried him, but, 'Dawn and Roger were quite scary, some of the schemes they brought to me to fund were just mad. Dawn in particular thought she could nearly get away with murder.'

CHAPTER 7

GATHERING STORM

George Peterson, the state Labor Member for Illawarra, began to push law reform for gay men in the NSW Parliament in 1981, but he didn't meet with great success. It would take another three years – 22 May 1984 – to get there, with an oddity being the introduction of laws in 1982 to prevent discrimination in the workplace against gay people. Garry Wotherspoon, writing in *Gay Sydney*, observed that although there was a broad change in community attitudes, 'right-wing groups, conservative politicians, and Christian fundamentalists' still considered gay men and lesbians in the same breath as other minority groups as a 'threat to their vision of what Australian society could be like'. Even incremental progress was a battle.

In early 1981, Kings Cross and the disturbing issue of child exploitation were on the agenda. The media had been snooping around the place and found children and teens operating as sex workers: at 'The Wall', the high sandstone wall on the perimeter of the court and prison complex in Darlinghurst Road near

Oxford Street; in the adjacent Green Park and in Fitzroy Gardens in Kings Cross where the Alamein Fountain is located; and in seedy pinball parlours, dank laneways and even danker boarding houses and squats. They were kids from broken homes, abusive families, families with drug problems and in some instances kids from well-to-do families who wanted an adventure, or just didn't fit in. Many were rapidly hooked on drugs provided by the pimps, clients and assorted low-life that were part of the Cross in its most miserable period. Prostitution and petty crime became the only way they could pay for their heroin addiction. The *Sydney Morning Herald* of 19 March 1981 reported that the reason for the outbreak in the Cross was 'partly the police success in combatting the drug traffic; prices had gone up and young people were selling themselves to get the money'.

Amid the furore, Premier Wran reacted predictably: he announced a crackdown and created a new CIB squad to deal with the problem, working closely with the Child Welfare department and community organisations. I was one of the first detectives selected for the squad, and we spent the next year working in the squalor and sadness. It was a fast learning curve; we found out which community organisations were best avoided if you had a teen in need of some care – most were terrific but a couple, well, we thought the kids would be better somewhere else. We also found which premises in the Cross were under police patronage, and that included a couple of brothels and the notorious Costello's gay club in Kellett Street, which was the focus of some of the seediest evidence in the Wood Royal Commission a decade later.

The gay community had also responded to the problem, focusing on young gay men working the streets. With our common interest, I arranged what was probably the first official meeting between gay organisations and the NSW Police. It wasn't a raging success – there was too much bad recent history on both sides and utterly the fault of our police colleagues. Not even my bonhomie turned to maximum could bridge the divide.

Adding to the mix of sex workers – both male and female, barely into their teens – and predatory males who were their clients, was murder. On 18 October 1981, the naked body of twenty-seven-year-old Gerald Cuthbert was found in his Paddington apartment. He'd been stabbed sixty-four times and his throat was slashed. Forensic examination found he'd had sex shortly before his death.

Two days later, the body of Peter Parkes, a forty-one-year-old teacher and member of the Gay Counselling Service, was found in his Potts Point apartment. The method of murder was different to that of Cuthbert. Parkes had been tied up at both hands and feet and gagged, then stabbed with a long-bladed carving knife. Investigators didn't know if the sex had been with his killer or killers, or an innocent party earlier in the night. In both cases, there were no signs of forced entry to the scene, and police surmised the murderer had been admitted by consent, and similarly the sex was also by consent. Parkes' apartment had also been ransacked and items stolen, along with his car, which was found abandoned nearby a few days later.

With lurid crimes against gay men and possibly perpetrated by gay men splashed over the front pages of the dailies, Fred Nile entered the fray in the Legislative Council on 28 October 1981. Nile posed the questions: 'Following the brutal murders of two alleged homosexuals, Peter Parkes, aged forty-one, and Gerald Cuthbert, aged twenty-seven, by alleged homosexuals, what steps does the Attorney-General propose to take to protect the homosexual community from this type of terror? Does the Attorney-General propose to increase controls over the so-called gay bars in Sydney? What does the Minister propose to do to enforce the existing Crimes Act which makes the abominable crime of buggery [sodomy] an offence?' All of which suggested the Reverend was more interested in political capital rather than the horrific crimes.

On 10 November 1981, staff from the Greek Consulate in Sydney made a grim discovery at the home of their boss, forty-six-year-old Consul General Constantine Giannaris. When the Consul hadn't arrived for work by noon, two staff members met his housekeeper, who let them into the harbourside Darling Point apartment. Inside, they found Giannaris, tied at the hands and feet and with a knife embedded in his back. A smaller kitchen knife had been used to slash his throat twice, which were the fatal wounds. The apartment had been ransacked and the man's Mercedes Benz was missing. Witnesses later came forward to describe two young men who had been seen driving it. The descriptions were similar to those of two men seen near Parkes' home around the time of his murder, and the murder scenes were only a brisk ten-minute walk apart. The tabloids dubbed the killings 'The Gay Blade Murders' and the gay community was on edge with what might have started out as simple and commonplace pick-ups of strangers for quick sex coming to such a violent end.

Police sealed off the area and later found the car dumped about one and a half kilometres away. With the murder of the Turkish Consul the year before fresh in their minds, their first fear was that it was a terrorist attack. However, when they found that Giannaris, described in Sydney's social pages as a 'bachelor', had also had anal sex, probably with his killer or killers, shortly before being murdered, they changed their minds on the terrorist angle and started to look at the likelihood of two murders by the same team who'd killed Parkes.

It was a high-priority investigation, with thirty-five detectives assigned to the case to drive an early result. The Homicide Squad had a slick and well-tried methodology: all crime-scene information was collated, along with detailed backgrounds of the people involved, including family, social and work histories, criminal history, intelligence reports – things like threats made against the Consul, people seen lurking near his residence and spoken to by police – plus incoming information from the crime scene, post-mortem, locally gathered evidence, statements, phone calls and so on. Each sliver was examined and leads followed then either finalised or earmarked for further investigation. One officer was responsible for collating the information and maintaining the running sheet. A murder investigation by the specialists of the period was detailed, comprehensive and seldom missed anything. It was this meticulous attention to detail, along with experience, dedication and long hours, that cracked cases.

Giannaris had often commented socially that, 'Consul generals must be like politicians – popular but guarding their privacy.' A canvass of the neighbouring houses revealed the Consul had a steady stream of young male visitors, so the first task was to locate and interview them.

The break in the case came when a pawnbroker reported two young men selling jewellery he recognised from information circulated by police as stolen from the Consul's residence. Police arrested nineteen-year-old Michael Caldwell and sixteen-year-old Andrew Tregurtha. The cold-blooded, calculated and vicious nature of the Parkes and Giannaris murders, committed by teenagers, captured the nation's attention.

Andrew was born in 1965 and was hyperactive in a time when understanding of the condition was in its early days. By the time he hit his teens he had a difficult life at school and at home; in his 1988 autobiography *Between Dark and Daylight* he said: 'Living at home was quite unbearable because someone was always arguing with me.' In his mid teens he ran away from home, lived in squats around Kings Cross and Darlinghurst and had been in and out of juvenile detention centres. He wrote of resorting to prostitution – 'cracking it' – when he'd run out of money and needed to buy drugs or food. Andrew was a heavy user of pot and pills, which in those days were uppers or downers available on prescription from a doctor. Dealers in pharmaceuticals got their supplies on prescription from dodgy doctors, directly from dodgy chemists or by using forged prescriptions written on stolen prescription pads. By fifteen Andrew was 'gay for pay', and because he had no home, he would take the dangerous step of getting into a car with his client and either doing the deed in the front seat or heading somewhere the client knew. He wrote of the men, from 'all walks of life': 'Some were married men with children my age and some were respectable businessmen flitting around. Many were heterosexuals just after cheaper sex.'

To dampen the impact, he self-medicated with drugs and alcohol, and wrote that in Kings Cross he'd found a life that, though tough, was one he preferred, 'free to do as I wanted than the more secure and physically comfortable life with my parents'.

He met Caldwell through a mutual friend, describing him as streetwise, a dominant figure, charismatic, and 'everything

I wasn't but would have liked to be'. The master and apprentice moved in together, sharing with two other friends and working the sex trade either jointly or separately. Michael made Andrew feel secure and looked after, ensuring he ate regularly and always had shelter – two basics denied to many of the Cross's street kids.

When the first police crackdowns started, targeting the highly visible Fitzroy Gardens, Andrew shifted to The Wall in Darlinghurst Road, which gave him a small amount of pleasure to be 'right under the authorities' noses' alongside the Supreme Court building – and it was there he met Peter Parkes. Andrew alleged Parkes was a 'bit of a weirdo' who had a fantasy of wrestling with boys. Parkes allegedly asked Andrew to introduce him to his friends and this is how Michael came into the act, with them meeting regularly for paid sex. According to Andrew, both youths were 'becoming sick and tired of earning money by degrading ourselves' and Michael thought robbery would be a better way to make cash – and if they had to kill to protect their identity, so be it. It is disturbing to note that Andrew wrote 'I placed such little value on my life that the thought of taking someone else's life did not seem as horrifying to me as [it] might to someone leading a more normal life.' Around that point a third person came into their lives, when Michael hooked up with a girl called Joanne, making Andrew a third party in the relationship – 'My life was going downhill fast,' he wrote.

On the day Peter Parkes died, Michael and Andrew had been drinking heavily with friends, and around one in the morning, Michael decided they should rob a client called Rodney, and if need be they would kill him. Though quite drunk, Andrew recalled he was shocked by the plan and not enthusiastic. After a few more hours of drinking he was more malleable, so as the party broke up around 3.30am, Michael went to the kitchen and slipped a long-bladed knife into his knee-high boots, then the two headed to Rodney's apartment in a security building. Rodney answered the intercom and told them he was engaged with someone else and declined to let them in – an act that saved his life. Peter Parkes was only a few blocks away and he was roused by tapping on the window; he let them in after Michael explained they needed shelter for the night.

While Parkes made drinks, Michael slid the knife from his boot. He menaced his host and, with the man terrified, told Andrew to tie him up while he put socks on his hands so he could ransack the place without leaving fingerprints. When the search revealed meagre pickings, Michael, not a master criminal, demanded Parkes write him a cheque for a hundred dollars, and so Parkes was briefly untied to sign the cheque, then retied. The two argued, with Parkes making the error of threatening to tell the police. Michael loaded the goods into Parkes' car and told Andrew, 'It's too late, now we have to kill him.' It was just on dawn when Andrew walked into the bedroom where they'd left the bound Parkes and put a pillowcase over his head. He and Michael then held the struggling man down and stabbed him, though Andrew later could not recall who stabbed first – not that in circumstances like these it really mattered. Andrew did remember that he cried as he left the apartment.

Michael and Andrew drove home in Parkes' car to collect Joanne. They were thinking of heading to Melbourne, but decided to stay in Sydney because, like so many criminals, they thought police wouldn't suspect them, and so dumped the car on the street. A few weeks later Andrew, allegedly consumed by the enormity of what he'd been a party to and drinking even more heavily, had confided in Michael and Joanne that he was going to give himself up. Both talked him out of it, with Michael's 'convincing' including a threat to kill him. It was, as Andrew wrote, 'a life ruled by alcohol, drugs and Michael'. After a subsequent re-bonding session that involved a large amount of beer and white wine, the conversation turned again to robbery and murder, and the first possible target that came to Andrew's mind was a regular client, the Greek Consul, conveniently located a short walk away. Giannaris had tried to short change Andrew on prior occasions, but he still 'seemed very rich because in the past he'd paid me to sit and talk to him. He had also made me do things with other people while he watched and then joined in.'

Andrew called their intended victim and told him he was bringing a friend. He arranged for Giannaris to pick them up at their usual rendezvous in front of the Gazebo Hotel across the road from Kings Cross Police Station. Michael selected a knife and insisted Andrew carry it.

A similar scene to that of the Parkes murder played out, with Giannaris being hospitable and making drinks, followed by Michael's menacing with the knife, then Andrew tying the man up, and Michael searching the house for valuables; in this case he found jewellery and stereo equipment. Giannaris was subdued by the two sitting on him, then Andrew plunged the knife into his throat. He wasn't sure whether it was him or Michael who tried to stab the man in the heart.

They packed their booty into suitcases and drove the Consul's Mercedes back to Kings Cross with Michael at the wheel. After unloading the car, Michael dumped it nearby and the two went for a drink at the pub and were there as the story broke around the world. In a brazen act, Michael decided to contact Rodney, their first proposed victim, and sold him the stereo equipment, a deal that netted them $500. Some of the jewellery was sold at a local pawnshop where, unfortunately for the two killers, the owner had read his police notifications of stolen goods.

Kings Cross was a small and astute community, and it wasn't long before the two cashed-up and indiscreet young men were prime suspects for what police now knew was a double murder. The killing of Gerald Cuthbert had a different modus operandi and was a separate investigation. Andrew Tregurtha was arrested in a Kings Cross strip club, and during a search of the room he'd been living in police found a sock full of jewellery stolen from Giannaris. He quickly admitted his complicity and that of Michael Caldwell.

Tregurtha and Caldwell were convicted in 1982 and both sentenced to life imprisonment on two charges of murder, and lesser terms for armed robbery. Tregurtha's autobiography, *Between Dark and Daylight*, written with assistance because he was barely literate, was published by Collins in 1988, a few days after he committed suicide in Berrima Gaol.

The victims of Caldwell and Tregurtha were gay men, both lonely and, particularly in the case of Giannaris, in need of easy, no strings, discreet hook-ups. Had the attacks not turned murderous, it was highly unlikely the victims would have reported the assaults, threats or thefts. They were easy targets.

CHAPTER 8

THE UNWELCOME ARRIVAL

One further issue that put the gay community into the front of people's thoughts around this time was HIV/AIDS. The disease came to light in 1981 and was first thought to be a rare form of pneumonia, but over the following year it became obvious it was a new and highly infectious disease. On 27 July 1982, it was named by the Centers for Disease Control and Prevention in the United States. In October 1982 an American tourist visiting Sydney became Australia's first diagnosed case of AIDS, with the first death occurring in Melbourne in July 1983.

The beginning of Australia's case of mild hysteria about AIDS probably started two months before the first death when the tabloid *Daily Mirror* in May carried the headline, 'AIDS: The Killer Disease that's expected to sweep Australia'. The medical profession added fuel in the June edition of the *Medical Journal of Australia* with a failed attempt at humour – or so they subsequently alleged – with an article describing AIDS as 'the black plague of the eighties' and stating: 'Perhaps we've reached a situation like this to show what we've known all along – depravity kills!'

Reverend Fred Nile followed up in the Letters page of the *Sydney Morning Herald* of 6 July, responding to the death by recommending the best way to deal with AIDS was abstinence.

From 1983 to 1985, 4500 cases were diagnosed in Australia, with Sydney and Melbourne as the epicentre and the victims mainly gay males and, to a lesser degree, intravenous drug users sharing their 'gear' (syringes). Just how infectious the disease was and how it could be passed on was unclear, and apprehension through to aggression and panic were common reactions. The pragmatic Fred Nile, writing in a December 1983 editorial in *Australian Christian Solidarity*, suggested the State Government should levy gay bars to pay for the hospital costs of gay men diagnosed with AIDS. In August that same year he'd asked the Federal Government to quarantine 800 gay men returning from a conference in San Francisco, on the premise that AIDS was thought to have a two-year incubation period.

Evan Whitton wrote in 'AIDS! The Media, Paranoia and the Wrath of God', published in the *Sydney Morning Herald* of 17 August 1985: 'The high level of AIDS induced paranoia may be ascribed to a number of factors: ignorance, fear – not of what has happened but of what might happen – medical scaremongering, media reportage and political overreaction.'

In the early days of AIDS, confusion was commonplace. Some men tested for the disease received false positives, which prompted sad, difficult and often destructive conversations with partners, sometimes wives, families, friends and employers, only to find on a subsequent test that they weren't HIV positive – they had ducked one bullet but their honesty might have caused a few wounds that might never heal. The HIV diagnosis could be a hand grenade, tearing some families and relationships apart. Parents turned their back on their children after getting the twin bits of unwelcome news that firstly their son was gay and secondly he had the disease that was all over the newspaper and the 'Grim Reaper' commercial on television. The luckier ones had families and friends that took the news stoically and were there for what would be a long and slow decline toward inevitable death – hoping that a cure was imminent, but knowing how unlikely that was. Some lost close friends, scared away by the proximity of someone with the disease. I recall a close and long-term friend who'd grown up around gay men and the occasional drag queen, meeting another friend of mine who'd been honest about his diagnosis. First came the glint of fear in the eyes, followed by a furtive glance at the hand he'd used to shake, then the normally gregarious man pulled his young son closer to him as he hunted for the fastest exit from the room. Our friendship of more than a decade ended that day through fear and ignorance.

As the disease bit hard, the daily routine for many included a visit to Ward 17 South at St Vincent's Hospital in Darlinghurst, which in 1989 became the first ward in the country dedicated to AIDS patients. Stop by, chat with friends and lovers, bring in a couple of bottles of wine or gin to add some civility to the hospital routine, then leave them behind, and home to dinner, often alone, or out to the Oxford Street strip. The community partied with the determination of the band on the *Titanic* after they'd got the bad news about the iceberg.

A generation of men learned not to begin a conversation with, 'How are you?' or 'Gee, you've lost weight.' AIDS is a cruel disease, attacking viciously and unpredictably, often targeting through some bizarre means the very thing that made the poor sod the most distinctive. One friend, a naval officer then dancer with a precise and detailed mind, was struck by early-onset dementia. Another, a gifted cook and passionate foodie, was unable to eat for months and starved to a point where he was so vulnerable, opportunistic infections took over. The only treatment the poor man had some brief success with was thalidomide, brought out of retirement after the horrendous effects it had on mothers and their unborn children decades before. It had a brief impact as an anti-nausea drug, but was soon overwhelmed. AIDS loved to taunt with a honeymoon period before coming back hard.

The last ingredient in the perfect storm to hit the gay community was a whisper campaign that started around 1988, which still pops up nearly thirty years later, linking prominent gay men to paedophilia. The public face of the campaign were Labor politicians Deirdre Grusovin and Franca Arena, described by Garry Wotherspoon in *Gay Sydney* as seeming to have 'an obsession with paedophilia'. Both women, he wrote, were 'apparently convinced children (boys) were turned into homosexuals by being sexually abused'. While their motives to protect children from paedophiles were genuine and passionate, their investigative skills were lousy, and the campaign had the fragrance of a witch hunt rather than an objective inquiry. Grusovin was a staunch Catholic and Labor royalty, with her brother Laurie Brereton serving in both NSW and Federal Parliament. As a contrast in attitudes in the same family, Lex Watson and the recently formed AIDS Action Committee in 1983 contacted Laurie Brereton, then Health Minister, who cut through the usual red tape and invited them to discuss the looming problem. Watson wrote in *Australian Left Review* in 1988: 'The bottom line was the Minister, for the first time had said, "I've opened the door; come in, sit down. Let's talk about it."'

Arena was mother to twin boys, and when they returned from an overseas trip at the age of twenty-three, Franca was doing the motherly thing and sorting their laundry. In an interview with the *Sydney Morning Herald* published on 27 April 2002, Franca said: 'I started taking the clothes out to the laundry, when a photograph dropped out of a pocket. It was a photograph of a young man with a loving dedication. It was not for the son who had said he might be gay, but for the other son. I was thunderstruck; I felt like my heart had stopped beating. I could not believe it. The idea that both of them might be gay I found really hard to accept.' It was, she said, 'the greatest sorrow of our lives'. She admitted in the same interview, 'I had deeply ingrained prejudices and I hadn't really been aware of them.'

The women had lists of men they suspected to be paedophiles, many of whom were openly gay. Some were closested or publicly heterosexual but in reality either gay or bisexual. Grusovin and Arena would use the privilege of Parliament to drop hideous allegations against judges, lawyers and prominent citizens – in one notable instance, based on information provided by the notorious paedophile Colin Fisk. The lists, discredited by any objective test, and by the Wood Royal Commission, were still being peddled to journalists as recently as 2015.

I had a personal brush with the whisper campaign. In the late 1980s I was part of the legal team defending Dawn and Anthony Deren on a range of abhorrent child sexual-abuse allegations that included ritual sacrifice. The case was known as Mr Bubbles, a name pulled from one allegation that involved a man dressed as a clown and blowing bubbles at a children's party. The fact that the allegations were not even physically feasible – they were focused on Dawn Deren's Seabeach Kindergarten in Mona Vale on Sydney's northern beaches and Tony Deren was sitting in the middle of Sydney's CBD surrounded by work colleagues – hadn't been considered by the detective leading the investigation. The hearing in the lower court ran for six hard-fought weeks and during that time the sources I'd developed over the re-investigation and hearing told me our team had been added to the growing list of men suspected of being paedophiles, because of our work for the Derens. We won the case and the Derens and their co-defendants were exonerated, and one key facet was the will to believe in a story rather than the facts. Good detectives take a step back and take an objective look, then draw up lists. It's lousy investigative practice to draw up the list then try to fit the facts, if any.

The assertions made by Grusovin and Arena were career defining and career ending. Grusovin's 1994 attack in Parliament on John Marsden, the prominent lawyer and former President of the NSW Law Society and Police Board member, in which she accused him of having sex with underage boys, was a disaster for all. The allegations were based, in fact, on a statutory declaration from Colin Fisk, which he later recanted, claiming he was under psychiatric care and couldn't differentiate fact from fiction. Given Fisk's appalling pedigree as a paedophile and amphetamine cook, his allegations should have been treated with a high degree of care and scepticism. Grusovin spent the rest of her career as a backbencher – she'd moved from the Legislative Council to the Legislative Assembly in 1990 in the seat of Heffron when her brother Laurie moved to Federal Parliament – before being rolled in the pre-selection by Kristina Keneally in 2002.

Marsden admitted to being a 'promiscuous homosexual' but denied being a paedophile, but Channel 7's programs *Witness* and *Today Tonight* broadcast stories on him, resulting in a long-running and combative defamation action won by Marsden.

Arena, when frustrated by the Wood Royal Commission's unwillingness to credit her allegations about paedophiles in high places, and in particular that former Supreme Court Judge David Yeldham QC and Wollongong politician Frank Arkell were among that odious group, attacked both men in Parliament on 31 October 1996. But first she alerted the media to her forthcoming speech. Yeldham responded to her allegations and admitted he was gay, and both men denied being paedophiles. Yeldham committed suicide a few days after Arena's speech. Arkell was murdered in June 1998. A sad and brutal end to a deeply destructive and misguided campaign. Arena's attacks isolated her in the Labor Party and she resigned in November 1997, but served out her term in Parliament.

Some light did come from the confronting times of the 1980s. The gay community became stronger, doing precisely what communities should do by supporting their mates emotionally, physically and practically, and for some, the strength of the community changed their lives. One man interviewed by academic Peter Robinson for *Homophobia: A gay history of Australia* said he'd always been attracted to men but had tried to comply with what was considered normal and acceptable. He was married for thirty years and had children, and said, 'I did not want to leave while the kids were growing up. In the end, we separated because the relationship had broken down. Brian and I met in 1983 and we moved in together in 1987. Brian was married too. I have no regrets. In fact my kids have been heard to say, "Dad has never been happier."'

In May 2005, Detective Sergeant Stephen Page, the copper responsible for uncovering crimes against gay men that had, in some cases, been passed off as suicide or misadventure, told ABC's *Four Corners*: 'There was a lot of violence towards gays back in that era. There was a lot of phobia against gays back in that time. In the mid 1980s it was still an offence for men to have homosexual intercourse with other men and you also had the hysteria of AIDS when it first came out. And, if everyone can remember the Grim Reaper ads and the repercussions that sent through society, there was a lot of fear and loathing of gays at that time.'

Page was speaking with a deep and detailed knowledge. He led Operation Taradale, which began in April 2001 with its focus on attacks around Marks Park in 1989. As the investigation dug deeply into the cases, other attacks, mysteries and disappearances emerged. One of them was the 1985 disappearance of a young Frenchman, Gilles Mattaini.

CHAPTER 9

THE STRANGE CASE OF GILLES MATTAINI

In the month leading up to the disappearance of Gilles Mattaini, violence against gay men had been prominent in the news. On 25 June 1985, the *Sydney Morning Herald* headlined with 'Fear On The Streets As Gay Bashings Turn To Murder', and told the story of twenty-three-year-old Ken Beckham, 'a homosexual living in the Oxford Street area of Darlinghurst, the centre of the gay scene in Australia'. Beckham had moved to the area from Brisbane only eight months before but had witnessed two murders and been attacked himself, by gay bashers. The article reported that in the two weeks prior there had been approximately fifteen reported attacks on gay men.

Beckham found the body of transvestite and sex worker Wendy/Wayne Brennan, who'd been shot to death in her Kings Cross flat in April that year, with the police believing the killer was possibly a client who'd got a surprise. Wendy's killer has never been found. Around 3am on Saturday 15 June, Beckham had been walking with friends, twenty-two-year-old Michael Stevens and twenty-one-year-old Graham Jones, in Palmer Street, Darlinghurst. The three gay men had been on a trawl of Oxford Street hotels and weren't sober and their last stop had been the Handlebar in Oxford Street. In Palmer Street, on the way home, they were attacked by a group of seven to eight young men who ran up behind them yelling, 'Faggots!'

Ken was bashed, but managed to get away, and as he ran off, he turned and saw that the gang had Michael on the ground and were putting in the boot. He said, 'They were kicking him for about twenty or thirty seconds but it could have been longer, but to me it didn't look long. When they ran off, I ran back, pulled him out of the gutter and called the police. Michael was just unconscious. He was bleeding from the nose and mouth and breathing funny.' Michael spent the next eight days in a coma with extensive head injuries before he died.

Detective Sergeant Steve McCann of Darlinghurst Police handled the investigation, and he got results. Eighteen-year-old Evan Tietie from Canterbury, seventeen-year-old Poasa Bolamatu from Liverpool, seventeen-year-old Atu Tulele from Annandale and sixteen-year-old Gordon Holmes from Homebush were charged with robbery and murder; they pleaded not guilty at their 1987 trial. Tietie told McCann, in an interview tendered to the court, that he'd screamed out to his fellow attackers that their victim 'had had enough, but they kept right on', and when they'd ignored him he'd run off.

The trial ran for twenty-two days, and on 27 March 1987 the jury found Tietie, Bolamatu and Tulele guilty of murder. Justice Finley described their crime as 'brutal and gratuitous' and noted the 'community's abhorrence' of atrocities like these being committed 'on a public street of this city'. Tragically, crimes against gay men were set to shift from the public streets to other places.

On 13 January 1987, only a few weeks before the start of the trial, Raymond Keam, a forty-three-year-old martial arts expert and technician working for the Department of Main Roads, was bashed to death in Alison Park, Randwick, a quiet middle-class neighbourhood a short drive from his home. The park was close to the Randwick Police Station; the beat was on the side furthest away from the police station, and operated on the premise that police on station duty were unlikely to walk out and head across the park. Police patrolling in cars, however, were a different issue.

Both this park and nearby Queens Park were popular beats, and ones where police had been known to hassle gay men. One man who frequented Queens Park recalled that after police helicopters had been fitted with dazzling searchlights, the men at the beat had to keep their ears attuned for the sound of the approaching chopper. The helicopter, with searchlight blazing, would sweep across the park, then try to herd the escaping men toward the police paddy wagon that was parked nearby. He said, 'We were awake up to that pretty quickly so we headed for the scrub. The helicopter couldn't spot us, and the coppers didn't want to get their uniforms dirty.'

Keam was tall, fit and skilled, so overpowering him was likely to need a combination of stealth and numbers. He'd trained earlier that night at the Balmain Leagues Club, then gone to his home in Waterloo for dinner. Like many men who used beats, Keam didn't think he was gay, and he could point to a female partner and their two-year-old son living in Canberra. It was around midnight when Keam drove his Holden Jackaroo to Alison Park, Randwick, and parked near the toilet block. An elderly woman walking her dog found his dead body the next morning at six o'clock. Raymond Keam had a fractured sternum, suggesting he'd been jumped on after being beaten to the ground, and signs of injuries inflicted by a baton, a piece of wood or one of the karate staffs from the kit in the back of his car. The car had been ransacked. His attackers were never found; however, in a gesture that restored some faith in human nature, soldiers from the nearby barracks offered to patrol the park at night to keep the gay men and any others in the park safe.

Gilles Mattaini was a shy and timid man, slight of build and on the shorter end of average at 170 centimetres. He arrived in Sydney from France in 1983 when he was twenty-three years old. He'd made the journey to be with his lover, Jacques Musy, whom he'd met in Paris in 1978. At the time the two met, Gilles was living with his parents in the outer Paris suburb of Goussainville, close to Charles de Gaulle airport, and starting his career in the finance market. Their developing relationship struck an early hurdle toward the end of its first year when Gilles was called up for National Service as an infantry soldier in the Chasseurs Alpins (Alpine Hunters). Military life was challenging for Gilles, and the idea of continuing in the Army for a year caused him such distress that he took an overdose of medication, which resulted in him being sent to a military hospital, then kicked out of the Army. It wasn't the first time the sensitive young man had attempted suicide; in his late teens he'd taken an overdose and cut his wrists while in bed at home, but had been found by his mother.

After his exit from the Army, the relationship with Jacques rekindled and by 1980 the two were living together and had a good life, with travel to exotic destinations such as the Maldives and Sri Lanka. Gilles was happy. In 1983, Jacques was offered a job in

Sydney, arriving there in March, and eventually gaining permanent residency. Gilles followed in September on a tourist visa, and found work at the Menzies Hotel in the city as a casual barman. They lived a slice of the Australian dream marketed to Europe by moving into a unit in Ramsgate Avenue, Bondi Beach, directly across the road from Australia's most famous strip of sand.

Jacques said, 'Gilles could speak English fluently, and tended to keep to himself. I would describe him as solitary and timid. He was law abiding and did not use drugs.' One of his great pleasures was to take long walks along the coastal headlands from their home and south to Tamarama; walks that included the edge of Marks Park. Parts of that walk were well known as a gay beat, especially Marks Park because it offered some shelter and discretion, but Jacques said of his partner: 'I do not think there was any sexual motive for him to have gone in the vicinity of Marks Park. Gilles was not promiscuous.' On these walks Gilles would have his headphones on, listening to melodic French songs, walking along in his own world.

In August 1985, Jacques headed back to France for a visit, and thought Gilles was apprehensive about overstaying his visa. He was in fine health. The two spoke every week, and Gilles was looking forward to a visit from Anthony Wyszynski, a friend of theirs from Paris with whom both men had shared a flat. He thought Gilles was lonely, but compensating adequately with retail therapy, buying furnishings for their apartment including bed linen, carpets, picture frames and indoor plants.

Toward the end of his visit to France, Jacques had a call from Vincent Ottaviani, a friend who worked with Gilles at the Menzies and lived nearby, to tell Jacques that Gilles hadn't turned up at work and was missing from home. Vincent and some friends had swung into action, calling hospitals, police stations, the morgue and the French consulate.

When Jacques arrived back in Bondi on 24 September 1985, he noticed no sign of forced entry to their apartment, and all their belongings seemed to be in place. Gilles' wallet, passport, credit cards and watch were still there, but his Walkman, house keys, a yellow spray jacket and white sloppy joe were missing. Knowing his routines well and the stiff, cold breeze along the coast in spring, Jacques assumed Gilles had gone for his usual walk and hadn't returned. By the time Jacques returned to Australia, Gilles had been gone for around nine days. A neighbour told him the last time he'd seen Gilles was on 15 September, and that he'd looked 'aloof' – the fifteenth was also Jacques' birthday. Around that time Gilles had spoken to Anthony, then still in Paris and preparing for his trip to Sydney. Anthony recalled: 'Gilles was very happy and looking forward to my visit. There was no indication about him being in trouble. This was the last time I spoke to Gilles.'

All their friends assumed Vincent had reported Gilles' absence to police; however, years later no record of a formal report could be found and by that time, Vincent had died of an AIDS-related illness.

Anthony recalled an incident a few years later in Marks Park, where he saw a group of more than four young men arrive in two cars and chase men doing the beat. Anthony ran as well, but carried a whistle with him for safety and he blew it long and hard to scare the men off, but he didn't report the incident to police. Neither the incident, nor lack of reporting, was a surprise to anyone who used the beat or lived nearby. The place 'worked' day and night, and users – and men just out for a stroll and mistaken for being gay – had been assaulted or chased with a bashing in mind. One older man told me he'd been there late afternoon 'just looking about' when he felt a stinging sensation on his buttock, and while fumbling around with his jacket found an air-rifle pellet lodged near the vent. He said, 'Some little bastard had shot me in the bum with an air rifle. Fortunately I was saved by Harris Tweed.'

The body of Gilles Mattaini has never been found, nor were there any reports of a scuffle around the Marks Park area around the time Gilles was likely to be walking. He simply disappeared. Friends later packed his personal effects and sent them home to his parents in Paris. Fifteen years later, the disappearance of Gilles Mattaini would be added to the list of men possibly murdered in a wave of gay-hate violence that gripped the city in that strangest of times.

CHAPTER 10

MANLY PURSUITS

The gangs of the eighties and early nineties who preyed on gay men at beats were organised and mobile, using their own cars to get them around multiple locations in the course of their hunt – a term I use specifically. They had a hierarchical structure, they planned, they had purpose and they knew where and when to find their targets. It was intelligence gained through experience and, as one alleged gang member disturbingly commented: 'We knew some of the other guys (bashers).'

Stephen Page, in his May 2005 *Four Corners* interview, said of the gangs: 'Gay beats had victims seen as easy targets. Offenders would walk away cashed up, and numerous people have called it the sport of the eighties. I'd probably lengthen it and call it the team sport of the eighties because there were no brave people in amongst that. They were all cowards and they would all act as a group.' Many had been students of the same high school who'd remained friends and drinking mates after leaving school.

Some beat users also moved in groups, and like the bashers they were mobile. Men from the eastern suburbs travelled around the city, sometimes together for convenience and safety. Arrangements for their adventures were made discreetly back in the days prior to decriminalisation. As one man said: 'We all had good jobs we didn't want to lose, so we kept it quiet, and some of the places we headed to had nicknames, and picking them was a bit of fun. We were out looking for a good, quick and anonymous time, and in the names, put our Catholic education to use. The nuns would have a fit if they'd known.'

Public toilets in Alexandria Park at Alexandria were nicknamed 'the Basilica' – a reference to St Peter's Basilica in the Vatican; and 'Stations of the Cross' on the northern beaches were made up of the venues at Narrabeen bus terminus, Collaroy Surf Club – where my first experience with gay-hate crime had occurred – and the Totem Shopping Centre at Balgowlah. The stations were arranged in a pleasant round-trip drive of the northern beaches, though the men avoided St Leonards Park at North Sydney and Milson Park in Kirribilli near the headquarters of Australia's submarine fleet – both were considered too risky. The men knew some of the cars used by the bashers, and the times they preferred to turn up. As one man told me: 'You can rely on them having tea at home with Mum and Dad, and after the news they'd head out.' They also knew that a come-hither look from someone needed to be considered carefully because of the risk of being beaten and robbed. A well-honed 'gaydar' was essential.

In 1987, police from the northern beaches patrols arrested one gang of youths who'd been attacking gay men. The gang was from the close-knit community of families from the former Yugoslavia who'd escaped to Australia and set up market gardens and glasshouses full of tomatoes in the Warriewood Valley, until a bit over a decade ago one of the few farming areas left within thirty kilometres of Sydney's CBD. One source said the gang was nicknamed the 'North Narra Boys'. They were from families that worked long, hard hours and kept to themselves, while the bulk of their schoolmates went surfing or carousing with their mates. On New Year's Eve 1986, police from Manly and Mona Vale ruined the festivities for a few gang members when they swooped on their homes and arrested them.

One of the men was Vojko Spadina, nicknamed 'Spud', and he was arrested at his home in North Narrabeen and taken to the Manly Police Station, where he was later charged with multiple counts of assault and robbery. Spadina was a notably ordinary young man who lived with his mother, father, brother and sister and worked part-time at the local Charcoal Chicken store. The police opened by asking about an assault on a man on Boxing Day that year at another popular spot, Reef Beach, then a designated nude beach set in fairly thick bushland and popular with gay men to cruise or get a bit of sun – or both. Aside from bashers, the other danger was local resident Rex 'The Moose' Mossop, notable sports commentator for Channel 7, former football great and resident of the dead-end street that led to the beach, and unhappy about the crowds. Rex once performed a citizen's arrest on a nude man who'd strayed out of the designated area, and commented to the media he didn't need 'male genitalia rammed down his throat'.

Spadina and two friends – Nick Janus and a juvenile who can't be named, so I'll call him John – had driven in Janus's mother's car, parked and headed into the bushland. He said, 'We walked around the bush track, [John] and I went one way and Nick went up another way. We came across a bloke and [John] punched him and I joined him and we bashed him and then Nick came in and he also bashed him.' They stole the man's rings along with the money in a bag he'd been carrying. The man was Laurie Levy, whom they left in the bush with lacerations, bruises and chipped teeth as the three ran back to Janus's white Toyota and drove to a snooker room in North Narrabeen. The assault and robbery had been part of a spree of attacks targeting gay men at known beats that had, as far they would admit, begun on 7 December, then again on 12 December, 24 December, the assault on 26 December and then two more on 28 December, with the charges for various crimes including assault and robbery, and assault occasioning actual bodily harm. What led to their downfall was that Levy had followed them down the track and made a note of their registration number.

The victim of 12 December was Stuart Blackie, a cleaner who had stopped at the Narrabeen bus terminus to answer a call of nature around 8pm on his way home. He went into the toilet and into a cubicle, shortly after which he heard noise in an adjacent cubicle so he decided to leave, but on the way out he saw another man waiting. Both men started to yell, 'Bloody poofter!' and Blackie yelled back. The moment escalated into a fight with fists flying – Blackie wasn't their average prey, though he recalled being scared. As he made a break for his car he was 'walloped by a bag' with something in it, which was later found to be drill bits. He finally managed to get to the safety of his car with blood pouring from a wound to his head that required stitches. The attacks were all similar in style, with the men splitting up, stalking their target and then converging and attacking, while yelling something along the lines of 'poofter'.

The only variation on the theme came in the final attack on 28 December; this time a little seduction was involved. One of the gang was sitting on the rotunda in St Leonards Park when the victim, Thomas Broderick, nearly fifty years old at the time, approached him and started a conversation about whether he was familiar with a few Oxford Street venues – a sure way of finding out if the young man was gay. When he responded he did, Broderick inquired if he'd like to come home, whereupon the young man attacked and two others came from out of the darkness and joined in, kicking, punching and yelling, 'I'm going to teach you a lesson, faggot!' Broderick screamed, 'Mercy! Mercy!' and told police 'after what seemed to be a long time, they ran off'. Broderick was treated in hospital for a dislocated shoulder, abrasions and extensive bruising. What was unusual was that all the perpetrators gave frank interviews to police. Their candour may have been prompted by self-interest and the hope of getting a lighter sentence.

While Spadina had been allegedly willing to be interviewed and admit his crimes without duress, the story changed at the lower-court hearing when he told the magistrate he'd made the admissions only after the interviewing detectives, Ray Peattie and David Patison, had 'touched me up', alleging the detective had kicked the chair from under him and hit him about the face and ribs. These were set-piece allegations of the time, and always denied by police.

The mobility of the gang was evidenced by their hunting grounds, which included the Totem Centre at Balgowlah, Reef Beach, Narrabeen, and then on a couple of occasions St Leonards Park. While they'd all made admissions of their crimes to the police, they'd pleaded not guilty in the lower court and were committed for trial at the District Court owing to the seriousness of their alleged crimes. Janus decided to plead guilty and was the first to be sentenced. He received five years' hard labour on 14 July 1988. Spadina followed on 15 December 1989, and received eighteen months' periodic detention. David Ashton, who'd been with Spadina's crew on a few of the attacks, including at St Leonards Park, went to trial on two counts and was convicted on one, receiving a $1000 fine on 18 April 1990. The juvenile 'John' pleaded guilty and received two years' probation.

In one of those odd coincidences, the North Narra Boys were in the Sydney District Court in King Street in the city for a procedural hearing on the same day the brilliant mathematics prodigy Scott Johnson walked to King Street to use an ATM, then on to Oxford Street to enjoy what he didn't know would be his last night on earth.

CHAPTER 11

A LONELY PLACE TO DIE

Scott Johnson probably died sometime on the late afternoon or early evening of 8 December 1988. He had celebrated his twenty-seventh birthday only eleven days before. His naked body was found on the rock below Blue Fish Point at North Head on the entrance to Sydney Harbour. The place was popular with rock- and spear-fishermen and was a sheer drop of about sixty metres from the edge to rocks below. While the area had a fine sea view, it was lacking in ambience thanks to the low scrub on the windswept headland and the unlovely adjacent sewage treatment plant that lent an unfortunate fragrance to the air if the wind was blowing in the wrong direction. It wasn't a spot for romance, but for some it was a discreet spot for a liaison. It offered ample parking in secluded bays; not much traffic came through from dusk onwards; the steep hill from Manly meant only avid walkers or joggers would come by and those who did were fixated on their exercise; and the added bonus was the proximity of the Army barracks and St Patrick's College, both of which had plenty of young men living strict lives who might just consider a bracing walk at the end of a long day and the hope of finding a discreet dalliance with a kindred spirit – either that or a combination of motive and opportunity – in relative safety.

As a young copper working with Manly as my first station in 1977, I got to know the area well. Uniformed police on patrol have a routine. Diligent coppers of the time were out on the road for as much of their shift as possible, patrolling in marked police cars or the classic Ford F100 paddy wagons – unruly, overpowered beasts with a cage on the back to carry prisoners. They were the workhorse of the NSW Police. Patrols would take you to areas where crime was common, such as around pubs at closing time, transport terminals and, in Manly, the beachfront and North Head. The two latter locations were popular spots for theft from cars, and what we called 'optic nerves', better known as perverts – people creeping around spots used as 'lovers' lanes' and getting their jollies watching others get theirs. North Head was particularly popular because it also offered some great views, fresh air – police are human as well – and on night shift, a place to catch a nap without being spotted by a supervisor or a member of the public who might dob you in.

The heart of good police work is methodology, observation and intelligence, and any copper working in Manly at the time and worth their fortnightly pay cheque knew that North Head and Blue Fish Point – the latter off on a side road just past Manly Hospital, where the scenic drive to the southernmost tip of the headland began – were gay beats. The location was ideal: men could drive and park their cars, then take a wander through the scrub, some of which was sufficiently high and dense to give them a degree of privacy.

Scott Johnson's siblings were, in age order, sister Teresa (Terry), brother Stephen (Steve) and step-sister Antonia Rebecca (Becca) and step-brother Sloan from their father's later marriage. Scott was born on 27 November 1961 in Glendora, an outer suburb of Los Angeles at the foothills of the San Gabriel Mountains. The family wasn't wealthy, and Scott's parents separated when the children were young, after which, Steve said, 'We lived on welfare for most of the time I was in high school and so Scott and I became much closer during those few years. We were really on our own. And Scott loved maths and was brilliant at it.' Steve delivered newspapers to add to the family income and they moved frequently during their childhood, with each move to a cheaper and cheaper property in neighbourhoods Steve described as 'ghettos', where street violence was common. Over their childhood they lived in twenty-five different houses, and money was so scarce they survived on boxes of Kraft macaroni cheese, tuna with macaroni and burgers with the meat eked out with the addition of protein-like 'hamburger helper'. It wasn't great, but it kept them fed.

Steve was no intellectual slouch either, and crossed the country to Harvard University. Steve would go on to become very wealthy after he wrote the algorithm that allows us to send photographs via email, and sold it to America Online. It was a revolution in the early days of the Internet, but his fortune came years after Scott's death. The brothers were the first in their family ever to go to university.

Scott was on the cusp of a brilliant career. In 1983 he graduated with high honours from the prestigious California Institute of Technology (Caltech). Of his brother's time there, Steve Johnson said: 'He was the centre of attention. He was everyone's friend. At Caltech he was surrounded by other extraordinary people and they all realised he was more extraordinary, so everyone was in awe of Scott and he was such a gentle, wonderful, nice, easy-going person. He felt totally comfortable for the first time in his life.'

After Caltech, Scott headed to Cambridge in the United Kingdom, where he attended a lunch for foreign students and met his soon to be partner, who was at King's College. At the time of writing, the partner's name has been suppressed by the NSW Coroner. Scott went back to California in 1985 to begin his PhD at the University of California at Berkley. Along the way he worked at Harvard, and at Caltech's Jet Propulsion Laboratory on the Venus Project.

Professor John Donahue of Harvard University said: 'Scott Johnson was in some ways the stereotypical math genius – quiet, shy, introverted. But the exception is that he had deep levels of sweetness that don't go with the stereotype. Steve and Scott were closer than most brothers are. They'd gone through a lot together.'

Though the two were exceptionally close, it took Scott a while to tell his older brother he was gay. Steve recalled an evening when the two brothers were working together on a programming job in Los Angeles, and had taken a break around 3am to go for a walk. Scott talked about a relationship and was having trouble telling Steve about the person, with Steve thinking Scott had got his girlfriend pregnant – a fairly common, but challenging, issue of the time. However, Steve was 'shocked' when Scott told him the problem was not an impending addition to the family, but the gender of his love – 'It's not a girl,' he said. Sometimes even those close to you can deliver a surprise, and at that point Steve hadn't met an openly gay man. Steve's shock didn't last long, though, and shortly after this revelation the two headed to Europe during a university break and climbed the 4000-plus-metre high

Matterhorn in the Swiss Alps. During the trip, Steve found out that Scott had fallen for an Australian musician and he was missing him desperately. Scott subsequently moved to Australia to study for his PhD at the Australian National University in Canberra. His partner was working as a lecturer at the Canberra School of Music. Another two lucky people finding each other in a time of exceptional challenges.

Scott and his partner divided their time between Canberra and Sydney, where they stayed at the partner's family home in Lane Cove, sharing his childhood bedroom. Both were careful not to 'out' his partner to his family. Scott also came to Sydney on his own, staying with his partner's parents, to work on his PhD at Macquarie University.

While in Sydney, Scott mixed his study with socialising and quickly made friends. He was a good-looking blond man with an engaging smile, a quiet and unassuming demeanour; and being a Californian who'd travelled, he was a little exotic in the Sydney gay crowd. Scott made up for the years of long study and discovered the numerous temptations the city offered young gay men. The awareness of AIDS meant safe sex was an imperative, but it didn't impede a good time.

Sydney in the late 1980s was a city in which sex often preceded conversation, a glass of wine or a romantic dinner. The saunas such as Ken's of Kensington on Anzac Parade (on the former site of the Purple Onion), Kingsteam (named after King Street, Sydney where it began before moving to Oxford Street) and 253 (unsurprisingly at 253 Oxford Street), were packed with a mix of men – tradies, hospitality workers, judges, politicians and notable faces around town – and were discreet and clubby. The sex-on-premises venues did a similar roaring trade, though usually in the early hours of morning when the pubs, including the Albury and Oxford, closed and men's minds turned to matters other than another drink or the dance floor of the Midnight Shift. There were plentiful opportunities for sex, and all you had to do was pay the entry fee at the door. For operators such as Dawn and Roger-Claude, who jointly and severally owned saunas and sex-on-premises venues, they were rivers of gold – rudimentary décor that could be hosed out, low light that offered ambience and covered up the scruffy interiors, minimal staffing, and profits from the sale of accessories such as amyl nitrate.

For those keen on an all-over tan, and the prospect of a little engagement while sunning, Obelisk Beach near Mosman in the Sydney Harbour National Park was exceptionally popular. It offered a lovely beach, superb harbour views and the option of plenty of secluded pathways and sufficiently dense bushland. It was more popular with gay men than Reef Beach and lacked the Mossop factor.

For Scott, Sydney was an adventure. He was an avid bushwalker and would come back to Lane Cove with tales of where he'd been and the fauna and animals he'd seen. He'd done his research on what gay Sydney had on offer, hitting the venues of the then bustling and vibrant Oxford Street, with the Midnight Shift and its crowded downstairs bar, and even more crowded and sweaty dance floor upstairs, a favourite. In the days leading up to his death, he also visited Obelisk. Fidelity wasn't a notable character trait for many of the gay men of the time, and Scott was going with the flow. Scott's partner was aware that Scott had dalliances outside their relationship, and his partner had also dabbled. Some men discussed these issues up front and established ground rules, which failed quickly when opportunity, interest and alcohol or a mix of all three came into play. One long-term couple I knew had a rule that neither strayed in Sydney, but when travelling, as both did extensively, it was permissible. The folly of that rule became obvious when both brought the same young man, an exotic-looking sex worker they'd found while thumbing through the personal classified ads of the *Wentworth Courier*, in a time before the Internet and Grindr (the gay smart phone app designed to arrange trysts – or to chat, allegedly), back to their home while the other was travelling. When the callow youth remarked he'd been in the apartment before, a terse phone call to the man's travelling partner followed – after the hour-long booking was completed. The aggrieved partner missed the irony. In Scott's case the catalyst for the conversation was a dose of crabs that needed an explanation.

In the lead-up to his death, Scott had received fantastic news on his PhD. He had dazzled his professor when he'd spoken at a conference at the University of Sussex in July 1988 and the professor had visited him in Canberra to discuss the PhD. The professor described him as a 'gentle, highly principled and brilliant young man'. When Scott came up with a major contribution to solving a math problem, the professor told him 'this would suffice for a PhD'.

On 7 December 1988, Scott headed into the city and used an ATM in King Street; his brother Steve thought he was likely to have then headed toward Oxford Street. The following morning the sister of Scott's partner, who was also a psychiatric nurse, said she'd been heading out the door around five-thirty or six o'clock for an early shift and while in the kitchen had seen Scott's legs poking out of the bed in her brother's old room. She said, 'I was the last person to see him alive', which in hindsight was possibly incorrect, but it was that human reaction – was there something I should have noticed? Something I could have done? And all spurred on by the police assertion that Scott had committed suicide, and wasn't the victim of misadventure or foul play. When she got home around 3.15 that afternoon she noted the bedroom was neat and tidy, the way Scott always left it before returning to Canberra, which is what she thought he'd done.

Scott called his professor that morning to arrange their next meeting. The professor said of this conversation: 'We discussed the possibility of meeting that afternoon [a Thursday] or Friday but decided it could wait to Wednesday fourteenth of December. I confirmed he had enough already for his degree. He was looking forward to telling me some of his new ideas. This was not meant to be; I feel a great loss.' Steve Johnson said of his brother receiving the great news: 'To my mind, Scott put his pencil down, said, "I'm going to see my professor next week. This is Thursday; I'm going to take the weekend off."' If you were looking for someone at risk of suicide, Scott Johnson would be a highly unlikely contender. Scott spoke to a few friends and colleagues later that day, the last of them around 2pm.

What happened to Scott after that remains a mystery that just won't go away. The weather during the days was perfect, so anyone with a penchant for bushwalking and a little naked sunbathing with a spectacular ocean view would find a pleasant spot and discreet location near Blue Fish Point. Around 10am on Saturday 10 December, a sergeant stationed at the Army base at North Head – a short walk through the scrub to Blue Fish Point – had gone spear-fishing with one of his subordinates, who had brought his teenage son. It was a fine, hot morning, so instead of taking the tricky path rock-fishermen occasionally used to get to their favourite spots, they had driven to Fairy Bower and walked back along the rocky path below the cliff face, and about 200 metres north of the point the son saw a body on the rocks. The drop from the cliff top to the rock was around sixty metres.

According to a police statement, he pointed and said, in what sounds like police speak, 'Look, there's a dead person.' The statement went on to note that the men had stumbled upon the grisly sight of Scott's body, 'naked, deceased and that fragments of his body had been scattered'. The sergeant stayed with Scott while the man and his son made the long trek back along the rocks to Fairy Bower and then the short drive to Manly Police Station. The son raced in while his father parked their car and though the police were dubious at first, they changed rapidly when his father confirmed the story.

The sergeant walked his dog regularly on the cliff tops and knew the area well. He recalled the weather the night before had been stormy and with driving rain and a strong westerly wind, but in spite of the turbulent conditions he and his wife had walked the dog and hadn't seen anything suspicious around the Blue Fish Point area.

Constable Troy Hardie, a uniformed officer then with four years' police experience, caught the case and headed to the scene with Probationary Constable Sylvia Roux, with other police following. The two arrived around 10.45am and made their way down to where Scott's body was found. A paramedic who also arrived at the scene told them Scott had been in that spot for up to two days. Philip Flogel, the scientific officer for the district, photographed the body.

The Army sergeant assisted Constables Ludlow and Taplin, who had arrived on the scene, in a search of the cliff top. Under a tree, directly above where Scott's body had lain, they found a pile of his personal effects, including his Adidas shoes with a black felt tip pen, a watch, comb and key inside a pair of light blue trousers, a bone-coloured long sleeved shirt with a plastic sleeve in the top pocket containing a ten-dollar note, a cashcard from the Canberra Building Society, a student travel concession card in the name of Scott Johnson of Downer, ACT, and a pair of green underpants and white socks.

Scott's body was lifted from the rocks by the police helicopter at around 1.50pm, a sight I had witnessed about ten years earlier as a young constable seeing my first dead body. The man in that case had decided to end his life by jumping off a spot on the south-eastern tip of North Head – a straight drop down to the rocks 100 metres below. There was no chance of second thoughts for that poor man, and in those days, and at the time of Scott's death, there were no safety fences or, if the light was poor, any indicators of where the edge might be. Lifting the body using the helicopter was not an easy task, with updrafts of wind and rocky debris falling from the cliff face into the rotors, but it was safer and faster than using the men from the rescue squad and their ropes and assorted climbing paraphernalia.

After a doctor went through the formality of pronouncing life was extinct – the routine term – Scott was taken to the morgue below the Glebe Coroner's Court for the post-mortem, a legal requirement even though the massive injuries from the fall gave a pretty clear idea of what had killed him. The post-mortem also looks for evidence of recent sexual activity and blood toxicology for drugs, alcohol and poison. The process of examining a death is detailed, thorough and works to a set of requirements, but it didn't shed any light on how Scott ended up at the bottom of the cliff.

What happened at the scene was curious. A healthy young male found naked at the bottom of a cliff, and with his clothes folded neatly at the top of the cliff, should have stirred a few thoughts in the minds of the police, and certainly enough to call detectives – but surviving records have no sign of the local detectives being contacted. In policing, one of the first rules you learn is to cover your arse, and having your actions signed off by senior police or detectives was something police of the time would have done in most cases. Various scenarios should have come to mind. While it's popular to think people planning suicide will leave a note, most don't, and someone who commits suicide naked is unusual. Other alternatives should have been considered, such as misadventure, either on his own while sunbathing or in an interlude with someone during which he overbalanced and fell or the other participant turned violent. There was one other possibility: that Scott was overpowered either physically or by threat, forced to remove his clothes and then thrown off the cliff.

Flogel photographed the clothes, which were still damp from the previous night's rain, but the investigation of the surrounding area for signs of a scuffle, blood trails, more clothing, a bag – at the time they didn't know what Scott had been carrying, if anything – were rudimentary. Flogel's report noted 'a lack of identifiable tracks or clearings in the area around where the clothes were found'; and 'looked over the headland in the area above where the body was found and saw no sign of a struggle such as scuff marks or breakages to the cliff edge'.

Suicide was the decision, and looking at it nearly thirty years later, it appears to be a decision short on objective facts. Steve Johnson commented that in his view the police 'promptly airlifted

Scott's body to the morgue, labelling his death a suicide with only the most superficial of investigative effort'.

The police should have considered the recent history of attacks on gay men on the northern beaches, including in the Manly Police patrol. Ignorance is an excuse that doesn't float. The police community on the northern beaches was a close one. Transfers were frequent between 14 Division (Manly, Dee Why and Frenchs Forest) and 29 Division (Collaroy, Mona Vale and Avalon), and there were strong professional and social networks between detectives, uniformed police and the criminal-intelligence officers for both divisions on the northern beaches. Manly detectives had been involved in the arrest of the 'North Narra Boys' and other incidents over recent years in both their patrol and further north. A young, naked man at the bottom of the cliff in an area known to be popular with gay men should have set alarm bells ringing, but there was nothing in the police behaviour to suggest it did. Scott's death seems to have been treated as a straightforward suicide, but was it? Flogel was reported to have investigated 'hundreds of scenes of suspicious deaths over a six-year period', which could lead the reader to believe Midsomer had come to Sydney.

Back at Manly Police Station at 6pm, Constable Troy Hardie prepared his occurrence-pad entry, the document that records incidents of note at the station, and arranged the most important part of any death like this: the sad task of telling the next of kin. It was going to be a long day for police, who had started duty at 7am and expected to be done by 3pm. The Australian Federal Police headed out to Downer and, finding no-one home, spoke to the neighbours, who confirmed Scott was a Californian but they hadn't seen him for a few months. The police returned later and found his partner home – he'd been in Melbourne for a few days staying with his aunt and attending job interviews. Scott's partner drove through the night and on the morning of 11 December identified Scott's battered body. These are moments no-one will ever forget, and that last glimpse comes back to many of us deep into nights when sleep is elusive. I can still clearly remember the faces of murder and suicide victims forty years later.

Police formally recorded that the partner was 'a very good friend and flatmate' of Scott, who was a man of 'exceptional character' and 'high integrity'.

The partner told police Scott was vegetarian, 'did not smoke or drink and was the model of health' and didn't 'take any type of drug, including aspirin', and that Scott 'had a successful relationship with no known recent personal problems, psychological or behavioural difficulties'. The partner allegedly mentioned that Scott was possibly part of a group of people at high risk of HIV/AIDS infection, and made reference to a prior suicide attempt around five years before, but didn't elaborate.

At no time in his conversation with police did Scott's partner mention the word 'gay' or the real nature of their relationship. In America, Scott's brother Steve got the sad news. He told *Australian Story* in 2013: 'I got a message that Scott's body had been found at the bottom of a cliff. We were both crying by that point, and I asked how it happened. And by the time I got here about thirty-six hours later, the police had decided that it was a suicide. And from then on, the wonder about what happened to Scott has always been there. I didn't know whether [chokes up] my brother had chosen to leave us. I didn't know whether someone had pushed him. I didn't know whether he had slipped. I didn't know why we lost Scott.'

The sister of Scott's partner was also surprised and told *Australian Story* in 2013: 'Well, I was shocked, absolutely shocked. We couldn't understand, I couldn't understand how that could have happened. He was happy, he was fine.' She recalled talking to him about becoming an uncle: 'We were in the kitchen one morning, and he was beaming and very happy that there was a new niece in the family.'

Following the notification and identification, police move on to the paperwork, which includes preparation of the P79A Report to the Coroner, and statements and reports for the brief of evidence for the Inquest. In Scott's case, suspicious circumstances had been discarded and so Hardie wasn't required to attend the grisly business of a post-mortem. Had there been suspicious circumstances, detectives would have handled the case and one would have been at the post-mortem to observe and collect evidence for analysis.

Two days after Scott was found, Steve Johnson arrived in Australia, leaving his wife and recently born child back at home. He flew from Sydney to Canberra, where he met with Scott's partner, who Steve recalled urged him not to talk to the police and accept that 'Scott's gone, there is nothing we can do.' The two men drove to Sydney, Steve bursting with 'all the normal questions you get from watching cop shows on television'. What Steve wasn't about to get was the answers he was looking for.

He met with Hardie, who, Steve recalled, was 'very sorry I'd lost my brother, but the first thing he told me was this is where people go to jump, especially homosexuals'. Hardie then asked if Steve knew that Scott was gay, and he answered honestly. It was an odd conversation, held in the context of no evidence – then or now – that gay men were notably suicidal and preferred

Blue Fish Point to end their lives. Sydney's gay community was then focused around Darlinghurst and the upcoming Newtown area, and crossing the bridge for any reason was not a decision taken lightly.

In Steve's view, the police felt that once they had taken statements from Scott's partner and his professor, the investigation was done and dusted. It wasn't a situation Steve Johnson was prepared to accept without strong reasons. While police were sympathetic, Steve was struck by what he perceived as their lack of curiosity about how Scott ended up naked at the bottom of a cliff. Steve wanted to know more but had run into the immovable blue wall of the NSW Police. He said, 'I was dumbfounded by the NSW Police's certitude that Scott had committed suicide. They said he had tried suicide once before, atop the Golden Gate Bridge, and that there was no sign of foul play. They had all the facts wrong and had not investigated the case at all. Scott did not drink, smoke or take drugs; he was extremely health conscious. He had never been depressed in his whole life. There was simply no way that it was believable that he would take his own life.' Steve hadn't known of the alleged suicide attempt until police had told him it had been found during their investigations.

One thing about policing of the time, and a cultural quirk that still exists, is that though officers are compassionate and decent, there is unwillingness to have their actions questioned. To borrow that awful phrase much loved by government spin-doctors, 'open and transparent' is not something our police do well, and it's more like 'put up or shut up'.

Steve, who had no idea what a gay beat was, formed his own theories of Scott's last moments. 'He rode there with some friend, was my working hypothesis, I guess, they took their clothes off and then somehow Scott slipped or got pushed off. Now my theory is this guy [Scott] came here 'cause he'd heard of this really cool beat that was kind of rustic and he liked to hike, and it was dramatic 'cause there were these great cliffs.' Police, however, would formally deny they knew the place was a gay beat, a denial they repeated for a decade and something that would become a long-running contentious issue with the Johnson family. Steve was also curious that Scott's wallet, which he usually kept in his left back trouser pocket, hadn't been found.

Steve spent the first few nights in Sydney staying in the Lane Cove home of Scott's partner's parents, sleeping in the bed Scott had slept in during his visits to Sydney. Under the pillow he found a letter he had sent to Scott in late October, telling him of the birth of his first child. Scott's funeral was on 15 December, and a few days later, Steve left for home with a head full of questions and few answers. He said, 'I knew Scott couldn't have jumped, couldn't have jumped for so many reasons. Certainly wouldn't have left, wouldn't have done it without a clue.'

Back at the Harvard Kennedy School, Steve chatted with a student of his who'd been a detective at Scotland Yard for twenty years, and he recalled, 'He had never heard of a naked jumper . . . you don't take your clothes off to jump off a cliff.'

Steve took his suspicions and frustration to his professors, some of whom had political connections, and in Massachusetts that often meant a Kennedy. Steve's professor arranged for Senator Ted Kennedy to intervene and get some answers, and the request bounced down the line through political channels until it hit the desk of NSW Police Commissioner John Avery.

In police terms, the Kennedy request was likely to turn into a 'blue' if not handled quickly, competently and decisively. The likely progress of the request was from Avery to a senior officer in headquarters, then to the Superintendent in charge of D District who had responsibility for a large slice of northern Sydney including Manly. He'd take one look at the file, mutter something likely to contain an expletive or two, then ring his officer in charge at Manly and explain that a file was coming and to 'pull your finger out' getting it finalised. The file finally landed on the desk of Paul Hulme, a senior detective at Manly.

Hulme, when I knew him back in 1979, was an avid smoker with a rumpled appearance and easy-going disposition. He gave the file to Detective Sergeant Doreen Cruickshank to handle. Cruickshank was from a farming family in Gilgandra in north-western New South Wales and joined the police in 1971. She spent her first fifteen months giving road-safety lectures to school children and was then one of the handful of women accepted for criminal-investigation training. We worked together at Mona Vale around 1980–81 and I admit a small bias. When a colleague committed suicide with his service revolver in our office, I was given the task of breaking the news to his parents. Delivering a death message is one of the hardest jobs a copper ever has to do, and in this instance even harder because the dead man was both a good friend and colleague. I remember sitting in the car, taking a few breaths before driving, when Doreen got in beside me and simply said, 'You shouldn't have to do this on your own.' Writing this decades later brings a bit of moisture to the eyes. Doreen was a competent and honest investigator, and having a woman work on the Johnson case, in their thinking anyway, added a hint of empathy.

Hulme's instructions to her, I fancy, have never been canvassed. The prospect of a detective overturning the original decision of suicide was remote. On 19 January 1989 Detective Sergeant Doreen Cruickshank became the officer in charge of the investigation into the death of Scott Johnson.

Her investigation was meticulous and she quickly ruled out the possibility of foul play involving his partner, who was definitely in Melbourne for a job interview and staying with his aunt. In an interview with the partner, he told her of Scott's alleged suicide attempt. He recalled that around 3 September 1985, Scott phoned him and told him he had 'made an unsuccessful attempt to jump to his death from the Golden Gate Bridge in San Francisco'. Cruickshank said 'the reason was he had contracted HIV/AIDS and was distressed for himself and for their relationship'.

In an investigation like this, the partner's information was a 'eureka' moment for Cruickshank: she had been offered a prior suicide attempt in a similar manner – jumping off a precipice with no opportunity for second thoughts. There is no record of the partner mentioning if Scott had been naked at the time – a scene that even in liberal San Francisco would have attracted a crowd – or how a person can make an 'unsuccessful attempt' to jump from the bridge. Scott also wasn't HIV positive.

Cruickshank now had what she believed was the key piece of evidence for her investigation, so all she had to do was tidy up, make a few inquiries, prepare for the Coroner's inquest and, most importantly, complete her report that would head back up the line, to be read and initialled by increasingly important police, until it got to Avery, and get the politicians off his back.

The Coroner's inquest was held in 1989. According to police reports, the Coroner Derrick Hand 'acknowledges Scott's family would naturally find a suggestion of suicide upsetting and unsatisfactory but that no other conclusion was able to be drawn on the evidence available before him'. He described the investigation as 'full and proper'. Steve Johnson, who'd flown in for the inquest and was legally represented, didn't give evidence – he was on the other side of the world when Scott died and arrived in Australia two days later, so he had little if any evidence that could be of use. Constables Hardie and Ludlow gave evidence at the inquest, but Roux and Flogel weren't called; instead, their statements were tendered to the court, which is not unusual in cases such as this – their statements were sufficient unless there was a need for cross-examination.

The Coroner considered the police evidence on the placement of Scott's clothing and no apparent damage to it presumably from an attack, absence of any signs of a struggle or of any evidence to indicate Scott wasn't alone, and said, 'There is no evidence implicating anybody at all in the death of the deceased, and there is no real evidence as to why the deceased would take his own life.'

At this point the Coroner considered the alleged earlier attempted suicide apparently based on HIV/AIDS, then broadly mused on the nature of suicides, motivations and the many who don't leave notes. In the absence of any evidence to the contrary, the Coroner had his rubber stamp poised over the police view of the death of Scott Johnson. He found: 'The deceased, between the 8th and 10th day of December 1988 at North Head, Manly, north of Blue Fish Point in the State of New South Wales, died of the effects of multiple injuries sustained then and there when he jumped from the top to the rocks below with the intention of taking his own life.' It was a decision the Coroner must have been satisfied to make, though he did have the option to leave the case as an open finding. However, it's likely the evidence, or lack of it from the cliff top, and allegation of a prior suicide attempt, nailed the Coroner's view.

Steve Johnson said of the inquest: 'Hand bought the police argument hook, line and sinker. I was in utter disbelief that the police and the Coroner would base their conclusions on so little thought about Scott and what might have actually happened.' He went on: 'Thus relying on nothing more than a series of stale stereotypes strung together, Coroner Hand ruled that Scott must have committed suicide because he was gay, introverted, highly intelligent and socially awkward. He also threw in the nonsense about the Golden Gate Bridge and a few other titbits, and that was it. The NSW Police said they were done.'

Steve Johnson flew back to graduate school in Boston feeling 'that a terrible mistake had been made' and that 'we had all failed Scott and there was a lot more to his death than we were seeing'. The two trips to Australia had ravaged his finances as well. 'As a graduate student with a wife and daughter, the cost the trips and an inquest attorney wiped out my savings. I could not afford an investigator or experts or anyone else who might persuade the police or the Coroner to take a more careful look at the actual facts.'

What no-one, including Steve Johnson, knew at the time was that Scott's death wouldn't be consigned to an entry in official paperwork or a sad memory for those who loved him. Steve Johnson wasn't prepared to let his questions go unanswered. In 2005, with stories running in the *Sydney Morning Herald*, Steve Johnson began his own investigation and this time he had the resources to fund it. The investigation wouldn't deliver answers about what happened that day but would raise more questions about what police might have done and offer credible alternative scenarios to suicide.

Around six months after Scott's death, a man was viciously attacked at a gay beat in Surry Hills, and his assailants may have been members of the NSW Police. However, just like Scott's death, this attack would lie dormant for decades, until publicity about Scott and other cases stirred old memories.

CHAPTER 12

WRONG PLACE, RIGHT NUMBER

Alan Rosendale remembers snippets of Friday, 5 May 1989 quite clearly because he's been able to refresh his memory from the diary he's always kept, and he still has the book written in neat longhand.

Alan was thirty-two years old and working as a manager at the Waldorf Apartments in Liverpool Street in the city, which involved shift work. He was gay, comfortable with his sexuality and enjoying a busy social life and the Oxford Street scene. In the diary he wrote: 'Finish work and home to more washing, drank vino and watch my TV shows, then to bed. Missed meeting at work. Up and watched TV with Shane [flatmate] then to the Oxford for a few, me to the club when pretty pissed not much happening, lots of people but tourists. To the Taxi and pick up trade. Begin to walk home but never got there, assaulted by a gang of about six guys, police and ambulance arrive and me off to St Vincent's.' Friends brought the diary to Alan while he lay in bed at St Vincent's recovering from a broken nose, shattered front teeth requiring a denture of six teeth across the front top of his mouth, bad bruising all over his body and severe bruising to his head, all of which kept him in hospital for a week, and off work until 24 May.

What Alan meant by 'Taxi' was the Taxi Club, formally known as The Grosvenor Club that opened in the mid fifties as a place where cab drivers could get their cars fixed and have a meal. By 1989 it was popular as a last-stop venue for a drink when many other places were closing; or for those who had started early and were fairly pissed, which meant its eclectic charms of large drag queens, assorted tough crims, drunk coppers, big Islander bouncers, poker machines that seldom paid out and a mix of gay and straight people in various states of disrepair was appealing; or it was on the way home, and 'one more won't hurt', and of course that one more did hurt. Alan recalled 'pick up trade' meant he'd met someone there and had a chat.

When his money ran out Alan decided it was time to head home to Rennie Street, Redfern, about a ten-minute walk down South Dowling Street. He walked south along Flinders Street to South Dowling Street. He said, 'I'm a creature of habit and I would have crossed over to the side of the road opposite the Taxi Club and walked down. When I got to about Bennett Street or Prospect Street I decided to cross over and go into Moore Park. I'd had a few drinks and I would have thought, "Oh well, I'll just pop over and see if there's anyone there."' It was a gay beat at the toilets and gardens at the tip of Moore Park near the tennis court.

The beat was well known around Sydney and very popular in spite of the occasional attacks on the men using it. John Stapleton, in the *Sydney Morning Herald* on 27 October 1988, wrote: 'Inside the toilets at Moore Park, a well-known meeting place for homosexuals, are the words "Slave wants Master". Next to this "poofs are dead" and outside in capitals "BEWARE BASHERS".' The article talked about the increase in bashings of gay men as the weather warmed, and of the seven bashings in Moore Park, two in Green Park (Darlinghurst), and two in Rushcutters Bay Park since January 1988 and observed: 'Police and gay groups agree that many bashings at any time of year go unreported.' Gary Cox of the Gay and Lesbian Rights Lobby told Stapleton, 'Many members of teenage gangs are insecure about their own sexuality, which is probably the major reason for assaults on gay men. You are seen as a real man if you go out and bash a poofter . . . Gays are one of the most hated sections of the community. While racist comments are no longer socially acceptable, derogatory comments about gays still get widespread approval.'

The article quoted Sergeant Gately of the Police Gay and Lesbian Liaison unit saying, 'we want people to report bashings' and 'there are 12 000 police, and there is obviously a range of attitudes, but amongst the upper echelons the attitude towards gays has become much more tolerant'. His sincerity wasn't enough to triumph over years of mistrust, but it was a start.

In the mid 1980s, when I was a detective at Internal Affairs, I was involved in an investigation of an incident at the same beat where Alan Rosendale was attacked in May 1989. Our victim, a middle-aged gay man on his way home from a night out, was inside the toilet block waiting to see who might amble by. The place was dimly lit, seedy, and with the strong scent of disinfectant that didn't quite mask the other odours. It was surrounded by a grove of trees and shrubs, which gave some cover from the road and provided a place for those who were a bit shy, as one man told me, or who liked their encounters outdoors in the fresh air.

In a beat, you need to be alert, both watching and listening, and he knew there was trouble coming his way when he heard a deep male voice bellow, 'Faggot!' as a big lump of a man ran into the toilet and started to belt him with what he thought was a short bat of some kind. The attack was brief and brutal, leaving the victim bruised but fortunately not seriously injured. He struggled to his feet and followed his assailant at a distance and saw the man get into a plain-looking sedan. He had the presence of mind to take down the registration details, and the next day reported his assault to his local police. It didn't take long for the alarm bells to start ringing when the registered owner of the car was the NSW Police. A 'flick pass' followed and it landed on the desk I shared with my senior partner at Internal Affairs.

First step was to interview the man – years later I can't recall his name – who told us he'd been asking around the community's very efficient grapevine, and heard the attack he'd suffered wasn't the first. We were walking in a political minefield and were careful to make sure our victim was properly looked after and reassured we were taking his allegations seriously, and that he wouldn't end up a victim for the second time. We didn't expect the man to trust us – there had been too much bleak history.

The linking factors of the attacks were the brevity and frenzy of the attack, and the scream of 'faggot' at the beginning. The man could also provide a description of his assailant: tall and quite solid, with a moustache a bit like Tom Selleck, then a gay pin-up in his long-running *Magnum PI* series. Detective work is more perspiration than inspiration, but I didn't break into a sweat tracking the car to Darlinghurst Police Station, which was followed by a call to the officer in charge to let him know we were about to drive up – police of the time seldom walked if they could drive, even though we were only a few blocks away – and what we were looking for. In this case it was the rosters of who was working that night and the diaries for each car, which would tell us who was driving, where and when. As we walked into the station's charge room, a senior constable with a large build and moustache was behind the counter. In a police force where beards were forbidden – less for someone to grab onto in a brawl, was the reason given – and moustaches were rare, it didn't take the skills of Sherlock Holmes to guess we'd found our man. The startled look on his face confirmed our suspicions.

Within an hour we had the documentary evidence we needed along with a tearful confession. In some instances it should have given us some pleasure, but not this one. It was obvious the man had some serious mental-health issues and, equally obvious, sexual-identity issues. A psychiatric professional confirmed our amateur view – the man needed therapy and medication – which brought us to the moment when we had to recommend what was to be done with him. He could have been charged with assault, the penalty for which could have been mitigated by his psychiatric condition, or we could have him dismissed from the force and get him some help. It wasn't a fait accompli, and we talked to the victim, who took the compassionate view. The constable was dismissed and took his therapy seriously and medication religiously. I met him years later and he'd turned his life around and was a happy and comfortably gay man, leading his life openly and working hard to help a community in the depths of the AIDS crisis.

Alan Rosendale continued his story, telling me he walked to the Moore Park beat. 'I was only there for a matter of minutes, and I didn't see anyone else around. After a minute or so I heard a male voice say, "There's one, get him!" The voice was definitely an Australian male and he was yelling aggressively when he said it.' Alan saw that the man was part of a group and they were armed with what he thought were 'bits of wood'. He continued: 'I remember thinking, "I'm outta here or I'm dead!"' Alan ran through the wooded area and jumped down the ledge to the footpath on the side of South Dowling Street and ran across the street. When he was near to the Langton Clinic he slowed down and thought he was 'in the clear and they would leave me alone and I'd be safe'. He was wrong.

Alan stumbled and fell just before he got to the footpath and thought, 'Oh my god I've fallen and they're going to get me.' The group of men, perhaps up to six of them aged in their twenties and thirties, were right behind him and they began to strike him with what he had thought were 'bits of wood'. 'They were all assaulting me. I remember feeling hits to my head and body. I saw the headlights of a car pulling up on the road and then I remember seeing the car drive past me slowly. I thought, "thank god, someone's here, they'll stop".' He thinks he then passed out. The next thing he remembered was being in St Vincent's Hospital on a stretcher in casualty, with police asking him questions, but he has no recollection of the questions or his answers. He said, 'I vaguely recall seeing a copper in casualty, but I was in emergency until mid morning and unconscious for most of it. I remember my flatmate came to see me about two-thirty and I was dopey for most of Saturday with terrible headaches.'

As he lay in his hospital bed for a week, literally black and blue all over, he thought the police would come back to interview him. They didn't.

The routine in cases like Alan's is for it to be followed up by detectives who would come on the day shift, so he was quite right to expect a visit to his bedside at St Vincent's. The only surviving record the police have been able to find of this case was a 'Crime Information Report' submitted on 6 May 1989. The report notes the attack was 'assault occasioning actual bodily harm', misspells Alan as 'Allan' and notes his date of birth as '10.12.43' instead of the correct date, which was a different day and fourteen years later. The report notes: 'The victim was walking home when he was attacked by four young persons possibly skinheads. He was punched to the ground then kicked. He lost consciousness for a short time. The victim was unable to provide any description of his assailants. The area where the assault occurred is one where there are frequent assaults which usually involve homosexual persons who particularly frequent the park opposite.'

Alan doesn't have any recollection of the conversation but years later was sure skinheads weren't involved. From my recollection, as someone living and working in the area at the time, 'skinheads' weren't a group commonly roaming around and attacking men in public toilets.

Alan is a robust bloke who understood how close he came to being maimed or killed, but he fully recovered from the assault and put it behind him. He said, 'It was a time when the community was full of guilt and shame. I thought the police would come to see me but they didn't, and I didn't want to cause trouble. I thought, "I'm alive and that's fine".' He said friends came to visit and all brought flowers, but no-one asked if he had been to the police.

But Alan's story didn't end here. Twenty-four years later he was reading an article about gay bashings and murders in Sydney during the eighties and nineties. Part of the article was a witness talking about an assault near the Moore Park beat in 1989, and Alan thought the man was describing the attack on him.

CHAPTER 13

GROSSLY INADEQUATE AND SHAMEFUL

Ross Warren disappeared on 22 July 1989 and his body has never been found. Like Alan Rosendale's case, the investigation by police would become the focus of questions, but again with few useful answers.

Ross was a good-looking blue-eyed young man with a face loved by the often-brutal television camera. He was twenty-five years old, reading the news on WIN TV in Wollongong and had a promising career in television ahead of him. He was adopted as a baby by an affluent Gold Coast family, and grew up with an older brother and sister. By mid high school, Ross had decided television, not university, was where his future lay. At nineteen he got his first job as a cameraman in Lismore in northern New South Wales, but it didn't take long for him to swap sides of the camera. What followed was a typical apprenticeship of many starters in the Australian media at the time, working in country television stations as a jack-of-all-trades, reporting on the weather, local events and news.

Ross worked in Mount Isa and Wagga Wagga until 1987 when he was spotted and offered a major step up the ladder as weatherman and weekend newsreader at WIN. He was hardworking, dedicated, popular and talented. But what Ross didn't broadcast was that he was gay. He'd had one close call when arrested at a beat in Southport on the Gold Coast, but fortunately his case had slipped through the court without being noticed by the local newspaper.

In the Australian media of the time, being gay wasn't a career-enhancing move. You lived your life discreetly and kept quiet about your sexuality. Ross kept clear of the few bars in Wollongong where gay men met up. Some of his colleagues knew of his sexuality, but it wasn't information for public consumption. He lived quietly, and had just given up sharing a flat and moved into a one-bedroom apartment on the ground floor of an old building in Smith Street, North Wollongong. Ross was lacking in domestic skills, so living on his own worked well.

Every second weekend, he drove up to Sydney where there was little risk of being 'outed' and he could have some fun. On Friday, 21 July 1989, he finished work at the station after the evening news bulletin, then pointed his chocolate brown Nissan Pulsar toward Sydney. He arrived at his friend Craig Ellis's house in Albert Street, Redfern, then a rough part of Sydney, around 8.30pm and settled in with Craig and his boyfriend Paul for pizza and a few drinks. Around 11pm, Ross headed out to Oxford Street, leaving Craig and Paul to their quiet night at home. Ross was wearing well-washed jeans that were chic at the time, a white turtleneck and black sports coat. The bitchy Sydney queens, who were out in strength in those days, may have whispered that Ross looked 'very Gold Coast' with the turtleneck and blazer on one so young.

Ross had parking karma that night, finding a space beside the law courts in Taylor Square. Outside the Oxford Hotel he met Phillip Rossini, a friend from Wollongong who also worked at WIN and was up in Sydney for a weekend of fun. The Oxford was favoured by older men who tended to wear flannelette or checked shirts. Younger men in tight T-shirts preferred the glitter, shirtless barmen and drag shows of the Albury just two blocks east. Above the more macho ground-floor bar of the Oxford was Gilligan's, the most stylish bar on the strip and named after the character played by Bob Denver in the US sit-com *Gilligan's Island.* The bleak wedge of park across the road with a few unhappy-looking palm trees was known as Gilligan's Island.

Ross and Phillip had a few drinks upstairs, with Ross drinking light beer and mineral water – he wasn't a big drinker and was mindful he had to drive later. The bar was packed as usual, but you could drink literally cheek by jowl with some of the best-looking men in Sydney, many of whom weren't as abstemious – the most popular drink was the Long Island Iced Tea, a lethal mix of tequila, rum, gin, triple sec and vodka. One was good; two was great; and three, well, good luck. If you had too much and wisely left your car in the Darlinghurst of those days, there was a fair chance it wouldn't be there the next morning. Stealing cars was a popular way to get home from the bars and nightclubs of nearby Kings Cross. Gay men and their cars were easy prey.

After Gilligan's, the pair did the traditional Oxford Street stroll, bypassing the dying days of disco on offer at the Midnight Shift, and heading to the Exchange Hotel, once owned by Dawn O'Donnell and Roger-Claude Teyssedre. Around 2.15am, Ross walked Phillip back to his car, with the two talking about the possibility of going to a dance party at the Hordern Pavilion the next night. With Phillip in his car, Ross walked back to the Pulsar that was parked close by. Phillip watched his friend depart but was intrigued when Ross didn't head for Redfern, but rather drove east along Oxford Street. Phillip recalled that Ross was 'in a good frame of mind and did not appear worried or depressed in any way'. Phillip was the last person who will admit to seeing Ross Warren alive.

Ross, with a life lived discreetly in country towns and more recently in Wollongong, was no stranger to gay beats. It was quick, easy and anonymous and ideal for other men with similar issues, and unlike sex-on-premises venues or a sauna, it was free. It was Friday night, he'd had a few drinks and mingled in the bars and like many blokes, gay or straight, his penis was doing the planning rather than his brain. Ross knew the cliff-top beat that ran from South Bondi through Marks Park to Tamarama well, and it was where he'd met Craig, his host for the weekend, around fourteen months before. He parked the Pulsar in Kenneth Street, Bondi near Marks Park.

On the cold, windy and desolate stretch of coastal cliff that was Marks Park, Ross Warren disappeared. It's likely that this location was where Gilles Mattaini disappeared a few years before.

At a civilised hour in the morning, Craig Ellis got out of bed, walked through his house and noted his guest hadn't returned from his night out – not unusual in Sydney's gay world where young men got lucky in the early hours of the day and spent a hazy few minutes in the morning trying to remember where they were and whom they were with. However, by the afternoon Craig was concerned. Ross hadn't come home and he hadn't called. Craig called Phillip, who told him he'd last seen Ross heading east a little after 2am. On dusk, Craig called the police, who told them they'd need to wait a little longer before the police would take a formal missing-persons report. Police are worldly and know that a young man can disappear for a day then re-emerge, often the worse for wear.

By 5pm on Sunday the alarm bells were ringing because Ross hadn't arrived at WIN to present the evening's news bulletin. It was something the diligent and punctual young man wouldn't do unless something serious had happened to prevent him from calling or getting there. Craig and Paul went to the Paddington Police Station and reported Ross as missing – under the circumstances police didn't demur. Constable Robinson prepared a Crime Information Report, listing Ross as a 'missing person' and noting: 'He is quite responsible and there are concerns for his safety and he is not the type of person not to notify work or his friends as to what he is doing.'

The two then went for a drive around the places they knew Ross liked, trying to find his car. Their first destination was Bondi, and they followed the web of narrow roads around the headland near the beat where Craig and Ross had met, and found Ross's car in Kenneth Street. They drove quickly back to Paddington and told police of their find, and police had some worrying news – the body of a young man had been found that afternoon in the water to the north of Bondi. What neither expected was a trip to the morgue at Glebe, in a police car.

However, the body at the morgue wasn't Ross. Hope returned, but Ross was still missing. To compound the growing mystery, Ross didn't call his mother Kay on the Gold Coast that Sunday night, and he was as regular as clockwork. The next morning she got a call from WIN wondering if she'd heard from her son.

Her next call was to the police and eventually to the officer in charge of the investigation into Ross's disappearance, Detective Sergeant Ken Bowditch. He had served at the squads of the CIB including the Drug Squad, and was one of the detectives involved in the investigation into the attempted murder of their colleague Mick Drury in 1984.

The Bowditch investigation didn't swing into action quickly. Both Paul and Craig took time off work to undertake some inquiries of their own and returned to Marks Park on the Monday morning, where they found Ross's car still in the same parking spot. It's surprising the car hadn't been towed to a secure holding yard and examined for any evidence that may have shed some light on the disappearance. The two men then did a canvass of local houses and the home units that overlook the park to see if anyone had seen anything, and then searched the park. On a rough staircase down to the rocks at Mackenzies Bay, on the southern side of the headland park, Craig spotted something silver glinting in the morning sun.

In a pocket in the rocks below the cliff and just above the waterline he found Ross's car keys on their distinctive brass key ring. They found a phone box and called the police. The call stirred police a little and they finally arrived and did their own canvass and search of the park, assuring Paul and Craig that the Water Police and the police helicopter would join the search. When police searched Ross's car they found his grey leather wallet that held $77.31, the usual receipts and cards, and an ANZ Bank transaction record dated 21 July for the withdrawal of $300.

Missing Persons circulated the story to the media and the public in a release stating, 'Ross was last seen driving his vehicle east on Oxford Street towards Paddington about 2am on 22 July 1989. Extensive inquiries were conducted by police whereby Ross's vehicle was located in the vicinity of Marks Park, Bondi on the morning of 24 July 1989. Ross failed to attend work, and family and friends have not heard from him. This behaviour is totally out of character for him. Grave fears are held for his safety.'

Seventy-two hours after he was last seen alive, Ross Warren had become news, with the *Daily Telegraph* on 26 July 1989 claiming 'Murder Fears For TV Weatherman' and Wollongong's *Illawarra Mercury* of the same day running the headline, 'TV Star Murder Fear'.

Not all the media attention was flattering. As journalists dug deeper into a story made for the tabloids, they found Ross's Queensland arrest. The likely source was an occurrence-pad entry at Paddington Police Station. As part of their routine inquiries police had done a criminal-records check and found that Ross had been arrested on 13 June 1985 for an 'act of gross indecency' in a Southport toilet. The tabloid articles included stock footage of Oxford Street frolics and became the backdrop of the story. Ross was posthumously outed.

Ross's parents, Kay and Alan, arrived on the Wednesday morning and spoke to police at Paddington, before heading to Wollongong to be present when Ross's home was searched. All they found was evidence confirming that Ross was lacking in domestic skills. Greg Callaghan in his book *Bondi Badlands* wrote of the contrast between the zeal of the Wollongong officers who'd thoroughly searched Ross's home, taken photographs and dusted for fingerprints, and the Sydneysiders who had failed to fingerprint either the car or its keys and whose interest in the case 'seemed to have stalled, if indeed it had ever really kick-started'. An appeal to the public for information didn't yield anything. A subsequent investigation into the actions, or lack thereof, by the Sydney team found no record of specialists being called to fingerprint Ross's car or keys, nor was there any record of the Water Police or police helicopter being called out to help the search.

What could have been treated as a possible homicide inquiry wasn't, and within a week the so-called investigation was nearly over. Given the history of gay-hate crimes around Marks Park that were either reported or part of the intelligence gathered in each police patrol and kept locally (and shared with the criminal intelligence-specialist unit in the city) to aid investigations – these were things like time, date and place of observations of cars and people; intelligence from criminal sources and so on – it was disturbing that Bowditch didn't treat Ross Warren's disappearance as a possible murder. By his own admission, he knew the area was a gay beat, but that didn't seem to move him to look seriously at the question of foul play.

Bowditch finalised his investigation on the morning of 28 July 1989, with a lengthy occurrence-pad entry at Paddington Police Station, in which he stated: 'Investigating police are of the opinion that the missing person has fallen into the ocean in some manner and it is anticipated that in the near future his body will surface and be recovered. I am not able to offer any explanation as to how he would have fallen into the water, only that the area near where the keys were located is a treacherous rock formation which at the present time is secreting a lot of water and moisture from recent rains.' He finished by saying 'further inquiries are continuing', but what they were remain a mystery.

In his final report on the case on 19 August 1989, Bowditch reiterated his earlier comments from the occurrence pad and added, 'There is nothing to suggest that Ross Warren's disappearance was the result of foul play or a deliberate ploy on his part to disappear. He was highly regarded by his employers and amongst his friends, and our inquiries revealed that he appeared to enjoy a fruitful and happy lifestyle.' This largely discounted the suicide theory they'd had as probable until the lack of a note and the positives from Ross's friends and peers became apparent – a contrast to the attitude of police investigating Scott Johnson's death. Bowditch didn't offer any theories as to why he thought a twenty-five-year-old man on his way home from a night out would take a six-kilometre detour in the opposite direction, park his car near a well-known gay beat and then make his way down a treacherous cliff path in the middle of a winter night.

On the first anniversary of the disappearance, an anonymous caller rang the Wollongong Police Station and said Ross was alive and living in South Australia with a man called Anton Astone. Constable Robinson, who had taken the initial report of the disappearance, located Astone in Western Australia. He was interviewed and denied knowing Ross and said he hadn't been in New South Wales for two years. Robinson was thorough and checked with South Australia Police, who couldn't find any record of Ross being in their state. In February 1991, a security officer on a payroll escort job in Bondi allegedly saw Ross at a 'homosexual strip joint or pick-up joint in the Bondi area' according to the police-intelligence report. The security guard, who didn't mention why he was in the establishment, told police he'd walked up to the man and said, 'I know you! You're the fellow off Channel 4 who's gone missing,' to which he alleged the man said, 'Get lost. I have my reasons, now get out of here.' The police decided the security guard wasn't trustworthy.

Bowditch later gave evidence in the 2003 coronial inquest, saying: 'I don't know what happened to Ross Warren. As far as I know, unless there is other evidence that I'm not aware of, he is still a missing person. There was always a possibility he had been murdered. But it was not my belief at the time.' One unnamed witness at the inquest gave evidence of the bitter reality of a view held by the gay community of the time: 'If there was a homosexual assault or a murder it wouldn't get the same privilege as a heterosexual assault or murder.'

The Coroner had a clear view on the investigation, describing it as 'grossly inadequate and shameful'. It was Ross's mother Kay who never gave up believing her son may have been murdered, and it was her persistent letter-writing to police that finally pushed them to review the case, and with a dramatically different result.

CHAPTER 14

ONE MORE TIME

The disappearance of Ross Warren from Marks Park didn't impact the traffic at the beat and nor did an article by journalist Paul Paech in the gay newspaper *Star Observer* headlined, 'Poofter bashing or first-degree murder'. In the edition of 17 November 1989, Paech wrote: 'In Australia, poofter bashing has usually been regarded as an amusing, childish and essentially innocent sport. Rumour has it that our esteemed police force has even indulged in a bit of it from time to time.

'For most people, the death of South Australia's Dr George Duncan was just "unfortunate", amounting to little more than a sad accident caused by a few well-meaning chaps being a bit careless because they'd had a few too many drinks.

'But now, after AIDS, poofter bashing has turned into something more sinister, something that leaves people with more than a few bruises and a few broken bones and the odd shattered notion about being gay. Today, poofter bashing amounts to first-degree wilful murder. AIDS means that people must now accept that most men really enjoy having sex, and that – one time or another – some of them are likely to do it not just with women but (gasp) with other men. And all the laws in the world won't stop them from doing it.' The last sentence was a dig at Queensland and Tasmania who were slow to get the decriminalisation message. The Sunshine State waited until 1990 and Tasmania 1997.

As summer approached the numbers of men using beats grew. It was busy, fun and if you were careful you'd be okay; at least that was the theory. The beat users, both regular and inquisitive one-off visitors, took what they thought was a calculated risk and at a time when many had more pressing issues to deal with, like the health of their partners and friends, escaping for just half an hour was enough sometimes.

John Russell was the antithesis of Ross Warren. He'd grown up in Bondi in the old family home in Ocean Street, just a short walk from the beach, shops and local pubs. The Russells were solid, working-class Bondi locals; they surfed, climbed around the rocky headlands and, in a nod to their parents' passion for ballroom dancing, learned that art form at a time when disco was king. One of John's early jobs was as a barman at Charlie Brown's in Pitt Street, then a popular spot with a largely gay clientele. He'd been on Oxford Street with a few mates the night of the first Mardi Gras parade but hadn't joined in the march that ended so badly with beatings and arrests. Over the next few years he worked as a barman at Patches, the gay nightclub owned by Dawn and Roger on the site of what had once been the infamous 33 Club, a large illegal casino favoured by the city's elite including Frank and Kerry Packer, and at Tropicana, which was the forerunner of the Midnight Shift. These were Sydney's premier gay nightclubs.

As he grew close to his thirtieth birthday, John took a step back from the frenzy of the gay scene and got a job at the BP service station in Rose Bay, and as a maintenance man at Rose Bay primary school. It meant he could spend more time with his recently divorced brother Peter and his young son Alan, and keep an eye on his grandfather who getting quite frail. They were all living under the same roof, and John relished his role in Alan's life. In his spare time, he coached the rugby league and soccer teams at Double Bay and Rose Bay primary schools. Socialising involved the occasional trip to Oxford Street or a beer with mates at the Bondi Hotel.

In September 1989, John's grandfather died, and their old family home was put on the market, so the boys moved into a three-bedroom apartment in Rose Bay, along with Peter's partner Donna. It was a temporary measure for John. With a $100 000 inheritance from his grandfather he'd bought a kit home to build on his father's property at Wollombi on the edge of the Hunter Valley wine country. John was going to give the rat race up completely and planned to start work on the house in late November. His future could not have been brighter.

On Wednesday, 22 November 1989, John had his bags packed and was ready to leave two days later, after a couple of farewell drinks with friends. Wednesday was beers at the Bondi Hotel with mates; Thursday, dinner and more drinks at the Waverley Legion Club; and then on Friday his father Ted was driving down to collect his son.

As planned for the Wednesday night, John went for drinks and dinner with his closest friend Peter Redmile at the Bondi Hotel. The two had known each other for thirteen years, starting with a brief affair that turned into a strong friendship – a very gay Sydney arrangement. Peter had lived occasionally with the Russell family over the years and caught up with Johnno, as he called him, a couple of times a week. Peter came to the apartment and then they walked to the hotel, getting there around 7pm. They talked about John's plan to build the house at Wollombi, do some travelling around Australia, and how he'd like to help Peter get into the Sydney property market by lending him ten to fifteen thousand dollars to help with a deposit. They 'reckoned there were happy times ahead'.

It was a serious night of drinking, with them having around twelve to fifteen middies of Powers beer. John shouted dinner and the drinks. Around 11pm, Peter left to catch a bus back to Darlinghurst, and John remained in the bar talking to one of the barmaids.

John didn't go home. Instead he headed toward the beat on the cliffs between South Bondi and Tamarama, which included Marks Park. John knew the place could be dangerous at night, and though of slim build and 175 centimetres tall, he'd done judo and boxing training and could look after himself. He'd also had a run-in with bashers in Darlinghurst and was alert to the dangers.

Stories from local people who weren't keen to make formal statements had it that around 11.45pm a man fitting John's description – a short-ish, slim man in torn jeans and a red top – was seen on the walkway that runs around the cliff tops near Mackenzies Bay to the south of Marks Park. The night was a quiet one, with few people out. Just before midnight one man heard yelling but couldn't discern what was being said. The man, who didn't report the incident to police, was probably hearing the last cries of John Russell as he was overpowered by thugs and hurled over the cliff. John wouldn't celebrate his bright future, or his thirty-second birthday on 28 November.

Around 10am the next day, Neville Smith, a personal trainer taking a break between clients and grabbing some fresh air on a beautiful warm morning, was out near Marks Park. His morning's peace was shattered when he walked down some stairs from Kenneth Street just to the north of the park, to join the walkway to Bondi, then down some rough stairs to the rock ledge near the water where you usually found fishermen or the occasional sunbather. Instead, he saw the battered body of a man in a red long-sleeved jumper, blue jeans and black gym boots, face-down in an indentation in the rocks, with some coins nearby and a crushed Peter Stuyvesant pack – John's preferred brand. As Neville got closer he saw that the red jumper was raised up exposing some of the man's torso and there was blood pooled beneath him. He clambered toward the body and checked to see if the man was breathing or if there was a pulse, but there wasn't. He left the dead man's side and climbed back up the cliff to a block of home units that were being renovated.

Fortunately Rick Saxby, one of the builders, had the latest piece of contemporary technology, a car phone, and called police. Fifteen minutes later the shaken personal trainer was guiding ambulance officers to the dead man. The post-mortem examination revealed John had massive multiple injuries including a tear in his heart and skull fractures.

Peter Russell had thought his brother had got lucky the night before and had spent the night with someone. However, when Peter came home in the afternoon and still no sign of John, he was worried. His brother wasn't the most punctual of men, but he was very responsible and probably would have called. Later that night, Peter rang the Bondi Police Station but got the usual suggestion: give it twenty-four hours and see if he turns up, if not come in and make a formal report. Coppers hear similar stories all the time and their advice is usually correct, but on this occasion, the constable hadn't put two and two together – a missing man and a then unidentified body in his patrol.

At the Legion Club, his friends waited but the guest of honour didn't arrive. Peter Redmile knew his friend very well and said, 'I wasn't really concerned because John is unreliable.'

The next morning, the police came to Peter Russell at 8.30 with that look on their faces that sends a chill down your spine. They drove him to the morgue at Glebe, where at 9.30am he identified the body of his brother. John's face had been badly damaged from the fall including a gaping wound near his left eye. Peter now had the sad task of telling his son Alan, his father Ted, and John's friends. With Ted driving down the next morning, Peter decided to break the news in person.

The police investigation got off to a respectable start. Crime-scene investigators comprehensively photographed the area around where John had landed. In John's back pocket they found his National Australia Bank card. They also found some light-coloured hairs clutched between the thumb and forefinger of John's left hand; these were collected and bagged, but unfortunately they were lost at some point after being logged in and were never scientifically examined. The investigators also didn't consider anything unusual about the position of the body or the trajectory it had taken. These important questions wouldn't be asked until years later. In criminal investigation, one of the early essentials is to make sure that what you have seen or been told could have actually happened in that manner. It's a basic objective test – stand back, take a deep breath, look and think.

With the history of assaults on gay men in the area, the hair, position of the body and John's pulled-up jumper, police suspicions of a murder should have been on high alert. However, just like Ross Warren's death only two months before, they weren't.

Detective Constable First Class Owens and Plainclothes Constable Sally Dunbar, then beginning her criminal-investigation training, were the local detectives on the scene. In those days they would make an examination of the scene, discuss the evidence with the forensic investigators and uniformed police, then decide whether the case was suicide, murder or misadventure. The common sense of policing dictates that if you can't decide, then you treat it as a murder until the evidence takes you down another path. Sergeant Adrian Ingelby, one of the uniformed police first on the scene, said, 'I already knew from previous local knowledge that the area was frequented by the homosexual element and on the patrols I could see many men in the area sitting, walking or cruising as it is known.'

The sergeant said he had interviewed men who used beats, and said: 'Contact between the homosexuals was not verbal but by body language or eye contact,' and, 'I had received information from a constable at Bondi that one method used for contact between gays was by rattling coins in the hand or rattling keys. When this was done, the interested persons would come out of hiding from the bushes.'

Ingelby was a former detective and a thorough investigator – the sort of copper you'd want as a mentor in your early days. In his statement of 26 February 1990, he summed up by saying: 'Assaults and assault-and-robbery on homosexuals is a popular pastime with the juvenile and hoodlum element. Unfortunately most of the victims, who are homosexual, do not report the incidents to police when they occur as they may not want the publicity or have a perception the police are not interested, that police may not be able to detect and arrest offenders. I believe that "unreported" assaults and associated offences on the homosexual element in the area (and other areas) would be extremely high.' Like any good police officer, he knew his patch thoroughly and while on night shift on 9 December 1989 had been taking names of young men loitering around the toilet blocks in the park near Bondi Beach.

On the death of John Russell, the sergeant said, 'From inquiries so far I am unable to say what caused Mr Russell to fall from the cliff top. It is known he'd consumed alcohol on the night before his body was located. Some of the homosexuals who frequent the area sit on the edge near the cliff top. It is not known if Mr Russell did so. It appears Mr Russell was in a normal state of mind, which rules out suicide. Crimes of violence on the homosexual element in the area are prevalent as it is in other parts of Sydney frequented by the homosexual community. I believe there would be a great number of "unreported" crimes of violence in this area. There is no direct evidence available at this stage proving foul play. The possibility of a dispute between Mr Russell and another homosexual is another potential hypothesis.'

Peter Bishop, a detective at Bondi at the time, recalled in a statement in 2001 that he had spoken to boys he believed were members of the 'Parkside Killers' or 'Bondi Boys' youth gangs around 1989 and 1990 and taken their details and submitted intelligence reports. He also recalled having a chat with a few boys in January 1990 about the graffiti around South Bondi, with one of the boys saying, 'The Bondi Boys threw a poofter off the cliff at South Bondi'; the detective thought they referred to Marks Park. His instinct made him think the boy might have seen the incident, and the detective remembered submitting a report on what he had learned.

Detective Owens was transferred shortly after the case started and the running of it appears to have fallen on Dunbar. In her statement of 16 February 1990, Dunbar said, 'I am aware the southern end of Notts Avenue is frequented by homosexuals and is known as a "beat". At this time there is no evidence to suggest the deceased committed suicide or there were any suspicious circumstances surrounding his death. There were no signs of violence on the body and personal property was located on his person. It is my opinion that the deceased fell from the cliff-top edge to where he was located. Whether this can be attributed to the deceased's level of intoxication will be clear with the results of the forensic tests.' It wasn't. John was quite pissed, but that doesn't mean he fell over. The problem with the investigation may have been Dunbar's lack of experience – a plainclothes constable is just out of uniform and at the beginning of a criminal-investigation career – and more importantly, a lack of supervision and perhaps interest shown by her superiors.

In July 1990, the coronial inquest took thirty minutes to find that John Russell had died by misadventure – an accident, not murder or an assault gone wrong.

However, the Coroner based his findings on a lacklustre police investigation. Fifteen years later, and after a highly competent police re-investigation, a Coroner found John had been murdered.

CHAPTER 15

FATAL AND ALMOST FATAL SHORE

David McMahon was a twenty-four-year-old chef living in Notts Avenue, Bondi Beach not far from the Icebergs Club. He was a jogger, and the walkway around the cliff tops was a challenging and beautiful track he knew well, and he'd run it often both day and night depending on the demands of long hours in the kitchen. Around 10.30pm on Thursday, 21 December 1989, he went for a run, dressed in trainers, running shorts and a white sloppy joe with the 'Molson' Canadian beer brand on the front. He started by heading north along the promenade to the barbecue area at North Bondi, then reversed direction and ran to the end of Notts Avenue to where the walkway south to Mackenzies Bay and Tamarama begins. After going down the stairs, he joined the walkway and ran along the water's edge to the first bay, then up a set of steps to a high point on the cliff where there is a landing. As he ran up the stairs, he saw a group of ten to twelve people he thought were approximately fourteen to eighteen years old, and included two females.

What David didn't know was that three days before, forty-six-year-old Alan Boxsell had gone for a walk toward Mackenzies Bay at around 10.40pm and was set upon by three people, who demanded to know if he was gay, and then overpowered and attacked him, punching and kicking, one of them swinging at him with a skateboard. Boxsell suffered a broken nose, fractured ribs, bruises and abrasions. They took his keys and after searching his car and taking the $5 they found, threw the keys off the cliff and then walked away. Boxsell reported the attack two-and-a-half weeks later. Alan Boxsell was lucky.

David recalled that one of the group he encountered, described as probably seventeen years old and on the shorter side between 168 centimetres and 172 centimetres, with short blond hair and dressed in an unseasonable combination of black tracksuit pants and white round-neck sweater, stopped him. David noticed the teen was carrying a blue 'Caribee' backpack, the same brand as one he owned. The teen was reasonably well spoken with an Australian accent, and said to David, 'What are you doing here?' to which David said he was out for a run. While the teen was quite relaxed, there was a feeling of menace in the air and David was tense. The reputation of the place was well known locally. One of the boys, who David thought might have been Maori, said, 'You got a cigarette for two dollars?' David ignored him and resumed jogging, very keen to put as much distance as possible between himself and this group. He pressed on as far as Tamarama and on the return leg he diverted through Marks Park, intending to jog down three sets of stairs to the first bay. On the second set of steps and getting close to the beginning of Notts Avenue, he said he was 'thrown forcibly onto the grass verge on the left side of the footpath. There is a grassed area leading to a rock face with small caves. The rock face leads up to the grassed area around the Notts Avenue cul de sac.'

It was an ideal spot for an ambush – empty and remote at that time of night. He rolled onto his back and saw the teen who had stopped him earlier and the Maori boy who was around the same age and height as the other, but a bit on the plump side. He saw approximately six others milling around behind them, and someone in the pack was yelling, 'Poofter! Poofter!' The first teen started to yell, 'You're gay!' over and over, and as David tried to get up, the Maori teen hit him in the face with a left-handed closed fist. The other teen joined in, with the two bashing David around the face and stomach. David was crying out for help, and one of the teens in the pack said loudly, 'Don't let him look at us, he knows me.' They rolled him onto his stomach and the beating continued with fists and kicks to the head and ribs. He thought he'd been hit to the temple at least twenty times. One of the cowardly gang entered the fracas and began to twist David's left foot, and while this was going on they were demanding money, with David pleading he didn't have any.

The first teen David had encountered began to drag him down the steps to the verge of a sheer drop of around fifteen metres to a rock platform. He said, 'I'm gonna throw you over the side,' and chillingly, 'Let's throw him off where we threw the other one off!' What David didn't know was that the scene was twenty-five metres from where John Russell had plunged to his death a month before.

David was resisting as strongly as he could, and managed to break the grip. Later, he said, 'I knew where the gravel area was. If we were there and they lost their footing, I could get away.' He seized the only opportunity he was likely to get, stood up and ran down the stairs. He could hear the sound of someone running behind him but didn't slow to look around. However, believing he had a gang on his tail, he started to yell for help, which, for a brief moment, he thought might be coming his way when a light went on in a home unit and a man shouted, 'I'm not going to help you, poofter!' David kept running as fast as he could toward his home, which fortunately was not far. His pursuers gave up.

David rang a friend and then the Bondi police, who visited his home, and after making a report he went to Prince of Wales Hospital, where he spent four-and-a-half hours in casualty being tended for extensive bruising, cuts, abrasions and loosened teeth. He thought the attack lasted for ten to fifteen minutes, and when he did an inventory, he found they had ripped the diamond stud from his left ear, and taken his signet ring and his Puma running shoes. In the commotion, he'd run home barefoot. The nightmares lasted for weeks after his injuries had eased. One other thing was clear in his mind – David could identify his attackers.

The New Year of 1990 got off to a violent start and change of venue when Richard Johnson, a thirty-four-year-old gay man, was beaten to death near toilets in Alexandria Park in Alexandria. Johnson wasn't the first victim at the toilets. On 28 December 1988, fifty-year-old school teacher William Allen was brutally beaten and stabbed with a screwdriver in the same place. Allen had managed to get to his home in Newtown Street, Alexandria, where he was found the next day, slumped dead over his bathtub. Police treated this one as a murder, but though there were suspects, no-one was ever charged.

Johnson's killers weren't so fortunate. Richard, who had a clerical job, was born in New Zealand, lived in seaside Coogee and was an occasional user of the Alexandria Park beat. He'd left his telephone number written amid the graffiti and other telephone numbers in the toilet block. In some beats, the toilet wall was a pre-social-media noticeboard. Richard had received a call on 24 January 1990 to arrange an assignation, and though potentially dangerous, he decided to take up the offer. Instead of the anticipated hook-up at 10pm he was met by a gang of eight boys aged between sixteen and eighteen, a few of whom had just finished a basketball game, and were either current or recent students from Cleveland Street High School. In a frenzied attack, Richard was kicked and punched so violently his liver ruptured and five ribs were cracked. They went through his pockets, stole his cash and left Richard for dead. A man walking a dog found his battered body outside the toilets the next morning. The man called an ambulance, and Richard was raced to hospital; however, his injuries were too severe and he died without regaining consciousness.

The Homicide Squad handled the investigation and had arrested members of the gang within ten days. The eight teens became infamously known as the 'Alexandria Eight', and over the following year, three were convicted of murder and five of manslaughter. In his summing up, Justice Badgery Parker said the young men had waited in nearby school grounds where they could see the arrivals at the toilet without themselves being spotted. When Johnson arrived, went in and found the place empty he walked out again and was 'set upon without mercy. One punched him heavily and without warning to the jaw and he fell to the ground. He was still conscious as most of the group assaulted him in various ways. At least two of them stomped with one heel on the right side of the victim's head and above the ear, causing a sub arachnoid haemorrhage and almost certainly unconsciousness.' He went on with the brutality, saying, 'many of them kicked him in the head and trunk. One at least jumped on the victim's right chest as he lay on his back, landing with his full weight on both knees.'

The Homicide Squad had a similar success in July 1990 with the murder of Krichakorn Rattanajurathaporn back at the Bondi beat. The slightly built thirty-four-year-old Thai man worked as a kitchen hand in a Thai restaurant on Campbell Parade, Bondi, across the road from the beach to pay for his university tuition, food and rent. He'd arrived in Australia in early 1990 prior to the start of the academic year and worked hard, long hours. He was a personable man who'd fallen for his new home.

On Friday 20 July he had decided against going home after his shift in the kitchen and instead took a detour to the walkway from South Bondi to Tamarama. It was a cold night, particularly so for someone adjusting to his first winter out of the heat and humidity of Thailand. In the early hours of 21 July, it was quiet at the beat and Krichakorn got as far as Mackenzies Point when he finally spotted a kindred spirit, Geoffrey Sullivan, who was sitting on a ledge near the cliff. The two struck up a conversation, swapping life stories, and Sullivan recalled Krichakorn telling him about his work, study, hopes and sending what little was left of his meagre income back to help his family in Thailand.

While Krichakorn was working hard scrubbing dishes, cutlery, pots, woks and pans during a busy service, the McAuliffe brothers – Sean, then seventeen, and David, sixteen – and Matthew Davis, also sixteen, were at the McAuliffes' semi in Redfern in the shadows of the multi-storey housing commission towers. The boys were drinking alcohol and getting themselves psyched up for a night of poofter bashing – something they'd done before. The beat around Marks Park was a favourite for them because it offered parking – an attraction for some of the gay users as well – and a steady stream of men who might have cash, watches and jewellery to plunder. Parental guidance for the boys that night was notably absent. Sean did the driving because he was the only one old enough to have a driver's licence.

Around 3am, Geoffrey Sullivan recalled hearing footsteps on the path and seeing a group of teenage boys emerge from the gloom. The boys were the McAuliffe brothers and Matthew Davis. Geoffrey and Krichakorn were terrified and outnumbered, and given their position on the cliff, they didn't have an escape route. Sean attacked first, demanding money and jackets, and threatening, 'I'll kill you.' Geoffrey handed over his wallet and jacket, hoping it would pacify the clearly hyped-up teens, but it didn't. Moments later, Geoffrey was hit on the head with a hammer that Sean had armed himself with for the night, and collapsed. Sean set to him with his fists and feet, cracking ribs.

David and Matthew attacked Krichakorn, who tried to fight back and landed a few punches before he was overwhelmed. Matthew had armed himself with a baton or stick and the two assailants took it in turns to hold their victim while the other used him as a punching bag. He managed to break free but didn't get far before being caught and the beating intensified. With Geoffrey close to unconsciousness, Sean moved to the now battered Krichakorn, kicking and punching. In the middle of this melee, Krichakorn again broke away, but Sean McAuliffe caught him and kicked him squarely in the chest to 'finish the fight', he said. He left Krichakorn lying in a pool of water near the edge of the cliff, and walked away. Davis was still beating Geoffrey Sullivan when the two brothers called for him stop and join them to go home.

Krichakorn, in his battered state and in the depth of night, stumbled over the cliff. He managed to claw at the edge of the precipice with his hands so valiantly he left blood-stained handprints on the rock before he fell, landing on a ledge two to three metres below. The ledge was two to three metres wide and recessed into the cliff face, and it was where police later found blood, vomit and pieces of paper, including part of a letter from Krichakorn's mother. At some point he rolled off the ledge and onto another below, and finally into the sea.

The three assailants didn't bother to check on Krichakorn's fate, or Geoffrey's condition, but instead drove home to Redfern, where they washed the blood off and shared a bong of marijuana.

Michael Connor came upon the crime scene the next morning when out with his partner walking their dog. The cliff top, he said, looked like it had been 'raining blood'. He recalled seeing a blue handkerchief 'stained with red', and 'fresh red marks' on the path. 'We wondered if a jogger had fallen,' he said. Michael looked over the edge but didn't see a body. His partner Kim, seeing blood on the very edge of the cliff, also leaned over to look and Michael headed home across Marks Park to call police. In an interview with the *Sydney Morning Herald* on 23 June 2015, he commented on the incident that still haunts him: 'Police officers were on the site within five hours but the investigation did not begin until well over twenty-four hours later. Like us the police also looked over the edge. Krichakorn Rattanajurathaporn may still have been alive when we were all standing on the site of the attack.'

Around the same time Michael Connor found the Rattanajurathaporn crime scene, two tourists out for an early morning cliff-top walk found Geoffrey Sullivan, the imprint of a shoe clear on his face. They called an ambulance.

Krichakorn's body was recovered from the water in the early afternoon of 22 July. Homicide Squad detectives were already nearby following other inaccurate reports of a headless corpse in the water off Bondi. A search of the Mackenzies headland found patches of blood near the edge of the cliff. This time, the occurrence-pad entry said the dead man might 'have been a victim of foul play'.

The investigation was led by Detective Sergeant Steve McCann of the Homicide Squad, and treated as murder from the outset.

One of the early moves in the investigation was to review reported attacks in the same area, prompting McCann to interview David McMahon. On 30 July 1990 they spoke to him at the cafe where he worked and showed him a portfolio of photographs – the selection was drawn from young men primarily from around the Bondi area and suspected of being part of the gangs – to see if he could identify any of them as his attackers. They met again two days later at Waverly Police Station and McMahon identified the person he believed was his attacker. Investigations cleared this man and his gang as suspects in the attacks on Geoffrey and Krichakorn.

The stupidity and arrogance of criminals is a boon to good police work, and in this killing, Matthew Davis provided both to give investigators a breakthrough. On the afternoon after the killing, he was in a Redfern butcher's shop when an acquaintance noticed what looked like blood spots on Davis's shoes; Davis bragged that they were from 'some faggot Chinaman's head'. He then announced: 'We beat up this guy in a park last night,' and expounded on the excellence of Sean McAuliffe's cowardly kicking skills. The problem was, the acquaintance's mother overheard Matthew's bragging. At that point there hadn't been any publicity on the case.

Later in the week he was at a party in south-western Sydney where he again bragged of his poofter-bashing exploits at Bondi. While the braggart was pumping himself up, McCann did something that was a first for the NSW Police – he appealed to the gay community for help, talking to the gay newspapers *Capital Q* and the *Sydney Star Observer*, and taking leaflets to businesses on Oxford Street. McCann wanted anyone who'd been attacked or witnessed attacks at Bondi to contact his team 'urgently, in the strictest confidence, to help identify the culprits'.

The first big leap forward in the investigation came from the mother who had overheard Davis's bragging. McCann now had what detectives yearn for: a red hot suspect. His team delved into Davis's background, starting, as police always do, by checking his criminal history, driver's licence – address, date of birth, traffic convictions because it wouldn't be the first time someone was given an infringement notice on the way to or from a crime – and criminal-intelligence files that could place him in the vicinity of other similar crimes, and his associates. Davis had had a few brushes with the law for break-and-enter and possessing illegal drugs. His parents separated when he was seven and he'd spent most of his life living with his father in Redfern before moving to Campbelltown in south-western Sydney, where his crowd of friends were similar to those he'd had in Redfern – disenfranchised young men with little clear sense of right and wrong, and influenced by peer-group pressure, which is the standard recipe for most youth gangs.

With the groundwork done, Davis was brought in for questioning and was one of those criminals who, when confronted, start talking. Crooks who tell the truth usually do so in increments, testing how much the investigators know and drip-feeding them with as much information as they think they need to. Davis, however, was more forthcoming. He admitted the attack was a gay bashing, that Bondi was well known to bashers like him as a gay beat and, more helpfully, he offered up Sean and David McAuliffe's names as the two with him. Davis also told the investigators how he and his mates had bashed men at various locations around Sydney, but later retracted that statement. In his record of interview, he told McCann: 'We bashed poofters before. We rolled them.'

It was an intriguing admission, because many years later a source told me the McAuliffes had mentioned they knew the 'North Narra Boys' and had committed gay bashings on the way home from South Sydney Rabbitohs games in other parts of the city or regional New South Wales, with the gang travelling by car or train. The men were passionate about their football.

Davis, a pleasant-looking kid, said the McAuliffes used him as bait to lure gay men. He said, 'I would talk to the gay men and make them feel at ease, and they got the impression that I was gay and interested in them.' Then the others would arrive and the assaults would start, using a baton, fists and feet, beating their victim to unconsciousness so they were easier to rob. Davis said, 'To be honest, I wanted to knock them out because I hated gafs [their term for gay men] at that stage.' The gang roamed locally around the beats of Centennial Park and Moore Park – the same beat at which police allegedly assaulted Alan Rosendale in May 1989.

The McAuliffes were arrested but didn't talk. Like Davis, they came from a dysfunctional home but neither had a criminal record. They pleaded not guilty at their subsequent murder trial.

Davis didn't fight the case and pleaded guilty. The McAuliffes were convicted, a prosecution based on the premise of a joint criminal enterprise. In sentencing the men, Justice Wood took into account their youth – they were sixteen and seventeen at the time of the attack – and the hope of rehabilitation. However, he also made it clear that gang attacks like this were 'brutal, cowardly and entirely reprehensible'. The McAuliffe brothers each received a sentence of twenty years with a non-parole period of twelve years; Davis got a discount for pleading guilty, and was sentenced to nineteen years with a non-parole period of eleven years.

Krichakorn's murder sowed a seed in Steve McCann's mind. Though there had been publicity of attacks on gay men, the police hadn't approached the issue with any vigour as a collective problem, in spite of numerous reported incidents and intelligence on unreported attacks. While there was evidence that could have suggested patterns in commonality of place, victims, attack methods and descriptions of the group, no-one had sat down and analysed the information and considered what could have been done to investigate the crimes and prevent others. Investigations were still treated on an individual basis, and the term 'serial killer', which is commonly used these days, only came into being in the mid eighties in the United States before it finally made its way to Australia in time for Ivan Milat's murder spree in the Belanglo State Forest that started in 1989.

In the months following the arrest of Davis and the McAuliffes, McCann thought about what Davis had said about other attacks at Bondi, and as he dug through the old paper records the names of Ross Warren and John Russell emerged. However, what was missing in both those cases was a detailed investigation at the time they had happened. Instead, the paltry files on Ross Warren had been boxed up as a missing person's case gathering dust and waiting for new evidence to appear; and John Russell's case had been signed off by the Coroner as 'misadventure' requiring, and to use the term police used in the Scott Johnson case, 'NFA' – no further action. One of McCann's early moves was to go back to the public. The media release of 3 April 1991 appealed for other assault victims to come forward, and included a comment from Sue Thompson, the NSW Police Gay/Lesbian Client Consultant. Sue said there were many now in the community who were open about their lives, 'however, there are many others who hide their sexuality for fear of prejudice or being ostracised by their family or friends. Sometimes these people may even be married and the only avenue to express their hidden sexuality is to meet other men anonymously.'

She estimated there had been a thirty-four per cent growth in attacks over the past year, with many men still not reporting them. The release was followed by stories in the mainstream press in which McCann talked of 'sensitive material' that 'involved similarities' between Ross Warren's disappearance and other incidents at Bondi and 'three other unsolved homosexual murders in Sydney'. On the back of McCann's public appeal, part of the gay community joined in, with a more radical approach. If they'd wanted attention, they got it.

In the early hours of 8 April, eleven prominent city buildings, including the front walls of Parliament House, entrance doors to the Sydney Tower, front doors of St Mary's Cathedral and St Andrew's Cathedral, the front of the Downing Centre court complex and offices of Channel Ten in Ultimo, Fairfax on Broadway and a News Limited building in North Sydney, were hit by red paint. In addition to the paint, the protesters left posters saying: 'We're over it. Stop the violence against gay men and lesbians.' The protesters wore surgical gloves to avoid leaving fingerprints. The attack coincided with the murder trial of the men charged with killing Richard Johnson – the gay man beaten to death in Alexandria Park in January 1990 – and a policy paper prepared by the Gay and Lesbian Rights Lobby, which claimed that 'youths found themselves at the mercy of the courts due to the inaction of the Department of Education', and demanded the addition of anti-gay violence to the curriculum. The protesters called themselves 'One in Seven', possibly based on a theory that one in seven people are gay.

In the *Sydney Star Observer* of the same week, the protesters published their manifesto, and the comment: 'Our blood runs in the streets and in the parks and in the casualty and in the morgue . . . Our blood runs because in this country our political, educational, legal and religious systems actively encourage violence against us. We are gay men and lesbians . . . WE'RE OVER IT and we're going to paint the town red!'

Later in the month, the police in Bondi had finally got the message, with the patrol's Gay Liaison Officer Constable Brad Scanlon telling the local weekly paper the *Wentworth Courier* that he was willing to meet members of the gay community in plain-clothes rather than his uniform, and, 'We are sure there are more incidents of gay violence but because of a fear of the police, the bashings are not reported, and this is dangerous. Violence against the gay community is usually caused by hatred and to stop the attacks the police need to know who is responsible. If violence is kept secret the offenders gain more confidence and feel they can get away with more daring crimes.'

Steve Page and Sue Thompson at Marks Park.
Rick Feneley/Fairfax Syndication

Vince Esposito at the NSW Coroner's Court in 2007.
Lee Besford/Fairfax Syndication

The late Ludwig Gertsch. *Fairfax Syndication*

Carmen at home in Surry Hills. *Edwina Pickles/Fairfax Syndication*

Gay rights demonstration outside Sydney's Central Court of Petty Sessions, June 1978. *Fairfax Syndication*

Ken Bowditch, who led the first investigation into Ross Warren's disappearance and the early investigation into the disappearance and murder of Ludwig Gertsch. *Simon Alekna/Fairfax Syndication*

Marks Park – a lonely place to die. *Michael Mucci/Fairfax Syndication*

Ross Warren. *Fairfax Syndication*

Ted (left) and Peter Russell at Wollombi where they buried John's ashes.
Jacky Ghossein/Fairfax Syndication

Steve Johnson (centre) and the best man at his wedding, brother Scott.
Photo supplied by the Johnson family.

Scott Johnson in the outdoors he relished. *Photo supplied by the Johnson family.*

Steve Johnson (centre) continuing the fight to find out what really happened to his brother Scott. *Photo supplied by the Johnson family.*

It was a bit late, but it was a start. Gay men of the time shared a similarly black sense of humour with police, and a friend of mine commented on Constable Scanlon's offer that 'he'd get more attention if he wore his uniform'.

Other gay community groups followed a more traditional style of protest when on 12 May, Mardi Gras stars such as the Sisters of Perpetual Indulgence and Dykes on Bikes were among 800 people who marched through Newtown and Camperdown to protest against the spate of violence. News reports spoke of McCann's public appeals and the chilling information that at least six gay men had been murdered over the past three years, and that the offenders for some of the bashings and killings were between fifteen and twenty years old.

Amid all this, Scott Johnson's death wasn't on anyone's list. As with Ross Warren and John Russell, the case was done and dusted. Like the other two, that would change, but it would take nearly two decades.

All the publicity since Krichakorn Rattanajurathaporn's death was soon overwhelmed by another murder in gay Sydney, and it was one that grabbed the nation's headlines with a compelling combination of sex, passion, family entanglements, greed and money. It would also be the catalyst for police to review the deaths of and assaults on gay men in the recent past, and to finally consider that they might be linked, and some of the deaths might have actually been murder.

CHAPTER 16

AN OPERA IN TWO ACTS

Ludwig Gertsch, a hairdresser by trade and heir to a large pile of money and assets by good fortune and good management, disappeared on Friday, 19 October 1990. That same day, the gay newspaper *Sydney Star Observer* had run an advertisement by the police asking for 'information on bashers and all bashing incidents. All details, even just the time and place of an assault or an attempted assault are important' and giving a contact number of liaison officers.

It was the evening before the annual Sleaze Ball, which was the other big party event in the year's calendar and made the Mardi Gras look almost family friendly. The event had been around since 1982, when the first party was held at the Paddington Town Hall, and the community dressed up in a range of costumes from the brevity of a G-string through to elaborate drag and leather ensembles. It was the favourite event for the infamous 'trough man', a party regular who spent most of his evenings lying on the disinfectant beads in the trough of the men's toilet. Fortunately for those wandering in, it was dark, so it was usually too late for them to notice an extra amid the yellow beads and stainless steel. Consensus was the gentleman must have lived close by because public transport home would have been out of the question, and the cypress tree fresheners that were popularly hung on the rear-vision mirror of your car wouldn't have been up to the task.

The theme for 1990 was 'Angels and Devils' and around 12 000 tickets had been sold. You needed to get in fast or risk missing out. Events like these and Mardi Gras had taken the gay community out of the closet. The mainstream media reported the costumes, hedonism and morning after with revellers stumbling home or stopping for a few beers at a gay pub to gossip and recover from the antics of the night.

Ludwig had been rolling in cash since the death of his millionaire lover Roger-Claude Teyssedre on 16 April 1990, and entertained lavishly at the large terrace house he'd inherited at Sutherland Street, Paddington – described by one source as decorated in Louis XIV bordello style. For his first Sleaze Ball weekend minus Roger-Claude, Ludwig intended to party hard and had a house full of friends from Melbourne to help him.

However, the party didn't start for Ludwig. When he hadn't returned home on Saturday 20 October, his houseguests assumed he'd had some luck the night before and was still out with his latest seduction, and so they headed out to the ball. His Sydney friends, however, many of them straight, decided it was time to get the police involved.

Just over three weeks later, on 11 November 1990, Ludwig's body – wearing Jordache jeans, size forty-two black leather boots with a side zip, red socks, Egyptian cotton T-shirt and a beige Lacoste sweater – was found wrapped in a grey doona in bushland just off the Hawkesbury River Road at Winmalee in the Blue Mountains, eighty kilometres west of Sydney. An elastic strap had been tied securely around his neck; a tea towel was in his mouth and taped there. At a post-mortem examination, forensic pathologist Dr Ellis found that Ludwig had died of 'mechanical asphyxia due to strangulation by ligature and obstruction of his airway by gag'. The doctor also noted 'the state of Gertsch's body was consistent with death occurring approximately three weeks previously'.

Gertsch's death was the second act of a two-act opera, which began when he fell into a relationship with Roger-Claude Teyssedre, who, with his business partner Dawn O'Donnell (or Irwin, the married name she used occasionally), were the dominant commercial forces in the Sydney gay scene. Roger died in circumstances initially assumed by police and his attending physician to be natural causes. However, within a few months a sinister story emerged.

Views on Roger-Claude were mixed. Denise Coussens, his long-time friend and later co-owner of Kingsteam on Oxford Street – a gay sauna nicknamed 'Chopsticks and Walking Sticks' because of the age and cultural diversity of its clientele – said he 'had the charisma of a Bhagwhan'. One gay community member told journalist Ben Hills in 1990: '[Roger] just seemed like evil incarnate to me, he used to make the hairs stand up on my neck every time I saw him.' I met Roger in the early eighties and agree with Hill's source. The man was a swarthy, deeply tanned and oily character, favouring caftans and, in summer, sandals instead of shoes. He was arrogant with the hauteur of a minor European royal, and a regular visitor to Tahiti for a winter tan and plastic surgery, with the nips and tucks giving his eyes a slightly unnatural cast – one tuck too many, was my first thought on meeting him.

In 1985, Roger joined a club of which no-one wanted to become a member when he was diagnosed as HIV positive; and full-blown AIDS, to use the term common at the time, followed in November 1989, rendering him susceptible to the opportunistic infections common to all AIDS patients. In Roger's case, pneumonia, thrush and skin diseases became part of his daily life.

A close to 100 per cent mortality rate, the likelihood of a brief future and the utter lack of a cure on the horizon, brought out some of Roger's more unpleasant character traits. His lavish and frequent dinner parties around the exquisite dining table at his home in Sutherland Street, Paddington, provided him with an opportunity to torture his circle. The house was described by Hills in his 1990 piece as 'the elegant Paris salon, with its priceless Aubusson tapestry, Persian carpets, its brass Buddha statues, Tiffany lamps and Donald Friend paintings', but there was a fair chance that some of the objets d'art were cheaper knock-offs. One occasional visitor reckoned Roger had 'more front than David Jones' and 'the paint was still drying on some of the old masters'.

By the 1980s, Paddington had cast aside its impoverished early-to-mid twentieth-century life and returned to the elevated social position it held in the Victorian era. Roger's home was a large terrace house, restored by him over three years and at vast cost. *Homes* magazine in winter 1989 gushed: 'An almost Ali Baba "open Sesame" experience awaits those who enter the home of Roger-Claude for the first time', and banged on about African slate floors, Chinese silks, Indian antiques (then very chic and looted in bulk from India for a pittance and flogged to the well-to-do of inner Sydney at huge mark-ups). Roger and

Ludwig shared the property with six Siamese cats and a daily housekeeper; and a granny flat at the rear of the property housed Roger's mother, Juliette. It wasn't a jump to envisage Roger sitting in a chair, stroking a cat and contemplating world domination. The house was opulent but taste was in short supply, with Hills nailing it as 'an altar to camp chic'.

At the dinner gatherings, Roger took malicious delight in playing one off against the other, promising gifts in his will to those who played along with him and threatening to cut out those who didn't. Roger, according to one of his circle, 'treated his friends like gold and his lovers like shit', but the source was an ex-lover, now friend, who hoped for an inheritance. Ludwig, whom Roger forced to get a driver's licence at age thirty-five so he could play chauffeur, was 'chief cook and bottle washer' according to the same source.

Ludwig Gertsch was the latest in a long line of live-in lovers chosen in part for their willingness to kowtow. Ludwig had been in residence with Roger since 1982. In November 1989 Roger had had his first opportunistic infection that usually accompanied the onset of AIDS, followed by a 'honeymoon period' where the patient resumed good health, put on weight and began to feel hopeful. The cruelty of AIDS is a plummet in health often following the honeymoon period. By April 1990, Roger was still enjoying the honeymoon and was, like any other man with his illness, taking a cocktail of drugs to deal with or prevent other opportunistic infections. He was feeling so good, he'd planned a trip to Paris with Coussens to celebrate Bastille Day.

On 9 April, he was feeling below par and consulted with his general practitioner, Dr Robertson, who referred him to nearby St Vincent's Hospital, then the hub of HIV medicine in Australia, for a chest X-ray. Seven days later, Ludwig found Roger dead in his bed at Sutherland Street. According to the bereaved, Ludwig had visited his mother in Redfern the night before and arrived home in time to tend to his lover's morning demands. The night before, Denise Coussens and her husband had dined with Roger and he'd appeared in good spirits and health, though a little tired as the night drew to a close. His death came as a surprise.

His friends were suspicious when they heard that Roger's normally dishevelled bed was quite tidy. When Dr Mutimer, another general practitioner from the same practice as Robertson, turned up to certify the body as dead – a mandatory requirement even if it's obvious – he noted that Roger had been 'laid out' with his arms folded over his chest, and when Dr Mutimer asked Ludwig about it, he didn't offer any explanation. Roger had either died very neatly, or someone had been tidying, and the Coroner later noted that Ludwig had 'seemed to convey the impression that he had discovered Teyssedre in that position'.

At the time of his death, concerns over the possibility of contracting HIV from bodies suspected of carrying the virus meant that post-mortems weren't usually performed on them, and this was the case with Roger. Dr Mutimer inadvertently added to the problem by signing a death certificate, assuming Roger had died of pneumonia – with his reasoning based on Robinson's clinical notes at the practice. The problem was, the chest X-ray results hadn't arrived at the general practice, and the X-ray had been clear. Roger didn't have pneumonia. With Roger's supposed medical history and a death certificate, the police, who were also required to be at Sutherland Street, didn't consider foul play, in spite of the oddity of Roger's bedroom and mutterings of his friends. Ludwig had added to the story by telling them Roger might 'do something to himself' because of his supposed declining health, and told the police Roger had been sent home from the hospital because he was beyond treatment. But this wasn't the case, and Ludwig's script was accepted by the police as accurate – not unreasonably given the medical certificate, the hysteria of the times and the bereaved Ludwig's yarn. The truth would take literally decades to emerge.

Roger's funeral on a rainy afternoon four days later was relatively tasteful. Ludwig played the grieving spouse. Black limousines left from the funeral directors in Oxford Street and motored to the Botany Crematorium, which was in the midst of a rush in business as the AIDS virus gnawed its way through the gay community in the five square kilometres of which Darlinghurst was the centre. Ex-lovers sat with Ludwig in the family pew at the front, and Dawn O'Donnell, in her raspy battler's Australian accent, praised her business partner for his warmth and as a man who could 'befriend prime ministers and ordinary people alike', though prime ministers and politicians were absent from the service. The coffin containing Roger slid through the curtains at the crematorium to the sound of Sinatra's 'My Way', and Edith Piaf's 'Je ne regrette rien'.

But there were regrets and more than a few, to brutalise the lyric Sinatra phrased so beautifully, as the drama ratcheted up at the reading of the will, not held in a bland lawyer's conference room, but in the dining salon at Sutherland Street. The master of ceremonies was Roger's solicitor Brian Barrington Roberts, who had acted for him since about 1985. Clustered around the table were a bevy of friends, ex-lovers, expectant assorted acolytes and domestic staff – and with the exception of Ludwig and Roberts, they were in for a nasty surprise. His 1988 will included bequests for large chunks of what was thought to be an $8 million estate to ex-lovers, with the amounts to each man based on the length of time he'd known them, with the longest getting the biggest amount. Michael Caccomanolis, whose services as lover and friend dated back to the sixties and had been around the longest, was to receive $200 000. Next in seniority were Alex Chit-Nat-Hi-Rout, an exotic and handsome Vietnamese refugee, and Edoardo Alderighi, whom Roger had set up in one of Sydney's briefly hot restaurants in Darlinghurst in the early eighties – both men believed they would get $100 000. Last was Michael Trikillis at $75 000. Roger's housekeeper Aspasia Astas was in for $50 000.

However, what the expectant gaggle around the table didn't know was that Roger had changed his will yet again, and the latest document was drafted by Roberts and signed by Roger a little over two weeks before he died, with his florist and next-door neighbour as witnesses. The first surprise was the estate wasn't worth the expected $8 million but instead a dismal $2.7 million, including $895 000 cash in bank accounts. Then came the really bad news. To his 'most adored Edoardo' he left $10 000, with the other expectant lovers, friends and retainers, including Aspasia who got $2000, sharing total bequests of $52 000. Ludwig got the rest. The stage was set for what would become more than two decades of intrigue, accusations, denials, investigative failures and successes, and one more death.

Roger was barely en route to meet his maker when the trouble started. The disgruntled beneficiaries gathered like cardinals plotting a new Pope, and muttered darkly about the likelihood of Ludwig hastening Roger's demise. Then in May came the curious news that Roger had transferred his half-share in the Imperial

Hotel in Picton to Wayne Dowling, who owned the other half. The two had bought the hotel in 1988 for $600 000. The only problem with the recent transaction was that Roger had allegedly signed the transfer document on 31 May 1990 – an interesting trick considering he'd been dead for six weeks. Dowling said at the time to a question from Ben Hills of the *Sydney Morning Herald*: 'Mr Roberts is handling it. There was definitely something weird about it if he was dead when he signed the thing.' Roberts declined to comment, though as the saga wound on he would be questioned further about documents and signatures.

Around this time Ludwig had put his widow's black in the wardrobe and was out and about. Cruising past new housing-commission units being built on the corner of Burton and Bourke Streets, Darlinghurst, just a few hundred metres north of the then glittering Oxford Street, he spotted a good-looking tanned and buffed young man laying bricks on the site. Ludwig drove slowly past quite regularly and one night thought he'd struck gold when he spotted the man, then around twenty-five, at the Albury Hotel.

The Albury was an art deco pub owned by the nuns who ran St Vincent's Hospital across the road. For years it had been a watering hole for older locals, where you could sit and mutter into a schooner from 10am to 10pm. While it wasn't rundown, it needed a spruce-up, and in 1980 the nuns leased it to former Tivoli showgirl Nanette Theakstone and her business partner Leigh Jennings. With a bit of paint, a good scrub, a mirror ball and some fresh carpet in the former ladies' lounge, the Albury became the city's premier gay venue. The winning formula included shirtless, muscled barmen and drag-queen shows in the public bar, lounge acts in the former ladies' lounge, and down at the far end of the lounge where you'd find the toilets or back entrance to the public bar was a dimly lit area nicknamed 'the killing fields' where older gentlemen and lads of South East Asian origins communed.

Ludwig sidled up to the man – Vince Esposito – and offered to buy him a drink, and when he declined, Ludwig persisted until he gave in. What was obvious to the predatory Gertsch was that Vince was big on looks but short on experience, and he was right. Vince was one of sixteen children who had migrated from Italy to Australia in the late 1960s and moved into a classic Australian three-bedroom bungalow on a quarter-acre block in Sydney's far western suburbs. Vince was also married, father of two boys – two and three years old – and on the cusp of coming to grips with his sexuality. His visit to the Albury was the first time he'd been able to summon the courage to have a look at the life that was so different to the one he had.

Ludwig's persistence also paid off in other ways, and he became Vince's first gay affair. Vince said, 'I'd broken up with my wife, I was very, very confused and he was very comforting, he was very understanding being that his lover had died, and so he explained to me that we were virtually in the same boat.' Vince came slowly to the view, that 'I considered him and I as good friends, but maybe in his eyes he wanted to interpret it as being lovers. That's where the friction sort of virtually started.'

The friction wasn't eased by Ludwig's showering him with gifts, from jewellery to a Subaru wagon, a birthday party costing around $20 000, and public displays of affection. Nor was it helped by him bringing home male sex workers picked up on The Wall in Darlinghurst in an attempt to stimulate some attention from Vince. Three- or four-way was better than no way in Ludwig's thinking. Vince, a good Catholic boy with enough to deal with already, was horrified. However, one of Ludwig's redeeming features was his genuine love for Vince's two boys, and they reciprocated.

According to Vince, Ludwig was possessive. 'He wanted to become Roger and I would become Ludwig the servant, but I'm not like that.' Ludwig took on Roger's old and unpleasant habit of playing the will game – even though he was young and in fine health he bragged he'd left his newly acquired fortune to Vince, an act that didn't endear Vince to the coterie. In the couple of months leading up to his death, Ludwig became what his close friends and Vince thought was paranoid. He complained of receiving threatening phone calls; a distrust of Brian Roberts, his solicitor, who was partially disabled by hemiplegia after an accident at the age of twelve and on whom he had relied heavily since Roger had died; and growing distrust of Vince to the point where Ludwig thought Vince may have been part of an elaborate plot to have him killed in a secluded part of road one night when they were heading to dinner at La Perouse. He massaged his concerns by increasing his alcohol and ecstasy use, and having the house turned, as Vince said, 'into Fort Knox' and even having a deadlock installed on his bedroom door.

Adding to Ludwig's problems was the inaccurate belief that Brian Roberts was having or planned on having an affair with Vince. The two had developed a close friendship after Brian had arranged Vince's divorce but it hadn't developed past that, at least as far as the still naïve Vince knew. Brian was infatuated, something Ludwig had noticed, and it deepened the rift between him and his once trusted solicitor and confidante. Ludwig added to the gossip swirling around him by telling his friends he was unhappy with both Brian and Vince and would be cutting both out of his will and getting a new solicitor to do it for him. This was an added misery for Roberts, who had been on a $2000 per week retainer, which he'd persuaded Ludwig to pay him shortly after Roger's death. In July, amid what was looking like a soap opera, Vince moved out to a home unit in Ashfield, where the bond and furnishings were funded by Ludwig.

In his first statements, Vince said Ludwig had contacted him earlier in the week before his disappearance and asked if he could come by to see the boys, who Vince had for the weekend. In spite of all their disputes, Ludwig's fondness for the children was resolute and he liked to see them every Saturday, but with the Sleaze Ball and a house full of guests, the usual timing would be tricky. Vince alleged Ludwig rang about 6.30pm on the Friday and arrived at the Ashfield unit about fifty minutes later. It wasn't long before Ludwig became amorous. Vince was upset with the advances, particularly as his boys were playing in the next room. The inevitable disagreement began, with Ludwig screaming, 'I'm sick and tired of not touching you, you know I want more!' The conversation deteriorated and Vince alleged Ludwig said he was leaving to find a prostitute or two.

The boys came into the room and the dispute fell silent. Ludwig then rang Brian Roberts, who lived a five-minute drive away, and demanded he come by and drive him into the city, a curious request because he had arrived by taxi and they weren't hard to get. Roberts later told police he'd driven the agitated and unhappy heir into Oxford Street, Darlinghurst and dropped him near the corner of Palmer Street. That was, according to Roberts, the last time he saw Ludwig alive. Roberts' story was corroborated by Vince when questioned years later by police. They also questioned him about why the carpet in the unit's bedroom had been removed shortly after Ludwig's visit, and Vince said it was because his sons had vomited on it. It was a story stuck to for almost fifteen years.

On the day Ludwig disappeared, Brian Roberts allegedly did a few curious things. He wrote a cheque for $89 000 – he had the authority – on Ludwig's account and payable to 'B Roberts, Solicitor', which he later explained was for professional fees for the calendar year beginning 20 October 1990. He also wrote a letter to the manager of Ludwig's bank, the ANZ in Darlinghurst, authorising him to hand over Gertsch's safety deposit box.

The next morning Brian did something even more curious. Before anyone had told Roberts that Ludwig was missing, he spoke to Angela Summers – a florist he used regularly and an old friend of Gertsch – and said Ludwig had disappeared. Summers knew her friend well and suggested he might still be 'out partying'. Roberts disagreed and, she alleged, said, 'Oh no, he's missing. There's something gone wrong.' The two then discussed Ludwig's 'paranoia' that had been stirred along by threats he'd received by telephone. Summers thought the threats were made by disgruntled beneficiaries of the late Roger-Claude who believed they were entitled to larger bequests and jealous of the fortune inherited by Ludwig. Roberts then said of Gertsch: 'He's mincemeat now.' The disappearance of a high profile gay man at a time of stories of gay-hate crimes, from vicious assaults to murders, was a wake-up call to the police and public. Oxford Street and its community were leading the news, and speculation was that Ludwig was yet another victim of a gay-hate crime. Ludwig's fate was the catalyst for the police to finally come to grips with the fact that the city was in the midst of attacks targeting gay men. But their first steps in the case were unspectacular.

CHAPTER 17

THE CASE OF THE MISSING HEIR

By midday Saturday 20 October Ludwig's houseguests and his confidantes with whom he chatted daily, and sometimes a few times per day, were concerned that their friend was in strife, rather than wayward. By mid afternoon the group, including Brian Roberts, had gathered at Sutherland Street and decided to report Ludwig's disappearance to Paddington police. Brian Roberts and Maria Hamilton, accompanied by a mutual friend Kerry who was a police sergeant, went to the police while the others stayed at the house hoping Ludwig would call or return home.

When they returned, Maria took George Fidirikkos, a florist and longterm Ludwig confidante, aside and discreetly told him of Brian's odd behaviour. George recounted that she said to him, 'I can't believe what Brian has just said in the statement about Ludwig that Ludwig was into bondage, that he was on drugs and had large sums of black money.' They called a locksmith to break into Ludwig's locked bedroom to make sure he hadn't had a heart attack. Around this time Brian, according to Fidirikkos, recounted his story of the prior evening's drama and dropping Ludwig in Oxford Street at about 8.15pm. The locksmith arrived and broke in, but there was no sign of Ludwig, his wallet or the large key ring he usually carried hooked to his waist in a style that was common around the time. Most of the friends stayed the night, waiting and hoping.

In police interviews with Maria Hamilton in March 1991, Hamilton said of her visit with Brian to the police station that she was surprised by Brian when 'he mentioned something to do with a harness that someone had asked Ludy to buy for them. That's for whatever reasons. And he suggested that Ludy was into some sort of game playing, some sort of S and M is it, some sort of weird sex.' She alleged Roberts told the sergeant behind the desk that Ludwig was 'more than likely involved in some sex thing the night before'. She thought: 'The whole picture he was presenting was that Ludy really was a shady sort of sleazy character and there wasn't really any reason to panic.' Maria told the sergeant Gertsch had 'some fears for his safety' prior to disappearing, and that she believed that Roberts was 'pushing this image of Ludy being sort of a sexual deviant and also mentioning this black money'. A racy yarn like this would have spread like wildfire through the local police officers and their networks on a dozy Saturday afternoon.

Maurice Joseph was the supervising sergeant at Paddington that afternoon and recalled the visit in a statement made around a year later. He said Roberts described Ludwig as 'paranoid' and said he had received death threats since he'd inherited Roger-Claude's estate, and his paranoia was so great he'd had an iron security door fitted to his bedroom. The sergeant recalled Roberts told him: 'Ludwig was a very active homosexual who would often pick up a number of men during the night and [return] with them to his home for sex and then [ring] Roberts or Hamilton and [give] them all the details of his "conquests".' Roberts then recounted his version of 19 October and reassured the sergeant that 'Ludy would have phoned one of them, and if not telling where he was, would at least say everything was okay'. Roberts also told the sergeant that Ludwig, 'despite his behaviour and lifestyle, he always honoured his commitments', and knew he had a meeting with Roberts on the Saturday morning to discuss litigation brought by one of Roger-Claude's aggrieved beneficiaries.

The sergeant prepared a missing-persons report, and checked the morgue, local hospitals and twenty-four-hour medical services. He sent a detective to Kingsteam, one of the businesses Ludwig had inherited a share in, to see if there was any substance to a rumour that Ludwig had been lurking there at 3am – there wasn't.

Over the weekend, a posse of Ludwig's friends, armed with photos of him, hit the gay venues both obvious and discreet, such as the sex-on-premises venues found in the laneways, cellars and dimly lit upstairs rooms of the shabby old Oxford Street strip from Hyde Park to Taylor Square. Ludwig had a high profile on the strip, and they'd hoped to find someone who'd seen him on Friday night, either being dropped off by Roberts, or later. They were surprised and their worries deepened when they all drew a blank. No-one had spotted the highly visible Ludwig Gertsch on Oxford Street on the night he disappeared.

Around 4pm on Sunday, Sergeant Joseph arrived at Sutherland Street, where he chatted to Roberts, who told him Ludwig had a preference for 'rough sex' and 'was known to frequent S and M bath houses The Den and Numbers, both in Oxford Street, Darlinghurst'. There wasn't a towel or bath in sight at either of these popular sex-on-premises venues, just a lot of men milling about in the hope of some action. The sergeant also rang Vince Esposito to see if he could shed any light on the disappearance, and had Redfern police visit Ludwig's mother, then in the early stages of dementia, at her flat in Regent Street, Redfern above the shop where Ludwig had once run his hairdressing business. With the likelihood of foul play dramatically increasing as Ludwig's disappearance entered the second day, the sergeant prudently handed over the investigation to the detectives.

On Monday 22 October with Ludwig still missing, Brian Roberts was at the ANZ Bank with the cheque made out in his favour and the letter dated 19 October. He deposited the cheque and left with the safety deposit box, which he later opened in the presence of Ludwig's friends. The following day, Ken Bowditch – who'd been the officer in charge of the investigation into Ross Warren's disappearance the year before and was leading this police investigation – took a short statement from Vince in which he gave a thumbnail of Ludwig's visit to his home on 19 October, the argument, then Ludwig's call to Brian to come to collect him.

The story took a turn for the stranger when a private investigator who was a former NSW Police detective came on the scene, employed by George Fidirikkos. The private detective either beat or paralleled the police to interviewing the key witnesses in what was then a missing-persons case. His interview with Vince was long and detailed, whereas Bowditch's handling of Ludwig's disappearance was becoming as baffling as his work on the Ross Warren case.

One thing television scriptwriters get right when writing of murder is the importance of the first few days of the investigation. Given the timing of his disappearance on the eve of the

Sleaze Ball, and with a house full of guests and vigorous social calendar coming up and the insight provided by his friends of Ludwig's fears for his safety, alarm bells should have rung loudly at Paddington Police Station. In the early days of a murder or possible-murder investigation, all the available information should be thrown on the table like a jigsaw puzzle, with each piece then tested and assessed before being included in the appropriate place.

Among the pieces of the puzzle that should have been critically assessed were the stories provided by Brian Roberts and Vince Esposito. They dovetailed and became part of the premise of the police investigation. No-one questioned their veracity; no-one went to Frederick Street, Ashfield to interview Vince at his home and ask him about the events and Ludwig's state of mind that night or to test his version against the version given by Roberts. No-one bothered to question the neighbours at the block of units, and it was intriguing to see the investigation motivated by Roberts' lurid tale of sleaze rather than the view of Ludwig's friends.

Instead of painstakingly amassing and testing all the available information, the Bowditch strategy was to head to Oxford Street. Bowditch and his detectives, aided by some local men to act as guides, trawled the heart of gay Sydney, and had some experiences not covered in their training. Bowditch told writer Sandra Harvey in the late 1990s: 'You go through things and suddenly you get exposed to a whole new way of life. Some of the things they do are unbelievable, like watersports!' Ken had obviously led a life sheltered from tales of the British upper crust. He was also horrified to state: 'The Federal Government is promoting it! There's a brochure put out by the Government "Safe Sex in Bathhouses".' Ken hadn't quite come to grips with the thrust of the campaign, which was to educate gay men at a time when AIDS was really a crisis tearing the heart out of the gay community, their families and friends.

Bowditch was also fascinated by the economics, saying: 'In bathhouses, they can go in, pay ten dollars for a towel, and they can wander around for twenty-four hours if they want. They can go into a steam room, and if they see someone they fancy, they can go into a cubicle, have sex, and then go back. I think it would be wonderful if they had it for heterosexuals.' Ken, his fascination to one side, also said: 'Without any disrespect to Ludwig, he was a crazy little faggot.' The NSW Police investigation was a stroll on the wild side and an abject failure, and it wasn't until the grisly discovery of Ludwig's body that it finally, and too late, gained some focus. Bowditch's investigation of Ludwig's disappearance had more vigour than his work on Ross Warren's, but was similarly lacklustre.

Three weeks after his disappearance, a bushwalker discovered Ludwig's body in the Blue Mountains. His body was wrapped in a doona cover and he'd been gagged. A post-mortem revealed Ludwig had been strangled by someone using an octopus strap.

Ludwig's funeral on 23 November was a low-key affair, beginning with a service at a funeral home in Bondi followed by a burial at Botany Cemetery. During the service his devastated mother Emmah wailed over the rose-strewn coffin that one man 'did it!' and 'the five ghosts will not rest until the killer of my son lies beside him', which is an old curse from Surinam, the tiny former Dutch colony on the Atlantic coast of South America where she'd lived at one point. Whether she had any genuine evidence on the identity of the killer became academic because five days later, Emmah, dressed in widow's black, collected her son's effects from the police station and then walked in front of a moving train at Macdonaldtown station, one stop past her normal stop at Redfern. The rumour mill immediately kicked into top gear. Was the elderly woman suffering from the onset of dementia lured to her death? Or was it suicide? Or an accident? It is a mystery that remains unresolved. A further addition to what was looking like a soap opera started in the week prior to Ludwig's body being found. Five of the seven beneficiaries of Roger-Claude's will began action in the Supreme Court challenging the validity of the document.

Around the tight-knit gay community, the rumour mill was working overtime with stories of Roger's death, brawls over money and Ludwig's disappearance then grisly find in the Blue Mountains. The question on most lips was, had Ludwig been the victim of another of the gay-hate murders that beset the city? It had the community looking over their shoulders as they walked home after a night out on Oxford Street.

My interest in the case was prompted for two different reasons. I'd read the racy accounts in the press, some of which I'd worked on with a journalist, and also in my mind were the murders earlier that year of Richard Johnson and Krichakorn Rattanajurathaporn. Was Ludwig's death another gay-hate murder?

A few days before Christmas 1990, I received a call from Dawn O'Donnell. We'd known each other for a few years socially and she knew my past as a copper. 'Love,' she said in her raspy tenor, 'I think I'm in the shit. Can you come and meet me, it's not one for the phone.' A short time later we met at Hanover's coffee shop in Oxford Street, a place with bentwood chairs, heavy timbered décor, ordinary coffee and cakes with lashings of cream.

It looked like they'd tried to re-create a slice of old Vienna but got the name wrong. Dawn was in her usual denim outfit, with her steel grey hair cut in a mannish style that was never boyish, and carrying a large pile of keys that opened the doors of sex clubs, sex shops, pubs and her spacious pile at Beauty Point with its Middle Harbour views and collection of fine paintings allegedly by great Australian artists.

What struck me most about Dawn that afternoon was that her usual composure was gone. She looked old, tired and rattled, but she was straight to the point. With coffee orders out of the way and waiters and patrons out of earshot, she said, 'Love, it's about Ludy's murder. A source of mine high up in the investigation reckons the bastards want a result and are going to fit me for it!' I wasn't surprised. Dawn had strong contacts in the NSW Police. She and Roger-Claude had run some of the shadiest businesses in town that featured the twin motivators for bent coppers of the time – sex and booze. Bribing police to turn a blind eye to the antics, or, in New South Wales, the cardinal sin of selling a beer without the appropriate licence, was a cost of doing business. Police also hadn't looked especially energetically when Capriccio's had burned down on schedule. Dawn also used Brian Roberts as a solicitor, and a few contacts of mine had mentioned that Brian regularly entertained NSW coppers at his home.

Dawn then launched into a long story, with occasional hand-wringing, during which she reiterated her sadness at Ludwig's passing, how bad it looked that Vince was the main beneficiary of the will and that she'd been helping him with a few business opportunities. Vince, she reckoned, wasn't 'the sharpest tool in the shed, love, but he's a sweetheart and in this life, love, the queens will be all over him'. She assured me she'd had nothing to do with the murder and was as 'shocked as anyone' when he disappeared. 'I knew he'd been worried, and some of Roger's old friends could be such bitches, but Ludwig was a drama queen, so I thought he was wrong. Looks like I was.' Reflecting on the interview, I thought Dawn's story was largely the truth or she was a better actress than an ice-skater. I reckoned she was a cold-blooded opportunist, but not a killer.

We wrapped up our coffee chat with some advice. I told her that while I didn't want to know who her highly placed source was – though I had a fair idea – she might consider that police will usually only arrest for something as serious as murder when they've got the case nailed down. I didn't mention I thought it likely she was bribing her source or offering some sort of contra deal – coppers don't give away information to someone like Dawn without an expectation of compensation – but I suggested her source might be in round one of a scheme to squeeze some cash out of her. If she bites, then round two is to squeeze a bit harder by offering to derail the investigation into her, for a suitably large payment. By the deepening scowl, she hadn't thought of that but was now reviewing the situation. We parted and I didn't hear from her again on the subject. She was never arrested.

If you've spent your life interviewing people involved in crime and skulduggery, one thing is constant: even the most honest do not tell the whole truth, and it's for a mix of reasons including memory failure, asking the wrong questions, concern for their own welfare or that of others, and my favourite, the witness who spoon-feeds you as much as they think you should know. The latter are the ones you hit squarely with hard questions so they get the message that you're in charge, you already know much of what they know, and you're not easily conned; it's a strategy that usually produces a resigned nod and flow of information. Dawn hadn't been frank in her discussions with me as I found out years later, which may have been because she was a very cagey human being.

Ludwig's will was probated on 11 January 1991, with Vince getting a fifty per cent share in Kingsteam, which he had Dawn manage for him. In late January/early February, Roberts, as executor of the will, paid the beneficiaries, including Hamilton and Fidirikkos, and persuaded Esposito to let him handle his chunky legacy. Vince later said he only saw around $140 000, which he spent on himself, his ex-wife and their children. Roberts 'managed' away nearly a million dollars, including steering Vince into a gym in Newtown in partnership with Dawn and funded by Vince.

A glimmer of hope entered the stalled murder investigation when Detective Sergeant Steve McCann of the Homicide Squad began to look at the case. In 1990 he had led investigations into the murders of Richard Johnson on 15 January and Krichakorn Rattanajurathaporn on 21 July. In an interview with the *Sydney Morning Herald* on 9 February 1991, McCann said he was 'mystified and intrigued' by the case and 'the only thing we feel sure of is that this was a professional killing'. McCann's level of intrigue was piqued by a criminal in custody, called witness X by police, who had contacted the investigators in late 1990 and said he'd been contracted to burgle the Sutherland Street house and murder Ludwig. The fee offered for the job was $60 000, which he had accepted, but the plan had been thwarted by the man's arrest for an unrelated crime.

The Supreme Court action by the short-changed beneficiaries who were alleging Ludwig had exerted 'undue influence' over his lover stimulated police to begin to look at the will. The classic investigative technique of 'follow the money' led them to Brian Roberts and Dawn O'Donnell. On 27 September 1991, the same pair got a windfall courtesy of the Supreme Court in an action brought by Roberts against Denise and Charles Coussens, who had declined to cede a directorship in the company that operated Kingsteam. Roberts won. A few days later, on the Monday of the October long weekend, Coussens received a disturbing telephone call from a person she thought was a 'young man', who refused to give his name but said he'd been motivated to call after reading reports of Roberts' victory in court. He had information about the murder, and Coussens gave him McCann's phone number and urged him to call him.

The already murky case became murkier, with Coussens recounting in her statement of 23 November 1992: 'He said something like, I can't go to the police because it was the police that did it. The solicitor had paid them fifty thousand dollars to be in Ludwig's flat and they murdered him. The evidence will be in the carpet.' The two spoke again an hour later, and about two weeks after that when the young man said he had contacted McCann and an ABC journalist Coussens had recommended. He didn't call again.

Roberts' dream run came to an end in December 1992 when McCann and his team arrested him for forgery of the will and other documents. His luck continued to slide at the coronial inquest into the deaths of Ludwig and Roger-Claude, which concluded in September 1994 with Coroner Gould finding that Ludwig 'died at the hands of person or persons unknown' and that Roger's death would remain a mystery because of the lack of a post-mortem. Professor David Cooper of St Vincent's HIV unit gave evidence that some of Roger's medication had been found, two years after his death, to occasionally cause heart problems. The professor also said that sudden death for people with advanced HIV like Roger wasn't uncommon, and tantalisingly, that without a post-mortem he couldn't comment on whether Roger's demise was due to his health issues or 'some other misadventure'.

Roger's close friends, having seen him in good form the night before he was found dead in his bed, were fans of the 'other misadventure' theory. The *Sydney Morning Herald* of 20 September 1994 reported that the Coroner observed: 'Mr Brian Roberts and Mrs Dawn Irwin, an entrepreneur, had both benefited more substantially' from Ludwig's death. McCann commented on the evidence given by Vince of the fight and flight of Ludwig, dismissing it as a 'feeble and intriguing excuse'. On 23 December 1994, the Legal Services Commission struck Roberts off as a solicitor, commenting his conduct was 'disgraceful and dishonourable'.

Roberts ended up facing multiple charges of fraud and was sentenced to four years in prison. At one of the hearings in April 1996, financial experts who'd pulled apart his handling of both estates told the court Roberts had directly benefited to the tune of $500 000, with a further $475 000 going to companies in which he had an interest. The judge described Roberts as carrying out a 'binge of criminality'. The only problem was the will, signed on 7 September 1990, was a forgery constructed by Brian Roberts. However, it's a story that had some life left in it, and it was rekindled thanks to Roberts' estranged wife, Leonie.

CHAPTER 18

WIRED FOR SOUND

By 1991, Detective Sergeant Steve McCann's pleas to the gay community for help hadn't yielded the solid evidence needed to have the 'reasonable cause to suspect' to arrest someone for the violence at Bondi, and for that matter, to shed light on the deaths of John Russell and Ross Warren that would turn them from misadventure into murder. Gilles Mattaini was still an unreported missing person. However, in the first quarter of that year the hope of a breakthrough came again from a braggart.

One of the juveniles convicted for the killing of Richard Johnson at Alexandria Park was in custody at the Keelong Detention Centre in Unanderra, and said in front of a social worker and other inmates that he'd pushed a gay man off a cliff at Bondi and onto the rocks, not the water. When asked by one of the inmates: 'Why do you hate poofs, it's not as if they have sex in front of you,' the teen responded, 'They do, they do it in the park, at school and in the Cross.' He also said he'd thrown the gay man's car keys into the water after which there had been a scuffle. Whether it was big-noting himself or factual, it grabbed their attention and was reported to the police. One of the inmates, who'd been in the audience, offered to wear a recording device to pick up any subsequent brags of murder or assault. Detective Sue Emmett, who'd worked with McCann, included the death of John Russell and the disappearance of Ross Warren in her April 1991 affidavit to obtain the recording device. She noted, 'Due to the large number of similar attacks in the same location it is unsure which attack' the teen was referring to.

At the same time, Detective James Bignell was heading down the same track, using an inmate of the Minda Detention Centre. He added to his list of inquiries the murders of Raymond Keam and William Allen, and also Cleveland Street High School social-science teacher Wayne Tonks, murdered in his home unit in Artarmon on Sydney's north shore on 19 May 1990. His body was found two days later when the school called police after the normally punctual and reliable teacher hadn't arrived.

Wayne met a grisly end, beaten with what police thought was a baseball bat, rendering him nearly senseless. Then came the truly horrific part. His killers used industrial-grade adhesive tape to wrap his ankles and knees, then pulled his arms around his back and secured them in place by taping his wrists. Then they taped his mouth and eyes closed, placed a plastic shopping bag over his head and taped it tightly at the neck, cutting off his air. Wayne slowly suffocated. Detective Malcolm Smith described it as a 'cruel and callous murder'. With Tonks struggling against his bonds and dying slowly, his killers ransacked the home unit, with police thinking they'd been looking for something in particular, but there was nothing to indicate any thefts. What also troubled police was no sign of forced entry to the unit, so presumably

Tonks had either been conned into letting them in or knew them. One bonus for the investigators was they found fingerprints at the scene, but they couldn't match them to any prints on file.

What linked Tonks to the murders at Bondi and Alexandria Park were the facts that Tonks was gay and the possibility that some of the offenders had gone to, or were still students of, Cleveland Street High School. Smith said of Tonks: 'He was highly regarded. He was a dedicated and conscientious school teacher. He taught at a school in inner Sydney, which was difficult in many respects. However, Wayne was highly regarded by both the students and the teachers and the school management. Wayne had a private life. He was a very lonely man and he certainly appreciated his privacy.' The police discovered that Tonks had a similar habit as Johnson and had left his telephone number on the walls of toilets, and they speculated that this was how his attackers might have arranged to get into his unit.

Unfortunately for the detectives, none of the recorded conversations in the juvenile detention centres provided any intelligence or useable evidence to advance the investigation. The police force is hierarchical and runs on process and detail – a great strength, and often a great failing if you're challenging them – and so McCann had to account for his actions, use of resources and budget to his superiors. The other characteristic of policing is the need to 'cover your arse', a skill mastered by the police hierarchy early in their careers.

On 15 April 1991, McCann reported on crimes and 'the possible connection involving victims in the homosexual community in the Alexandria and South Bondi area'. His report covered the successful investigation of the murders of Richard Johnson and Krichakorn Rattanajurathaporn and the assault on

Geoffrey Sullivan, and noted that a taskforce had been set up to look specifically at crimes against gay men. McCann followed up on 10 August 1991 with a report in which he discussed the death of William Allen, John Russell and Raymond Keam, and the disappearance of Ross Warren. In Ross's case, McCann had been hopeful of getting recordings to pinpoint the involvement of specific youths, but without this breakthrough he'd had another idea and spoken to Crown Prosecutor Mark Tedeschi QC about the possibility of getting indemnities to persuade some of his suspects to turn; the prosecutor told him he was 'unlikely to get blanket indemnities for these offenders having in mind the overall circumstances for their incarceration'. He then mentioned two women from Nowra who'd come forward as a result of the publicity, and given statements that a female acquaintance had told them about three weeks after Ross's death that she'd been present when Ross was thrown from the cliff.

One of the women said the acquaintance told them: 'We bashed and killed him. You know, the guy who reads the news and weather on TV.' She said the woman bragged, 'There was a group of about eight of us, a Lebanese gang from Kings Cross. We got him and threw him off the rocks. We go poofter bashing all the time.' The woman's daughter was interviewed separately and had a similar recollection, telling McCann's team she had been getting ready to go to a soccer game when the acquaintance came to her home and said she knew something about Ross Warren.

She told the witness, 'We go poofter bashing all the time,' and, 'Do you know the one off the news that does the weather reports. The good-looking one?' The witness said she did, and the woman continued: 'We happened to find him and his boyfriend. We took him somewhere and bashed him.' The witness said, 'Although she is a bragger, she had no reason to brag about this. I believe she was telling the truth.'

The only way to obtain convincing evidence was for both witnesses to wear a listening device, and they flatly refused. McCann noted the suspect was a woman who had a 'lengthy criminal history for violence' and it was 'strongly felt she would not be open to police interrogation'. Even if this were not the case, she was 'nomadic and her present whereabouts are unknown'.

A possible witness in the Keam case had also refused to wear a listening device, thus putting that angle of inquiry on the backburner. As for John Russell, nothing new had come to light. McCann's summary at the end of the report caught his frustrations and the lousy relations police had with the gay community. He wrote, 'Throughout the course of this inquiry it was obvious that little help was gained from the homosexual community in reporting incidents of bashings to police.' McCann went on: 'This was largely supported by the lack of reported assaults in the relevant areas'. Or reported and never followed up, like the attack on Alan Rosendale.

He finished by saying: 'The reluctance of witnesses to assist police in their pursuit has prevented criminal charges from being laid against any individual.' The lousy police treatment of the gay community over decades had adversely affected both the police officers investigating the case and the community, who wanted results, and so the police moved on to other cases. A glimpse of what the gay community thought about police came in a letter to Sue Thompson of the NSW Police Gay/Lesbian Client Consultant and published in the *Sydney Star Observer* on 7 September 1990. The letter was about the February 1986 possible murder of Wollongong man William 'Bill' Rooney.

The letter writer was Rooney's partner Wayne Davis, who wrote 'to express his appreciation of the work undertaken by Detective Sergeant David Ainsworth'. Davis said: 'The reaction to this of the original investigating detectives was to put Bill's death down to an accident. The treatment I received from the police during the investigation was, to say the least, less than sympathetic. I was of the impression that as a gay man, I was a lesser human being and that Bill's death didn't matter because he was gay.' He went on: 'In the inquest into Bill's death I was of the distinct impression police were trying to secure a verdict of "death by misadventure".' Ainsworth, however, didn't go with the flow, and according to Davis's letter 'continued to investigate the circumstances of Bill's death and of the subsequent gay bashings'. Ainsworth, he wrote, had a 'sympathetic and caring attitude'. He ended the letter: 'Finally, it is indeed heartening to know the New South Wales Police Force has officers of the calibre of this man.'

Rooney's suspicious death came just a month before a sexual predator began a series of vicious rapes and beatings of men in Wollongong that would last until his arrest in September 1989.

CHAPTER 19

DOWN IN THE 'GONG

When Wayne Davis, a thirty-one-year-old TAFE teacher, got home from work on Friday, 14 February 1986, he expected to find William 'Bill' Rooney, his partner of four years, waiting for him. Wayne had spent the night before at a friend's place and had gone straight to work from there. Bill was a thirty-two-year-old Scotsman who had lived in Sydney when he first arrived in Australia, and met Davis at the 1982 Mardi Gras. Not long after that meeting Bill moved in with Wayne in Wollongong. Rooney was on a disability pension supplemented by occasional cash jobs, and Wayne described his lover as an easy-going, affable and highly intelligent man who was a 'party animal'.

Rooney liked a drink, so Wayne did a quick tour of their favourite hotels to see if he could find him, but when that plan failed, he returned to the house, opened a beer and watched the news on WIN television. One of the stories on the broadcast told of a young man without any identification found unconscious earlier that morning in a laneway off Crown Street in Wollongong's CBD. Police had taken the man's fingerprints and found that his name was William Rooney, an identification made possible because Bill had been arrested a few years earlier for stealing a bottle of whiskey. Wayne was horrified, but knew the relationship between some police and the gay community in Wollongong was poor, so he thought it prudent to take someone with him when he spoke to the police.

Davis called his friend, gay activist Levinia Crooks, and the two went to the hospital where Davis identified Rooney as his partner, and got the bad news that Bill was quite likely to die from severe head injuries. He recalled noticing, aside from other injuries, an abrasion above one of Bill's eyes and what he thought was the imprint of a fist on his stomach.

After spending time with Bill, Davis and Crooks went to the Wollongong Police Station, where Davis said he was seated in a small room with detectives crowded around him. Their initial questions tried to identify Bill's wife or girlfriend, but when Wayne explained that Bill was gay and he was his partner, the crowd thinned quickly, and he gave a signed statement to the detectives. At that early point it was likely he was a suspect – a reasonable assumption based on statistics and experience. However, he was eliminated rapidly after explaining his movements of the night of the thirteenth, and they were quickly verified.

Wayne told the detectives that on 13 February Bill had phoned him at work around 5.45pm and suggested a beer, so Wayne drove home to Gwynneville to pick up Bill – who didn't drive – and the couple went to Tattersall's Hotel in Crown Street, Wollongong near the train station. They drank around six schooners of Fosters and at around 10pm Wayne headed off to a friend's place in Keiraville; Bill said he was going to nearby Annabel's Disco in Crown Lane, which attracted a mix of gay and straight clientele and where the barman was a friend. He said Bill was 'in extremely good spirits and wasn't overly affected by liquor to any degree as he drinks quite a bit and can hold his liquor'.

At 8.40am the following day, Harvey Finch, who managed L&B Discounts at 250 Crown Street, Wollongong, went to the rear of his store, where he noticed a man – later identified as Bill Rooney – covered in blood, lying between the store and a concrete wall. Finch called the police, who arrived swiftly, and he was taken to Wollongong Hospital, where he was found to have massive skull fractures.

Detectives and scientific investigators arrived at the yard around 9.30am; however, the original police hadn't secured the scene and someone had hosed it down and most of the blood and physical evidence was gone. The examination included a few photographs and not much else. Looking at the surviving documentation thirty years later, there is no mention of the position of Bill's body – face-down or face-up – or where precisely in the yard it was, or a description of the location. One of the doctors who treated Bill had been told by ambulance officers that he'd fallen down a short flight of steps that led from the lane to the place where he was found. Wayne Davis recalled taking a look at the scene and thought that Bill's fall was six to eight feet. Wayne said Bill's main injuries were to the back of his head, indicating he'd fallen backwards.

Dr Mason Ramsay, head of intensive care at the hospital, confirmed massive skull fractures. For four days Bill was kept alive using a ventilator, but by the afternoon of the nineteenth he was brain dead, and Wayne, who'd got consent from Bill's family in Scotland, agreed life support should be discontinued. Bill died at 2.35pm the next day.

The investigation into what had happened to Bill was hampered by the lack of forensic evidence and an unspectacular investigation. Detective Senior Constable John Tait visited the hospital that morning and noticed abrasions to Bill's face, bruising on the inside of his left forearm and just below his right nipple, lacerations on his right thumb and 'considerable bruising to his right knee'. What the detectives didn't request was an examination for sexual assault.

Detectives checked around hotels for anyone who'd seen Bill; they found witnesses who'd noticed a drunken man passed out on the grass not far from the scene, and a local garbage man who'd seen a young man with what he reckoned was a broken arm around 6am. He had offered to drive the man to the hospital but his offer was declined and the young man wasn't Bill. Police checked the hospital but couldn't find any record of the man being treated. Detective Tait said he'd made some inquiries with 'members of the gay community' on 15 February but 'none were prepared to offer any information to the police'. Relations between the gay community and the police were toxic at the time.

The uniformed officers who submitted their P79A 'Report of Death to the Coroner' noted: 'Suspicious circumstances are related to this deceased.' However, in his statement for the Coroner, Tait said, 'I am of the opinion that the person Rooney was under the influence of liquor and sustained his injuries as a result of falling.' Wayne Davis recalled 'they [police] were keen to adhere to Tait's view of an accident while drunk; however, Dr Ramsay was adamant that the severity of Bill's head injuries wasn't easily explained by a fall.' On 15 May 1987, Coroner Warwick Soden found that Bill died from head injuries, 'but whether such injuries were received accidentally or otherwise the evidence does not allow me to say'.

However, a few of the detectives at Wollongong didn't agree with their colleagues, and thought the case was a murder. Though their views and suggestions of a more detailed investigation were overruled by the police hierarchy, the detectives did some discreet snooping. One of the ambulance officers who'd been at the scene recalled that Bill's fly had been open and when he tried to zip him to afford him some dignity, the severely injured man resisted. To one detective this was either an instinctive reaction or the act of a man trying to prevent a recurrence of an attack. The detective was even more surprised to find that there was no mention of Bill's fly being at half-mast in any of the police observations, nor had he been examined for evidence of a sexual assault. As in the Johnson, Russell and Warren cases, so much could have and should have been done on day one. Case closed, which was a decision that should have been overturned in the light of what happened less than a month after Bill's death.

The first reported attack happened in the early hours of 8 March 1986. A twenty-one-year-old apprentice spray-painter, still living at home with his parents, went out for a Friday night drinking session with friends and it turned into a pub/club crawl. The young man had no memory of what happened after he'd been refused entry to the Illawarra Leagues Club. His next recollection was waking up in a 'critical but stable' condition in Wollongong Hospital, after being admitted with severe head injuries. A medical examination, ordered by a thorough detective, found that the man had injuries to his anus 'consistent with a sexual assault'.

Later that afternoon, the detectives went to the Kenny Street car park close to McCabe Park, where they found a patch of grass covered in blood. The scene was examined carefully, evidence was collected and photographs taken. Over the next three years, a total of twelve sexual assaults on young men were reported, and all shared a similar modus operandi. The attacks were usually in the hours shortly after midnight, the men were often on their way home from a long night's drinking in the pubs and clubs in central Wollongong, and a couple had walked through McCabe Park, about 500 metres from the train station, where they were attacked. Some were hit on the head from behind with a rock, or threatened with a beating with a rock held in the attacker's hand if they failed to comply.

The attack involved the man pulling down his victim's trousers, oral sex – either performed on them by the attacker, or the attacker demanding it be performed on him – followed by him anally raping them. Some were robbed. One of the victims recalled the attacker, a taller than average, well-built and good-looking man in his early twenties, had a small penis.

The last reported attack was on 22 September 1989. The victim was a twenty-eight-year-old storeman who'd gone out for drinks with his mates around 7.30 the night before. They were celebrating the birth of a friend's child and started the night at Tattersalls Hotel and then moved to Pips nightclub around 10.30pm, where they kept drinking until the early hours of the next morning. The group broke up after an argument, leaving the victim drinking alone. He reckoned he was 'fairly intoxicated' when he left the club and walked up Crown Lane, and that a man 'started to punch me about the head viciously and I fell to the ground. This man then had something in his hand like a brick, rock or a piece of concrete and he hit me in the face repeatedly.' The victim was then anally raped.

Detectives visited him in hospital on 26 September and showed him a book of photographs. The man pointed to one and said, 'It's still a bit cloudy; all I know is he did have a red face like that guy.' Around 5.30 that afternoon, the detectives arrested twenty-four-year-old Mark Anthony Scerri at his home in Berkeley. Back at the Wollongong Police Station, Scerri denied the allegations of sexual assault and beating and said he'd never been in McCabe Park. As the detectives painstakingly took him through the long list of attacks, Scerri went from denial to refusing to answer questions. Police contacted his solicitor, who agreed to visit his client the next morning before court. Scerri was charged with the sexual assault and beating of one man.

At court the next morning, Scerri walked through a crowd of forty or so people. He wasn't handcuffed or flanked by police, but he was spotted by two of his victims who'd been brought to court to see if they could pick their attacker out of the crowd, and they did. Scerri was arrested again after his brief court appearance and this time he wouldn't walk free. The police investigation led to Scerri facing twenty-nine charges including attempted murder, kidnapping, sexual assault, assault inflicting grievous bodily harm and robbery against twelve male victims. The crimes were mainly in Wollongong, with one in Nowra and another in Jindabyne. His arrest prompted protests outside the police station by his friends and supporters, claiming he'd been set up by the police. Scerri stirred the dissent, claiming police 'wanted to load me up with everything', a common theme for criminals of the time, but in this case he was ignoring the similarity of all the attacks. As the extent and brutality of his crimes became apparent, the protesters dwindled.

Scerri left school at fourteen and worked as a builder's labourer, in the motor trade in workshops and later for the State Rail Authority, and admitted to being a binge drinker from the time he left school. His only criminal record was for drink-driving, minor assaults and offensive behaviour – crimes indicating problems with booze rather than a dangerous criminal streak.

At the first trial, the jury was discharged after failing to reach a verdict. One source reckoned it was because the good-looking and charming young man managed to sway some of the jurors into doubting his guilt. The prosecutors later took a truncated case to the court, proceeding only on the attacks on three men. The men were described in court as victims C, L and M.

On 19 February 1993 Scerri was found guilty by a Supreme Court jury of five counts of sexual assault, one count of maliciously inflicting grievous bodily harm, one count of maliciously inflicting actual bodily harm and one count of stealing. After listening to extensive psychiatric evidence and pleas for leniency including an assertion that alcohol motivated his crime – the credibility of which took a hit when a cab driver who'd driven him home after one of the attacks said he'd appeared 'quite sober' – Justice Greg James QC sent Scerri to prison for sixteen years. An appeal failed, with the judge commenting that Scerri had committed a 'horrifying sequence of serious crimes'. The *Illawarra Mercury* of 20 February 1993 had Scerri on the front page with the headline 'Sex Monster Gets 16 Years', and described him as 'the region's worst criminal'.

The detectives visited Scerri at Long Bay on 20 May 1993, and they had one old case to clear up – the death of Bill Rooney. The similarities between Bill's injuries and the methods Scerri had used in his attacks, along with the timeline and locations, were compelling. Plus, they had one other piece of evidence. On the evening of 18 December 1986, a thirty-two-year-old man had driven to McCabe Park and parked. Shortly after midnight a man whom he had seen standing near the toilet block approached him and asked if he wanted to go for a drive to Stuart Park about 2.5 kilometres away and on the beachfront. The man agreed and he recalled they drove there, got out of the car and as the man started to walk toward the beach, his passenger directed him to a spot above the beach. He told police: 'We got there and then started to cuddle and fondle each other with our clothes on, then we both took all our clothes off and he asked me to give him oral sex. I noticed this man had a small penis. I started to perform oral sex on him and while I was doing so this man just hit me to the side of the head. After he did this I backed off and said, "What the fuck is going on?" He punched me to the ground again and said something along the lines of this would be the last time I get to pick up anybody.'

The man ran, but was 'football tackled' by his attacker. The two struggled on the ground and the man was finally overwhelmed. He said, 'I couldn't see very well, and I was very scared.' The attacker forced him to 'crouch on the ground on my hands and . . . then he started to have anal intercourse with me'. The rape continued, broken only by brief pauses in which the attacker 'would go to the bush looking around as if he was looking for something'. After one of these moments, the attacker returned 'holding a large rock'. Using the rock to threaten his victim, he resumed his sexual assaults.

The man recalled: 'While he was doing this he was very abusive and he said to me something about my car, I think he was going to steal it and I told him it was my parents' car and that

I had to have it home and my parents would be worried. He said to me, "I'll kill you like I did the other poofter in the laneway."' The victim recalled: 'At this point I was crying, upset and very scared and when he said this to me I thought of a friend of mine who died in a laneway in Wollongong about six to twelve months earlier. I made out that I didn't know what he was talking about. He then put the rock in my hands and said, "I'm going to smash your head in with this rock."' The victim begged: 'Don't kill me, you can do anything you want to me, just don't hurt me, don't kill me.' When the assaults finally ended, the attacker drove his victim to the car park of the Tattersalls Hotel and left him there in the car. The victim waited until he thought he was safe, and went to police. This attack resulted in some of the charges heard at Scerri's first trial.

Armed with detailed knowledge of how Scerri operated, the detectives met Scerri in a conference room in the remand centre of the prison. He opened the conversation by demanding, 'What's this in aid of?' When they told him they wanted to interview him about the death of William Rooney, Scerri said, 'You can both stick it up your arse, get fucked, fuck off,' which ended the interview. The detectives took their brief to a senior Crown Prosecutor who, while sympathetic, told them what they expected to hear – without a confession, witnesses, the evidence to prove Bill's death was murder, and evidence to implicate Scerri, there was not sufficient case to arrest him, let alone put him in front of a jury.

Wayne Davis stirred the case along in an interview with the *Illawarra Mercury* on 30 September 1993. He appealed for any witnesses to Bill Rooney's death to come forward and took aim at the police who'd investigated the case, saying, 'The police were initially very keen to pin it on me, that was traumatic. Had I been home alone that night I could very well be in jail. It would have been an easy solution. The police weren't that interested – it was just another "poofta"; however, I do believe Dave Ainsworth is serious and I respect him for it.'

Scerri was released from prison in November 2001 and at the time the officials thought his chance of re-offending was 'moderate'. He had received treatment in prison and written letters of apology to his victims. On the outside, he developed a relationship with an old girlfriend, who thought he was 'very caring and loving' and got on 'terrifically' with her young son.

However, on 12 May 2002, Scerri struck again. His victim was a twenty-four-year-old man who'd left a nightclub in Wollongong's CBD around 5am and was planning to get either a taxi or a train home. Scerri crept up behind him, put his right forearm around the man's neck and then dragged him to a grassy spot near the station. He forced the man to the ground, then pinned him down by sitting on him. He punched him, then pulled the man's trousers down and performed oral sex. Scerri was enraged when the man didn't respond to his ministrations, but the young man saw an opportunity and gouged Scerri's eyes, then pushed Scerri off him and stumbled away, trying to pull up his trousers as he escaped. He reported the attack to the nearby Wollongong Police Station, and then went to hospital, where he was treated for a broken nose, abrasions and damage to his neck.

It didn't take inspirational police work to put Scerri at the top of the list of suspects, and when they raided his home they found boxer shorts that, when examined, had traces of the victim's DNA on them. Scerri went straight back to prison and on 12 September 2003 pleaded guilty at the District Court. In one of the reports tendered at the sentencing hearing a psychiatrist commented that 'his erotic sexual fantasies involve dominance over the victim'. Scerri was sentenced to eight years, and was released in February 2011.

The mystery of Bill Rooney's death remains.

CHAPTER 20

THE TOLL RISES

Back in Sydney, the murders and attacks on gay men continued through the early nineties, with the focus moving away from gay beats like Marks Park. Police thought some of the murders were domestically motivated and a couple either willingly or grudgingly acknowledged as possibly involving gay hate. The Reverend Fred Nile didn't help to moderate the problem with a speech given in the Legislative Council on 24 October 1991. After quoting at length some grisly details of gay bashing and prejudice detailed in a *Sydney Morning Herald* 'Good Weekend' piece from January that year titled 'Extreme Prejudice', Nile took aim at the victims. He told the chamber the violence in Sydney had no comparison to the nation's other major cities, and said: 'I present the case in this motion that there is a direct association between the provocation of a homosexual–lesbian Mardi Gras parade and what appears to be a backlash in the form of violent attacks.'

The Reverend lurched on, talking of the murder of Richard Johnson, then Ludwig Gertsch, of whose death he said, 'Not every murder or assault is part of anti-homosexual feeling, but obviously the majority are carried out by people who strongly reject homosexuals and their lifestyle.' Nile then mentioned the arrest of Scerri, so it's likely he hadn't bothered to research the allegations against Scerri.

William Duffield, a forty-one-year-old former jockey, was bludgeoned to death at his home in Mosman on 20 November 1991. The weapon was a sticky-tape dispenser, and topping the police list of suspects was a long-term friend. Police believed the likely culprit was someone Duffield had had sex with but declined to describe it as a gay-hate murder.

There was a similar finding in the murder of Kenneth Brennan, a fifty-three-year-old school teacher. Brennan was stabbed to death at his home in Elizabeth Bay and was found by his partner when he returned home on 12 June 1995. The two men had been at a dinner party in Bellevue Hill on Saturday 10 June and had a disagreement, so the partner had stayed there for the weekend. Brennan had gone home by train to Kings Cross Station. The walk to his apartment, if taking the straightest possible course, would have taken him through seedy Fitzroy Gardens, then still used by sex workers, drug users and thugs. There was no sign of forced entry at Brennan's home, but there was evidence he'd had sex prior to his death. In both the Duffield and Brennan killings, no-one has been arrested.

One of the strangest deaths was that of sixty-four-year-old Cyril Olsen who drowned in Rushcutters Bay on 22 August 1992. Olsen liked a drink and had been indulging heavily earlier that night, probably in Kings Cross at the gloriously sleazy Bottoms Up Bar at the Rex Hotel in Macleay Street, beside the El Alamein Fountain. The bar was in its final years – it closed in 1994 – and had been a gay watering hole for decades. In its latter days it featured strippers strolling around the bar top, sex workers hunting their prey, and the prey hunting sex workers for a keener price, and men who liked a schooner for brunch and then kept going until the final cleansing ale before stumbling out into the night. It was sleazy but it was an institution.

On his way home, Cyril diverted to the toilets at Rushcutters Bay Park. The toilets are now a chic cafe but back in the seventies, eighties and nineties it was a beat notable for a high volume of traffic in the late evening, and for bashers. You took a chance that either good or bad luck would come your way. That night for Cyril, fortune wasn't on his side and he was attacked and viciously beaten. No witnesses to the attack came forward, and it's likely that other beat users ran as the bashers swept in. What happened is appallingly sad. Cyril, likely befuddled by the attack, stumbled around the park and unfortunately took a northerly route toward the harbour. One local, out walking, saw Cyril near the wharf and recalled he had a bloody face. They spoke briefly and the witness thought Cyril was 'significantly intoxicated' but declined the man's help.

Cyril's body, without pants or shoes, was found in the harbour the next morning. Police believed it was a gay-hate crime and at the subsequent inquest said he was 'the victim of gay bashing and due to his injuries and level of intoxication was disoriented resulting in him falling from the wharf and drowning'. The Coroner found that Cyril 'drowned after accidentally falling'.

No-one was ever arrested for their part in Cyril's death, but police did get an anonymous tip-off from a male who said he'd been told by a cellmate in prison that he'd been out with mates to 'roll a poof tonight' around the time of Cyril's death.

Professor Stephen Tomsen wrote in his 2002 paper 'Hatred, Murder and Male Honour' that Cyril's response to people offering help may have been due to what he believed was 'tenuous claim [as victims of attacks at beats] to a status as legitimate victims seeking help'.

On 23 December 1993, Crispin Dye, the forty-one-year-old road manager for AC/DC, was bashed and robbed in Little Oxford Street near Taylor Square. Witnesses reckoned it was around 4.30am when they saw a man being beaten by three young males of 'Islander' appearance. The assailants bashed him, stole his wallet and then left him bleeding in the gutter. He died in St George Hospital on Christmas Day.

When not on the road, Crispin split his time between Cairns, where he kept away from the winter, and Willoughby on Sydney's north shore with his mother. On the night he was attacked, Crispin had been out on the town with friends to celebrate his maiden outing as a singer/songwriter with the release of his CD *A Heart Like Mine.*

Celebrations started with drinks at Gilligan's until about 1am, then moved to the Flinders Hotel about 500 metres away in Flinders Street – a common route for many men. Crispin kept drinking until the Flinders closed around 3am, then walked to the Courthouse Hotel at Taylor Square. Again it was a common route, and if you were heading to the Courthouse at that time it was likely you'd drunk enough to not be making decisions with any clarity. While there was a reasonable description of the three men, and a rumoured admission by a prisoner – often of dubious merit – that he'd 'knocked off' Crispin, no-one has been arrested.

The case was originally thought to have a gay-hate possibility, not unreasonable considering that you wouldn't head to

Oxford Street to find a straight man to rob. Crispin had been candid with his mother, telling her, 'People say I'm gay, Mum, but I don't know what I am.' When the Homicide Squad reviewed the cold case in 2014 they thought 'all the circumstances' pointed to robbery as the motive. More recently they've changed that view – perhaps motivated by context – and reckon 'based on perceived homosexuality and the incident location, this is a possible gay-hate crime'.

Professor Stephen Tomsen wrote in his 1996 research paper 'Gay Killings in New South Wales: Victimisation and the Legal Response' that from a search of murder and manslaughter records in New South Wales from 1980, there had been seventy-four homicides that could have been 'termed gay killings', and his analysis of the court records of 'thirty-one gay-hate killings recorded by the New South Wales Police Service from 1986 suggest the evident motives for this violence reflect both elements of homophobia and violent conceptions of heterosexual masculinity'. The figures didn't include cases where the victim's sexual preference was apparently incidental to the crime, or domestic murders. What was disturbing was that around twenty-five per cent of all victims of 'stranger' killings were gay men.

Nicholas Parkhill, the Chairman of ACON, which started life in 1985 as the Aids Council of New South Wales, wrote in the *Sydney Morning Herald* on 16 April 2015: 'The facts are that there are dozens of deaths and hundreds of bashings of men in and around beats between 1985 and 1995 that remain unresolved. During this time gay men lived in an atmosphere of extraordinary fear.'

One of the few positives is that by the mid 1990s what looked like an epidemic of violence against gay men seemed to have passed. There was still violence, but the frequency and ferocity was on the wane. Sydney, and particularly the gay scene and attitudes to it, was changing. AIDS/HIV didn't and still doesn't have a cure but it was on the cusp of becoming manageable rather than a death sentence – a combination of drugs introduced in 1996 literally saved lives and saw men with a life expectation of a few months return to good health and the expectation of a long and productive life. The mystery and terror of the disease was gone; and with around 16 000 diagnosed cases in Australia by 1996 and 5100 deaths, the brutal fact was that we had grown accustomed to it and knew how to handle and prevent it.

One of the few good notes to emerge from the AIDS crisis was that a strong sense of community emerged and it was a 'brand' that was being assimilated into the broader community. The Mardi Gras shift from being a political protest to one of the biggest events on the Sydney calendar is a prime example. Closet doors were being kicked open at last.

The culture of the NSW Police was also changing for a variety of reasons. The Wood Royal Commission was in full flight, exposing corruption, dodgy practices and horrible crimes involving the police; a generation of coppers from the bad old days were retiring and in some cases as quickly as possible, while some had decided to stay on and were 'born again' – the slang for forgetting their dodgy pasts and extolling the virtues of honesty, integrity, community spirit and taped records of interview rather than unsigned documents and verbals.

In Parliament, Franca Arena and Deirdre Grusovin were reaching their use-by date. Few were buying their 'circle of friends' stories about a coterie of powerful gay men who doubled as paedophiles. The public had grown tired of the repetitive allegations and the absence of any credible or useable evidence. 'Put up or shut up' was the consensus around Darlinghurst. Senator Bill Heffernan and Charlie Lynn from the NSW Legislative Council would recycle allegations years later.

Acceptance of the gay community by mainstream Australia was advancing, and the hatred Gary Cox spoke of in 1988 was consigned to the past, fools or bigots. Tasmania was the last state in the nation to decriminalise sex between consenting gay adults, bringing in the legislation on 13 May 1997, twenty-two years after South Australia.

One issue that did gain some prominence at a time when the decade of violence against gay men was drawing to a close was the 'Homosexual Advance Defence' or 'gay panic' as it was popularly known. It would have an impact on one of the 1990 murders. Malcolm Green first used the defence at his trial for the 20 May 1993 murder of Don Gillies. Green, twenty-two at the time of the killing, had visited Gillies, then thirty-six, at the Mudgee home Gillies shared with his mother. The two men had been close for six years, and Gillies acted as confidante and confessor, and occasionally loaned the younger man money.

On the night of the killing, Gillies' mother was away, and the two men had dinner, drank quite a bit of alcohol and watched television. Gillies suggested Green stay the night and offered his bed, and said he would sleep in his mother's room. In the early hours of the morning, Gillies slipped into bed with Green and became affectionate, but Green didn't reciprocate and instead started to hit Gillies. Green recalled seeing a pair of scissors on the floor beside the bed. He told police, 'He touched me around the waist and shoulders area and said, "Why?" I said to him, "Why, I didn't ask for this. I grabbed the scissors and hit him again.

He rolled off the bed as I struck him with the scissors. By the time I stopped I realised what had happened. I just stood at the foot of the bed with Don on the floor lying face-down in blood.' Green told police: 'Yeah I killed him but he tried to do worse to me.' When asked what, he said, 'He tried to root me.' *The Age* on 16 August 2002 reported: 'Gillies had apparently made some unwanted advances to his straight friend, Green, but there was no question of force. Green smashed in his skull and stabbed and beat him to death with a pair of chicken shears. Police said they had never seen such a battered corpse.'

Green was convicted of murder, and after losing his appeal in New South Wales he took his case to the High Court. In 1997 our highest court gave the thumbs-up to the panic defence. His lawyers told the court that one of the triggers was that Green thought his estranged father had sexually assaulted his sisters and was thus 'particularly sensitive to matters of sexual assault', and was a 'latent volcano'. Chief Justice Brennan, in a majority decision, said the earlier trial judge was in error by telling the jury to ignore the evidence of Green's father's alleged behaviour and a member of the jury 'might accept that Green found the deceased's conduct revolting rather than amorous'. Justice Michael Kirby dissented, but the case went back to the NSW Supreme Court, where Green was acquitted of murder but convicted of manslaughter and sentenced to ten years' imprisonment.

The High Court decision in Green's case provided an opportunity for the defence of the two men who allegedly murdered Wayne Tonks. The two were Peter Kane and Ben Andrews, both sixteen at the time of the murder and students at St Gregory's College in Campbelltown on the south-western edge of Sydney. One teacher said Ben was different from the other boys at a school where many were from the country and rugby league was a passion. Teacher Mario Ghezzi said he was 'artistic, creative', a boy who 'wrote poems, short stories'. At the end of Year 11, Peter Kane moved to another school, and Ben Andrews remained as a boarder, and his teachers noticed he was becoming more troubled. At a school retreat in 1991, he told Ghezzi, 'What if I tell you it's not so hard to kill a man,' which Ghezzi passed off as a flippant comment from a boy trying to shock. Not long after, school cook Frances Collins was talking to an obviously troubled Ben, who said he couldn't talk to his father and when she asked what was troubling him he said, 'I bashed a man to death.' A stunned Frances asked him where, and he replied 'on the north shore'. Ben also worried fellow student Brendan O'Hara; when the two were mucking around after dinner, Ben showed him his hands, turned serious and said: 'These are [a] killer's hands.' Both Ghezzi and Collins reported the conversations to police, but the information didn't get as far as the Homicide Squad or Chatswood detectives who were still investigating the now cold trail of the Wayne Tonks murder.

Peter Kane's father later learned that Ben had visited a doctor to have an HIV test and Peter had gone with him. The story Kane senior was told was that another male had sexually assaulted Ben. The two boys remained close friends throughout, and four years after the Wayne Tonks killing, Peter Kane married, with Ben Andrews as his best man. The marriage produced two children, lasted for three years and ended in a custody battle, which is when the story of the murder finally emerged in full. Peter Kane told *4 Corners* in 2005, 'I told her [Kane's wife] that I'd been involved in bashing a man and that he'd died later on. She also knew from Ben's side because Ben and her had become good friends. Ben was the best man at our wedding, and they'd also known each other very well before the wedding, obviously, and Ben had also told her exactly what the situation was.' Peter's wife told her mother, and both women went to the police.

In May 1997, Kane and Andrews were arrested and charged with the murder of Wayne Tonks. The two alleged that Tonks and another man had taken them back to his apartment, where they'd been raped, but their stories then varied. Justice Brian Sully, who was the judge at their separate trials, said of the case, 'The versions given at their respective trials by the two prisoners were as different as the proverbial chalk and cheese. What is beyond any rational dispute is that both of those versions cannot possibly be truthful.' Kane was convicted of murder, and Andrews of manslaughter. Both successfully appealed and a re-trial was ordered. While on bail Ben Andrews attempted suicide by hanging himself from a tree in the backyard of his parents' Port Macquarie home – he failed. At the subsequent trial Kane was convicted and sentenced to ten and a half years, and Andrews was acquitted.

In the trials, Tonks was portrayed as a paedophile. Detective Malcolm Smith said, 'I believe it's a ludicrous situation . . . Having investigated this matter for seven years, I felt at times I knew the victim better than his own family, and to suggest that Wayne, a well-respected high school teacher, would rape someone – there's no way.'

Alison Young, in 'Into the Blue' published by the *Yale Journal of Law and Humanities* in August 2013, commented on the Kane and Andrews case, saying of Andrews' defence that it 'played out in ways similar to that in Green. Familial abuse in Green, HIV infection in Andrews. In both cases this legal narrative of betrayal produces an anti-portrait of a dead gay man.'

The 'gay panic defence' for non-violent advances was abolished in all states and territories with the exception, at the time of writing, of South Australia and Queensland. In the year following the arrest of the two men for the murder of Wayne Tonks, another old case was poised to emerge, and the driving force was the mother of a young man who'd disappeared. The NSW Police had failed her son dismally – she wanted answers and she wouldn't be fobbed off.

CHAPTER 21

NEVER GIVE UP

Trying to get a police force to change its mind once a decision has been taken is an uphill battle, and few are successful, but that didn't stop Kay Warren. Since her son Ross's disappearance in 1989 she'd been writing to the NSW Police Force asking for a proper investigation. The brief hope that Steve McCann and his team might get a result had faded as the years passed, but she kept writing, sometimes not even getting an acknowledgement.

In July 1998 Kay had been told by the Coroner that only the police could ask for an inquest, and so on 15 July she wrote to the Commissioner: 'It is now nine years since Ross disappeared and we feel it is time for an inquest to close the case. We know there is no way he is still alive and the family feel it should be official so we can put the matter to rest.' She didn't get an answer, and wrote again on 5 September with no luck. She followed up on 1 December 1998, and again on 26 May 1999 and in this last letter, she made the point that Ross's sister was soon to have a baby and needed some financial assistance, which could come from Ross's estate, but standing in the way was the lack of inquest and the formality of declaring him dead. She didn't get a response.

In December 1999, Kay gave up writing to the Missing Persons Unit and Commissioner and instead tried the Crime Manager at Rose Bay Police, enclosing her prior correspondence and noting, 'If there is something about my son's disappearance that we have not been told, then I'd like to be informed. Sergeant Steve McCann who was investigating the case at the time told us that after about three months there was nothing much more that could be done and the case would be put on file. Will someone please do something to finalise this matter to enable this family to put the matter to rest, ten years is far too long.' This time she did get a response, which assured her that 'as soon as various inquiries are complete you will be notified immediately' – but she didn't hear again. Records later produced to the Coroner confirmed that police had made a few inquiries including with Missing Persons, recommending on 1 June 1999 that Rose Bay police get started on a brief to the Coroner. Unfortunately no-one told Kay, and the recommendation to get the brief started seems to have fallen through the cracks.

On 26 April 2000, a frustrated Kay again wrote to the Commissioner, enclosing copies of the unanswered correspondence and saying, 'I realise to the police my son is just another statistic but he was a very important part of our lives and we want to put the matter to rest.' Finally someone noticed, and may also have noticed the whiff of a public-relations problem. Her covering letter and the pile of unanswered letters were sent to Rose Bay Local Area Command for action. She was about to get the first piece of good fortune she'd encountered in the long and sad ordeal.

Her file of letters went to Detective Sergeant Stephen Page, who was based at Paddington Police Station, where Ken Bowditch had launched his investigation into the missing Ludwig Gertsch. Bowditch had subsequently resigned from the police force and was carving a career doing investigations in the corporate sector including being the sleuth of choice for the NRL and providing security for the sons of Libya's late Colonel Gaddafi. Page is exactly what you'd want in a detective – compassionate, smart, experienced, meticulous and streetwise.

His first action was to pull together the large number of reports that hadn't been disturbed since Steve McCann had finished his investigation a decade before. Page was pleased to find that so much of it had survived – old faxes and telexes fade, dust and water damage in police stations with the bare minimum of maintenance is common, or zealous records officers can destroy records as soon as their allotted lifespan is reached.

After he worked his way through the paperwork, which included crime reports, running sheets – the documents that detail every piece of information that arrives in an inquiry and what happens to it – occurrence-pad entries and statements, his instincts told him there was much more to the case. Though Bowditch had left the police on 30 August 1996, Detective Gordon Sharrock, who'd been part of the original investigation, was stationed at City Central. Page thought Sharrock with his background could get the investigation moving quickly, and sent him the file on 11 May. Nearly a month later, Sharrock sent the file to the police office at the Coroner's Court stating he hadn't investigated the matter and only knew what Bowditch had told him during the week of his alleged investigation.

Plan B was Constable Robinson who'd taken the original report, but Robinson wasn't an operational officer and didn't have the necessary skills to undertake the investigation, and so it was back to the Rose Bay Local Area Command, and Stephen Page's desk. He commented, 'I saw the investigation was complex, and took the responsibility as case officer.' It was one of the best decisions in the recent history of NSW policing.

One of his first calls, and certainly the hardest to make, was to Kay Warren. It didn't take long for an investigator approaching a case with an open and objective mind to get the strong impression that Ross hadn't committed suicide. His mother was clear that she knew Ross was gay and comfortable in his own skin, but at the same time, discreet. He wasn't a man who suffered bouts of depression; he was full of life and knew he had a fine career in front of him. Like Scott Johnson, Ross had everything to live for. Kay told Steve they spoke every Sunday – a ritual the two observed since Ross had left home. Kay made the point clearly to Steve that what her family wanted was to have Ross declared dead to bring an end to eleven years of uncertainty. What Page was rapidly coming to realise was that he had a very cold murder case on his hands.

Page and his team worked their way through Ross's friends and colleagues. Television personality Susie Elelman, who'd worked with Ross at WIN, had spoken with Ross in the April before he'd disappeared, and said, 'He was very career oriented and keen to move to Sydney to pursue a career here.' The two had discussed Ross putting together a showreel (a compilation of a TV presenter's best work) for upcoming jobs at Channel 7 and Prime television, and the two planned to catch up when the showreel was done. She said Ross was 'full of life' but that 'his one fear was that his homosexuality would be found out and it would jeopardise his career'. She remembered hearing the news of his disappearance and thinking, 'No way, there must be more to it.' Elelman's view was reflected in all the interviews.

Page took the fundamental step for a detective investigating either a new, or old and cold case, which is to go to the scene and get the feel of the place. You notice things such as landmarks, topography, views, wind direction, compass points, proximity of houses and thus potential witnesses, traffic flow, shadows and sun position for daylight incidents, and lighting either from street lights, the moon or buildings. After getting acquainted you can literally walk through the crime and consider options. An important facet of criminal investigation either at a crime scene or listening to evidence is to take an objective view and keep challenging yourself with the question, *Can this have happened this way?* You look at what you've been told, then consider other possibilities.

For context, in a useful move given the passage of over a decade since Ross's disappearance, Page spoke with Sue Thompson, the NSW Police Gay/Lesbian Client Consultant who took on the job in 1990. Thompson had started her career as a lawyer and had worked for the NSW Ombudsman. Thompson had also published academic papers on gay-hate crimes and she had some strong points to make.

In her formal statement of 31 July 2001, she said that in a study from 1989 to 1999 there were a 'disproportionate number of gay-hate homicides perpetrated by teenagers and young people with their predominant characteristics being white Caucasian, single unemployed males; most common cause of death being beating with high levels of brutality'. She also found that 'the involvement of strangers as offenders was significantly higher with gay-hate-related murders compared to other male homicides', and followed that chilling finding with: 'The second most frequent scenario for gay-hate homicide involves an offender or offenders attending a public park or public space where men are known to meet other men for social interaction or anonymous sexual encounters.' She also found that lesbians were six times more likely to be assaulted than other Sydney women, and gay men four times more likely. Homophobia caused seven out of every ten attacks. With the low rate of reporting of attacks at around 18 per cent, she observed that 'gay men were significantly less positive about their experiences with the police service'.

After looking at the evidence on Ross's disappearance, Page decided that to get a better grip on what had happened – suicide, misadventure or murder – he needed to look at the cases of Krichakorn Rattanajurathaporn and John Russell and links with the assault on David McMahon. The meticulous investigation tripled in size, and a potentially major piece of evidence was missing – the hair found in John Russell's hand. Back in 1989 DNA evidence was in its infancy, but the technology available back then to examine hair could have provided useful evidence. Page chased the crime-scene police and the analytical laboratories but neither had a record of receiving the hair sample. All he could confirm was that the sample was collected then disappeared. Adding to his problems was the fact that John had been cremated, so using contemporary technology to re-examine his body wasn't an option.

In the absence of any remarkable leads, the police went back to basics – virtually taking a blank sheet of paper and working their way through the incident and the investigations, or lack thereof. They re-interviewed witnesses, even speaking to the wife of the security guard who'd allegedly seen Ross Warren in 1991. Margaret Pillon said her late husband Arthur had done payroll runs into the city but a 'homosexual strip club' in Bondi Junction wasn't on the list. While she believed his report was probably genuine, she added that he 'did tell lies', and 'at the time he saw Ross Warren I would have been with him'.

One witness who hadn't been interviewed in the earlier investigations was Craig Frew, who gave a detailed statement to Page's team in April 2001. Craig's story started in Wollongong and took the investigators into Marks Park – it was one of those interviews that gave a stark view of what life as a homosexual in the eighties was like. At the time of his interview Craig had full-blown AIDS and was one of the unlucky ones who hadn't responded to the therapies that restored many to good health and the prospect of a long life. In his own words he candidly told the young police: 'I have no immune system anymore and my doctor has given me six months to live.' Craig was then forty-seven and known to audiences in Wollongong and Sydney as his drag persona 'Sadie', and even though he was desperately unwell, he still did charity performances for the AIDS organisations.

Craig told them he'd 'tried to be straight in my younger years and had girlfriends and was engaged to be married three times'. Craig came out at twenty-one as 'publicly gay. I am not bisexual'. He started working as a drag performer in 1978 in Wollongong where he'd grown up, and in 1983 he was offered a contract at the famous Les Girls in Kings Cross, and kept performing in Wollongong at Kennedy's nightclub – a straight place that had drag shows; in the absence of any dedicated gay venue, it attracted local gays and lesbians. At Kennedy's, Craig met WIN TV personalities including Ross Warren. In a small gay community, the two men also bumped into each other at private parties. 'We weren't what I'd call extremely close friends,' but he recalled that Ross wasn't publicly known as gay, but 'we all sort of looked after each other around the traps'.

Craig moved to Sydney in 1990 when he was twenty-three, where he lived around the corner from the Marks Park beat and became a regular visitor. He'd known where it was and what happened there since he was twelve years old, but his statement doesn't mention how he got that knowledge. Craig said: 'It was often the case I'd meet a guy in the park and we would have sex.' While there was a toilet block, there were also 'quite a lot of honeycomb caverns or sandstone caverns around the walkway' that were popular for assignations. He gave an insight into the park's lure saying, 'It's also the case that most of the time gay men go to the park to pick up men who are termed "straight" because they might have female partners or be closeted homosexuals. In any case the rock area around the outside of Marks Park and the bushes on top of the flat area of the park are where people go because it is not as open to the public.'

He was attacked twice in 1990. The first was in early January, not long after he'd arrived in Sydney and it was in broad daylight. Craig had been to the bank in Bondi Road where he withdrew about $150 in cash to pay his rent. It was back in the days when landlords would visit and collect. Craig walked back to his home in Carlisle Street, using a lane as a short cut to the gate at the back of his house. As he reached the gate he was belted to the back and neck, and when he fell to the ground he saw three pairs of feet, two in white trainers and one in red gym boots. One of the attackers took his wallet, and the three ran off. There was no conversation and fortunately no further beating. Craig reported the attack to police but no-one was ever caught. It's highly likely the three had seen the bank transaction and followed Craig to a quiet spot for their attack.

In the early hours of Saturday, 13 January 1990, Craig was attacked again – and this time it was horrific. On the night before, Craig had been drinking at the Bondi Hotel from about 10.30pm to around 12.30am. He'd had four schooners of full-strength beer and was happy but not drunk. He recalled it was a hot night and he was wearing black cycle shorts with a G-string underneath and a white Bonds singlet. At the time he had long blond hair down to the centre of his back and was very thin at only forty-five kilograms. He left the pub and decided to walk home via the cliff-top walkway, pausing at a seat at the northern end of Marks Park to watch the moon rise. Another man – aged in his early twenties, Caucasian, wearing jeans and a shirt open enough to show some chest hair – sat beside him. Step one in the Marks Park mating ritual. The man asked him for a light, and after Craig had lit the cigarette the man intercepted Craig's hand and gently guided it to his crotch. Step two. After a companionable few moments, the man led Craig down the hill to some low scrub that offered a modicum of privacy.

Craig took off all his clothes, and the man dropped his trousers but kept his shirt on. There was sufficient light from the full moon for Craig to recall the man's genitalia and a large tattoo on his left calf. At this point the oral sex, with Craig doing the giving, was consensual. Then two men, who Craig thought might have been naked, came out of the shadows. He was overpowered, and what followed was a brutal sexual assault lasting for what seemed like an hour as the three men took turns raping Craig. One used his cigarette lighter to burn the hair from Craig's scrotum, and then burned his nipples with either the lighter or a cigarette. Throughout the attack he was verbally abused, called a 'slut' and told 'all poofters should be exterminated'; the attackers also told Craig they knew where he lived and if he talked, they would be back. The assault ended with the men ejaculating then urinating on him, followed by a few kicks and punches just to add to the humiliation. Craig said, 'I lay there some time. I was crying hysterically. I didn't want to move.'

No-one came to his aid, and when he finally collected himself, he put his clothes on and walked the short distance to his home. His mother was staying with him for a few days and he told her what had happened, then cleaned himself up and took a taxi to St Vincent's Hospital. Craig's physical injuries were severe and included four cracked ribs, a fractured right forearm, two cracked vertebrae, a deep laceration to the back his head that required stitches, and extensive bruising to his entire slight frame. Craig couldn't give a clear description of his attackers and was so terrified by their threats he didn't tell the doctors what had happened other than it was 'a bit of trouble'.

All he could recall of the men was that they were Caucasian, relatively smooth-skinned, and they didn't have accents, so he thought they were 'Aussie boys'. Police contacted him the following day after a Good Samaritan found a small wallet containing Craig's identification near the Catholic Church in Wellington Street, and handed it in to the Bondi police. When Craig called in on the following day to collect his property he told police he'd been the victim of a 'poofter bashing' but didn't want to make an official complaint. The constable on duty was thorough and made an intelligence report, including the extent of Craig's injuries.

Craig moved back to Wollongong and didn't visit a gay beat again.

He told his story after Page and his team contacted him in early 2001. They'd found the young officer's report of the assault and robbery as part of their Warren investigation and followed up. It was then Craig decided he should tell the whole story. They took him back to where it had happened. He told police: 'Nine times out of ten these incidents are not reported. A lot of people who've been through this type of thing would be dead now and so couldn't tell anyone about it anyway.' From what I could find, Craig kept going past his doctors' expectations and died in 2004.

CHAPTER 22

A FRESH SET OF EYES

One positive for the new investigators were the tapes McCann and his team had recorded of the Alexandria Eight. Page had the tapes transcribed and went hunting for clues that might link the talkative killers of Richard Johnson to what was now looking like a crime spree, with the cliffs of Bondi as the hub. The scope of his investigation was expanding rather than contracting and he thought it highly likely he had unsolved murders on his hands. The links were diverse: from the taped conversation of a juvenile in custody bragging that he had been part of a crew who'd pushed a man off a cliff at Bondi; to suggestions that some youths were part of a larger group who may have killed William Allen; to sources that named one man arrested on an unrelated crime of being involved in a cliff-top murder. One damning piece of evidence was a pawn slip in the name of one of the boys convicted of the Richard Johnson murder found in David McAuliffe's pocket at the time of his arrest for the murder of Krichakorn Rattanajurathaporn.

Page wasn't under any illusion about the quality of some of the initial investigations – prior to McCann's arrival – and in particular the death of Ross Warren, where his car and possibly crime scene hadn't been properly secured, some key witnesses were not interviewed, and no report of the possible death was made to the Coroner. He was also concerned by the loss of the strands of hair from John Russell's crime scene, and the failure to consider the fate of the two men in the context of other crimes. These were points made clearly to his superiors.

By April 2001, Page had assembled his results and began to prepare an investigation plan, along with the most important factor in any major investigation: the request for a name for the proposed operation. The names are computer generated after a formal request is made. It's bureaucratic but avoids names that seemed like a good idea at the time – like on pay night at the pub. Page filled out a form requesting a name for a 'Major Overt Operation' and it was faxed to Field Services and on 23 April 2001 'Operation Taradale' was born. Page was appointed to head the investigation and the terms of reference were to investigate the disappearance of Ross Warren, the assault of David McMahon and the 'suspicious death' of John Russell.

That same day Page sent a request for crime agencies assistance for a 'large scale, complex and sensitive investigation' that would need staffing and assistance from specialists. His investigation plan was state of the art, and included profiling of all 'persons of interest' – an investigative tool not available to McCann back in the early nineties – a media blitz in both traditional and electronic forms, Gay Liaison Officers to canvass the crime scenes at night to identify local residents from 1989–90 and then trace and interview them, and a detailed trawl through police records to see if there were any other crimes of the time that might provide some clues. One significant move was for physical and electronic surveillance of the suspects at the time of the media campaign. On the wish list for investigators is always that suspects will hit their phones or email to discuss what they'd heard – and all recorded by the police. A respectable back-up is for physical surveillance to track them to a meeting then film it; film of a meeting can be a handy tool to persuade a suspect identified by the profiler as the most likely to crack, to turn on his mates, because few criminals put loyalty before self-interest. The result of Page's electronic surveillance operation was 17 022 calls recorded from twenty different numbers over six months starting in September 2001.

One of the factors occasionally overlooked when investigating crimes that involve falls is trajectory and position. The death of Bill Rooney in Wollongong back in 1986 is an example, as is Scott Johnson's death in 1988. Position of the body is a critical element – too far to be practical or in an odd position, and you should ask questions, which is what Stephen Page did.

Among the experts he called upon was forensic pathologist Dr Allan Cala, who began to review John Russell's post-mortem results, photographs and police statements about the scene. In his August 2001 report he noted Russell had been found after a fall from an eleven-metre cliff. He said that John must have died quickly from the impact, extensive injuries leading to 'immediate incapacitation of the deceased and subsequent death'. The injuries, Cala noted, were 'unsurvivable'. Cala was unable to determine if John was conscious or unconscious when he left the edge of the cliff, but he was alive. Upon impact at the bottom, though: 'The deceased would have been immediately unconscious.'

On position, Cala said: 'Bodies may bounce after a fall, but a fall of eleven metres is not particularly great, so the amount of bounce may be zero to several feet. However, the position in which John's body was found is unusual in case of jumping or falling from a height. The body is facing toward the cliff, which is unusual given the small height of the cliff, implying if the deceased acted alone, he has been able to twist his body 180 degrees to rest in the position depicted [in the photos]. I do not believe he would have been able to move after the fall.'

Cala noted the position of John's red jersey and commented: '[I] would expect the clothing to have that appearance had it been in the standard or usual position at the time of the fall' rather than the pulled-up position depicted in the photos and observed by police who'd been at the scene. Moving on to the mystery of the now missing hairs from John's hand, Cala said: 'It would be unusual to find hairs on the hands of persons who have jumped. This finding is suggesting the deceased might have pulled them from the head of another person at the time he fell, implying the presence of another person or persons at the time of the fall. This raises the possibility of foul play in relation to this man's death.'

Wrapping up, Cala said he couldn't explain the cause of the fall, but, 'I cannot exclude foul play based on the crime-scene photographs and description of the injuries in the post-mortem report. I am not aware if there was any evidence to support suicide.' He noted he wasn't aware of John's blood alcohol level or if there were drugs in his system, but they 'would be of relevance in this case', and though there weren't any injuries that could 'indicate definitely the deceased was assaulted prior to the fall, there are some injuries to the face and hands which are suggestive of an assault'.

His last line nailed the case for Page and his team: 'The possibility still exists that this man has been met with foul play and might have been forcibly thrown off the cliff.'

Cala also offered his expert opinion on the scant information available in the Ross Warren case, telling Page that when a human body is immersed in a large body of water, like the ocean, it will initially sink; then, currents, tides, flow and local environmental factors such as rocks, waves, water depth and so on, take over. He said: 'The body may, but not always, rise to the surface after some period of time,' and 'clothing may be stripped off by waves and currents'. Enter Robert Brander, a lecturer from the School of Geography at the University of New South Wales.

Brander, a Canadian with expertise in rip currents, arrived in Australia in 1993 to study for his doctorate. In 1995, he moved to the Tamarama Surf Club as caretaker, patrolled the beach as a lifesaver, and surfed and snorkelled the often treacherous waters around the beach and Mackenzies Bay. If you surf at Tamarama you'd be wise to slip a $5 bill into your swimmers because there's a good chance you'll end up by accident in Bronte, one beach to the south. Struggle out of the surf, have a coffee, then walk back to 'Glamourama'. In August 2000, Brander began a long-term survey of the sediment and waves around the beach, so Page calling for advice was timely.

Brander examined the wave and current data for the period 21 July – the day before Warren disappeared – to 20 August 1989. He said, 'In my opinion . . . around Bondi/Tamarama headland, it is unlikely that a body in the water off the shore platforms or on the bed would move landward over the time frames and climatic conditions described.' Bowditch's belief that Ross Warren's body should have washed ashore in a few days was completely wrong.

By the beginning of November 2001, Page reported that most of the investigations into the Russell and Warren cases were nearly complete and it was time to begin face-to-face interviews with six 'persons of interest' they'd narrowed down from their investigations and assessment of the evidence. He also took the media work up a notch, inviting them to a re-enactment of John Russell's fatal fall conducted on 9 December, an event coordinated with telephone intercepts targeting the suspects.

The media campaign, plus investigators knocking on doors and interviewing suspects, produced a flurry of phone calls. One call captured the feelings of those who were targeted as possible perpetrators, with one man saying: 'Probably just barking up everyone's tree to try and scare someone into saying something, you know what I mean.' One man rattled by the police interest said in a recorded conversation that he'd assaulted and robbed a man at Bondi Beach who'd been at an ATM, but, 'The guy got up, he was fine. If it comes across the papers and the news I'm being charged with murder, make sure you tell everyone I'm innocent. So shitting my pants. I am not a murderer.'

By the end of January 2002, police had completed more than forty interviews with the 'persons of interest'. Some interviews were based on the old recordings commissioned by McCann. The new telephone intercepts, while not helping the investigation into the death of the men, had revealed that some of the targets were embroiled in an ecstasy importation ring. Police charged Sean Cushman with drug crimes. Cushman was on a bond for his role in aiding and abetting in the assault of English backpacker Brian Hagland at Bondi Beach in 1996. After the assault, Hagland fell under a bus and died.

In the month following Cushman's drug charges, another five men were charged with drug crimes for supplying cocaine, ecstasy and cannabis, bringing the total of drug charges to forty-eight. Over the next few months another six people were charged with drug crimes. Unfortunately, there was still insufficient evidence to charge any of the men or women with gay-hate crimes.

The disappearance and likely death of Gilles Mattaini remained a challenge for Page and his team. With only minimal information on record and the death of Vincent Ottaviani – one of the few witnesses – years before the investigation, evidence was scant. On 12 August 2002 Page went public with a plea for help.

Operation Taradale's investigative phase was winding down, and Page was preparing his brief of evidence for the Coroner – the brief that would result in an inquest at last for Ross Warren and Gilles Mattaini and possibly a fresh inquest for John Russell. Page's conclusions in his epic-length statement, and brief of evidence, were to the point. Ross Warren was dead and his body went into the surf near Marks Park. His keys were placed on the rock shelf either by Ross or someone who'd found them; but placed there, not thrown. Neither Ross nor John had gone to Marks Park to commit suicide, but were likely there for 'clandestine sexual encounters', and 'both men met their deaths at that location as a result of violence'.

From all the evidence in the 2685-page brief, Page concluded that gangs including the Bondi Boys, the Tamarama Three and the Alexandria Eight had been involved in crimes at Marks Park and Tamarama in which gay men were targeted. What he couldn't do was point the finger at the culprits – there wasn't sufficient evidence. The prime suspects for the case had been talking to each other, by phone and face-to-face, and one by-product had been solidarity. No-one had turned on their mates, no-one had slipped up, and there wasn't that great moment police joke about when a suspect puts their hands up and says, *You're too good for me, Mr Detective, I give up.*

One of the main reasons for the inability of Page's team to nail their quarry was the calibre of the original investigations. For Ross Warren, there were a litany of failures, most importantly the elimination of foul play as a possibility early in the investigation in spite of the knowledge of the numbers of attacks on gay men in that location and around that time. For John Russell, foul play was similarly discounted early in the investigation, combined with the loss of the hair sample and the failure to take the position of his body into account.

For Gilles Mattaini, Page considered his early suicide attempt – which Page thought might have been stimulated by issues over his sexuality and being required to do national service, both issues long past – and concluded that 'homicide cannot be excluded' as the reason for his disappearance.

For all three men, the next step was over to the Coroner.

CHAPTER 23

JUSTICE AT LAST

Jacqueline Milledge was the Coroner appointed to handle the report of Operation Taradale. Milledge is different to her colleagues who are lawyers, usually from the government or private practice. She entered the NSW Police Force in 1972 as just one of three women in her initial training class. After graduation she didn't join her male classmates and get experience working in general duties; instead she was consigned to the fate of all new policewomen at the time: lecturing school kids on road safety. It was a mundane task, occasionally spiced by undercover work when a woman was required, or to interview young children or female victims of sexual assault. In 1974, she broke the gender barrier when she and a colleague became the first women to join the Prosecuting Branch. In the late 1980s she left Prosecuting and started in general duties at Maroubra. She told the *Sydney Morning Herald* on 7 December 2013 that when she arrived: 'I was given the highly specialised job of sticking pins in a map of the surrounding suburbs, charting where the break-and-enters had taken place.'

Milledge completed her law degree and left behind the challenges of general-duties policing in 1996 to take up an appointment to the Bench; she described telling her former boss in Prosecuting Branch as a 'really wonderful up-yours moment'. She was appointed Deputy State Coroner in 2000, and she told the *Australian* on 16 December 2006 the Coroner's Court 'was perhaps the last court where ordinary folk can come and express themselves without feeling shackled by the rules of evidence'.

She came to the evidence of Operation Taradale with an insider's knowledge of how an investigation should be conducted, a nose for what was right and wrong, a well-honed bullshit detector and first-hand experience of police culture of the seventies and eighties. The inquest began on Monday, 31 March 2003 at the Coroner's Court in Parramatta Road, Glebe. It was the second inquest attended by John Russell's father Ted and brother Peter. Ross Warren's mother Kay decided against being there, but she knew that at last her son's disappearance and presumed death were getting their day in court. It wouldn't bring Ross back, but at least it would bring the years of uncertainty to a close. Ross's friend Craig Ellis, with whom he'd shared a pizza and a few laughs before heading to Oxford Street on the last night of his life, was also a court regular, sitting on his own, watching the proceedings. On Page's subpoena list were the 'persons of interest' David and Sean McAuliffe and Matthew Davis, all convicted of killing Krichakorn Rattanajurathaporn in 1990. The McAuliffes and Davis were out of prison by this time and their release from prison hadn't attracted any media fanfare.

The early witnesses who gave evidence were victims who had been fortunate to escape their bashers. They were followed by the persons of interest, including Matthew Davis. Page had interviewed him back in April 2002, and shown him a photograph of Ross Warren and of John Russell; Davis had denied recognising the men. Davis, who'd confessed to Krichakorn's murder and pleaded guilty, told Page he had been living in Sydney's outer south-western suburbs in 1989 and was a student at Airds High School. Back then, he said, he had a 'very strong loathing for anyone that was gay' and traced the cause back to abuse he had suffered as a child. Davis had made the error of grouping 'gay' with 'paedophile', and told Page that because of psychiatric treatment and counselling he'd received during his imprisonment, he realised his mistake. He said, 'Cause I realise it's not gay people that, you know, do that, you know, it's paedophiles . . . there's a huge difference there, you know. And I'm well aware of that now, you know. If I had . . . dealt with this stuff earlier, you know, I could have prevented my last twelve years being lost.'

Davis spoke of his involvement in Krichakorn Rattanajurathaporn's death: 'He was backing away and, like, he's gone, there's the cliff face there like that and as he's backing away he's fallen off the edge of the cliff and then he's apparently hit the ledge of, of some description, then from there he's gone to a second one where he was, where he was still alive apparently and then he lost consciousness and then he's gone off that and ended up in the water.' Davis paused, trying to gather his words, then said, 'Where, where he apparently drowned.'

Page wanted to know if the McAuliffe brothers had spoken about their involvement in other attacks around Tamarama and Marks Park, and Davis said, 'There may have been some teenage bravado back then, but I think, I think it's just like I said, teenage bravado, but no, David and Sean weren't bad kids, the same as me, you know what I mean, they aren't killers, man, you know what I mean, they aren't maniacs that are going to go out and bloody kill people all their lives.'

At court, Davis's evidence was similar, telling Milledge he'd been a victim during his childhood but when he hit his teens he reached a point when he thought to himself, 'Fuck this – sorry about the language – I am never going to be a victim again. No-one is ever gonna hurt me again.' It was an attitude that changed over his lengthy prison sentence. He made the point that with both time and maturity he'd realised his error of lumping gay men in with paedophiles. He denied being involved with Ross Warren and John Russell, and when he finished his evidence and walked from the witness box, he stopped where Ted and Peter Russell were seated and reiterated he had nothing to do with John's death.

The evidence from the other persons of interest wasn't as enlightening, and aside from denial of involvement, little else of use emerged. Sue Thompson, who'd played a major role in trying to bridge the antipathy between the police and gay community, and who'd worked with both McCann and Page, gave evidence on the culture of the gangs that preyed on gay men. One witness who grabbed attention was Ken Bowditch. He'd been interviewed by Page on 19 February 2001 and had given a statement for the Coroner's brief. After outlining his investigation, including the use of the Air Wing and Water Police – which Page was unable to confirm – he said: 'There is nothing to suggest that Ross Warren's death was the result of foul play or a deliberate attempt on his part to disappear,' and,

'I stress there is nothing to suggest that his disappearance is or was gay related.' Bowditch re-affirmed his original theory of an accidental fall and observed that while there had been a full moon on the night of Ross's disappearance it had also been overcast and there had been a high tide – no surprise as there were two per day. Bowditch added, 'I inspected the scene during the initial investigation and I am extremely familiar with the area, as I walk regularly between Bondi and Bronte.'

Bowditch adhered to his line in the witness box, and insisted he'd done a thorough investigation. When pushed about the procedural flaws, such as not getting Ross's car fingerprinted, Bowditch became testy, never the recommended approach for witnesses, and said, 'I will not be a scapegoat for the inadequacies of the department, which was responsible for losing all the records.' When questioned about his dismissive attitude to some of the witnesses, he said there had been an 'extreme effort' but didn't elaborate on what that entailed. When questioned by counsel assisting the Coroner on evidence and documentation such as Ross's credit card details, dental charts, and police records such as diaries, he reckoned some were put into police records systems and others left at Paddington Police Station. Bowditch, when told many of the records couldn't be found, said, 'Now where it is I have no idea, and I am appalled the department has lost it.'

The Coroner would later give a clear view on Ken Bowditch's investigative vigour. Other police witnesses trooped in, painting a picture of investigations riddled with errors and omissions. One experienced officer who'd been involved on the edge of the initial investigations said to me, 'It wasn't the finest hour for The Job. Some of us offered advice on what should be done, but no-one was paying attention. There were too many assumptions and not enough suspicion or investigation. Leads just fell through the cracks.'

Forensic pathologist Dr Allan Cala was called and gave riveting evidence of what may have been John Russell's fate. With the hair from the Russell crime scene long gone, Cala had only the photographs to work from, and he believed that the hairs in John's hand weren't his, though he couldn't be definitive. It was likely, Cala said, that the hairs were 'tugged out' from someone else. He added, 'I've seen many people who've jumped from great heights. The finding of hairs is unusual and would raise questions with me.' Cala commented that the position of John Russell's body – with his legs pointing toward the sea and head facing the cliff – was unusual, and that most people found around North Head or the Gap – two Sydney locations well known for suicide, and in the same police division – are usually found with their head facing the ocean and feet toward the cliff. Cala reiterated his findings and said, 'The case would make me wonder whether he's been deliberately thrown off the cliff perhaps.' He noted Russell's blood alcohol level was high at .255, which could 'suggest Mr Russell could have met his death accidentally', but added that decomposition 'could also account for an increased alcohol reading'.

The hearing phase of the inquest ended in late September 2003; Milledge had what she'd heard in the courtroom and Page's brief of nearly 3000 meticulously ordered pages to consider. For a cold-case homicide with the volume of evidence, and a Coroner with her normal workload in addition, a result wasn't going to be quick.

Barrister Patrick Saidi, representing the Commissioner of Police at the inquest, made a closing submission to Milledge in which he said, 'The climate which then existed, which was a climate I think no-one in society could really be proud of, and that is the culture of gay hate, of gay-hate crime. The Police Service, whatever defects it may have suffered from during that period, was no more than a reflection of it, and was exhibiting the broader values and principles of the then society.' Saidi was acting under his client's instructions, and those instructions gave testimony to the habit of the NSW Police to ignore or try to deflect the unpalatable moments of its past. The cold hand of Commissioner Colin Delaney was more persuasive to their attitudes in the eighties than community sentiment.

On 9 March 2005, Coroner Milledge delivered her findings to a packed courtroom. Stephen Page, who'd left the police the year before, was there. It was a morning he wouldn't have missed. Milledge began with a recap of the circumstances of the death or disappearance of Gilles, Ross and John, followed by a description of the park, what a gay beat was, and gay crimes of the time – motivations, lack of reporting and why, the murders and assaults that had been investigated, painting a vivid picture of a brutal time. After listing the men killed or injured she said, 'All these victims were homosexual men. All assaults and killings were unprovoked and vicious.' Then she turned to the investigations 'past and present'.

Ken Bowditch and his investigation of Ross Warren's disappearance came first, and she noted: 'He was insistent that his brief of evidence was submitted to the Coroner in 1990. No such brief of evidence was received by this office.' She found a similar problem with his assertions that the Air Wing and Water Police had been called out to aid the search; and also looked to a document in which he had nominated being assisted by three policemen – in this case, one of the officers was on annual leave at the time, and the other two denied involvement. She said that even though Bowditch was aware Marks Park was a gay beat, Bowditch had 'paid little or no regard to the possibility of foul play'. On his being appalled by evidence that had gone missing, she made her view clear, saying, 'He's right! It is appalling that no documents allegedly struck during the course of the investigation have been found. There were no records of any of the specialist police Bowditch asserted he'd involved in the matter having been "activated". This state of affairs defies belief. To this day, no documents have surfaced, nor has their supposed disappearance been explained. This was a grossly inadequate and shameful investigation. Indeed to characterise it as an "investigation" is to give it a label it does not deserve.'

Milledge then moved on to John Russell, and said it was a better 'investigation' but 'far from adequate'. She said, 'Had police paid careful attention to the crime scene and the vital evidence presented to them, the perpetrator of that brutal act may have been identified, or at the very least Mr Russell's death would have been seen differently and not simply as a result of "misadventure".' Milledge acknowledged good police work by Sergeant Ingelby and Constable Scanlon, who'd raised 'the possibility that these were more than just disappearances and more than accidents'.

Milledge then made her view of the investigation clear, saying the loss of the hair in the Russell case was 'disgraceful' and the police who pointed the finger at each other for the loss was 'not good enough'. Milledge, as an experienced former officer, knew the imperative to safeguard and maintain the provable continuity of custody of crime-scene exhibits and the systems in place to do so – they'd been part of standard police procedures for years, thus heightening the failure.

She listed the similarities in the Warren and Russell cases, and then said: 'Yet investigating police believed Mr Warren and Mr Russell met their death by "misadventure". The earlier investigations into these men were inadequate and naïve. Not so the current investigation that triggered the inquests into the death of Mr Russell and the suspicious deaths of Mr Warren and Mr Mattaini. Not only was the investigation thorough it was impeccable.' There is usually a 'however' moment, and Milledge didn't disappoint when she said, 'General admissions were made by some "persons of interest" during conversations with family and friends. Details of Mr Russell's death and the disappearance of Mr Warren were discussed. These brutes that prey on people are known to be cowardly and boastful. Whilst a lay person could get quite excited about hearing one of them boast they had some involvement in the matter, without any independent evidence linking them they could not be prosecuted successfully for any crime.' Her experience was notable when she observed that Page and his team's work could be 'an excellent source of evidence should other matters come to light. Relationships between these thugs do not always remain "solid".'

On attitudes of the time, she said that beats were notoriously dangerous but that 'some offences went unreported because it was felt that police would judge the victim and nothing would be achieved'. One witness, unnamed in her judgement, had struck a chord when he said, 'If there was a homosexual assault or a murder it wouldn't get the same privilege as a so called heterosexual assault or murder,' but in the balance that same witness acknowledged some 'hard-working and decent officers that do make a difference'. Milledge echoed his observations and said, 'It wouldn't be unreasonable for the gay community to believe that as a group they don't warrant proper police attention. It's hard for the New South Wales Police Force to be seen as progressive and equitable when some officers fail in their duty to the community they're meant to serve.'

Milledge found that Ross Warren 'died in Sydney on or about 22 July 1989'. She added: 'Whilst the cause and manner of death are unknown, I am satisfied the deceased was a victim of homicide perpetrated by person or persons unknown.' Moving on, she found: 'John Alan Russell died at Marks Park, North Bondi between 22 and 23 November 1989. The cause of death is multiple injuries sustained when he was thrown from a cliff onto the rock by a person or persons unknown.' Finally, she turned to the third case and found: 'Gilles Mattaini died on or about 15 September 1985 in Sydney. The cause and manner of his death remain undetermined as the evidence before me does not enable me to say.'

The Coroner's findings and strong criticism of the police grabbed media attention, and Stephen Page was in demand. After court, he was interviewed on ABC Radio's *PM* program and said, 'Gay bashing was seen as a sport, particularly for young single men, predominantly of Caucasian background. And it appeared with a lot of them that they couldn't differentiate the difference between paedophiles and homosexuals.' He credited Kay Warren's persistence, saying, 'She was a mother who'd lost her son. She didn't have the opportunity of burying her son. There was no body. And I wanted to help her by giving her a little bit of closure.' For Page, the lack of things such as crime-scene photos and canvassing of witnesses mean that Ross Warren's disappearance was 'almost [as] if the offence had happened yesterday' – meaning he'd been called to a fresh scene. He ended his interview with a note of hope, saying, 'I've been involved in matters before which have been cold for many, many years, and then all of a sudden a witness comes out of the blue, and we can just keep our fingers crossed.'

The following morning Leonie Lamont in the *Sydney Morning Herald* covered the case in a story with the headline 'Detective Exposes Apathy in Gay Murder Cases'. She wrote that Page's work on Ross Warren's disappearance 'unearthed evidence of police investigative ineptitude', and also that the Russells had been in court each day listening to 'awful evidence of violence and hate'. Lamont quoted Page's comment made on the steps of the court just after the matter ended, when he said, 'I think if we'd managed it a lot better back then, we wouldn't have been giving evidence before a Coroner. It would have been before a jury and we would have had true finalisation for the families.'

On the other side of the world, reports of Jacqueline Milledge's decision stimulated another family in search of true finalisation. But first, there was one old gay murder case that was going to grab the headlines.

CHAPTER 24

A VERY THICK PLOT

The high public profile of Operation Taradale put crimes against gay men in the public eye, and a by-product was a rekindling of interest in the Ludwig Gertsch murder. No one had been charged.

The failure of the initial investigation to cover investigative basics had diminished the chances of a result for the investigators that followed, and Roberts, Esposito and Dawn O'Donnell were sticking to the stories they'd first told in the early summer of 1990. The subsequent conviction of Roberts for fraud was accepted by police as the best result they were likely to get.

For Vince Esposito, the case was still a deep wound. In the years following the murder he'd accepted his sexuality, and though the relationship with his former wife was strained, he was very close to his sons. Socially, it was a bit trickier, with stories of Ludwig's murder a perennial conversation favourite in some of Sydney's salons. Vince had been passed over for jobs when his name twigged a memory of his high media profile in the early 1990s.

The suicide of Brian Roberts' daughter Yasmine on 21 October 2002 was the flashpoint for a renewed look at the old crimes. The case was to be one of the first of the newly formed Unsolved Homicide team.

On 1 September 2003, Leonie Turner – formerly Leonie Roberts – sat down with detectives and told her story. Her electronically recorded interview formed part of the 'Brief of Evidence' for the Coroner's Inquest that would follow.

She covered the tale of Ludwig ringing the Roberts home on the evening of 19 October 1990 – the day Ludwig disappeared. He was, she said, 'really upset and angry', but what she added was that Brian answered the phone, which was 'unusual for Brian to answer the phone because he was hemiplegic' and 'doesn't walk or do any extra physical exercise that he doesn't have to do'. Brian told Leonie what had allegedly happened and left immediately. A short time later Vince and his two boys arrived at the Roberts home in Haberfield, and Vince told her the story he'd stuck to for years. She said, 'I ended up with him in my house, unannounced, uninvited with his two children who I couldn't stand, who would destroy your house in ten minutes.' She noted: 'If Ludwig snapped his fingers, he meant money, Brian would go. But that was the same for Dawn [O'Donnell].'

Leonie described Ludwig as 'not the most stable person you were going to meet.'

She told police of the antipathy that had been confected between Brian and Vince to lessen Ludwig's jealousy, saying: 'Brian would see Vince was there [at Ludwig's home] and scream and pretend he didn't like Vince and say "I'm not coming in there" and then Vince would scream and yell and say, "If that bastard comes in I'm leaving." Brian would leave, then Vince would storm out shortly after and the two would meet for coffee in Paddington.' She described the covert friendship between the two as 'a really weird mix. Vince was pretty much illiterate and innumerate and Brian has three degrees, so he's a really smart person hanging out with someone who's illiterate and can't put a sentence together.'

She also described her former husband as a 'social climber' who would spend large amounts of money to buy tables at the Black & White balls – then a feature of Sydney's old social world. She reckoned their marriage was loveless after Yasmine's birth, and crumbled after Brian's arrest. Following his release from prison, contact was minimal and she was aware he was working for the Institute of Traditional Chinese Medicine in Leichhardt and running a gay brothel in Kings Cross – a market in decline with the arrival of online offerings and the rapidly growing integration of the gay community into the mainstream. Brian had passed off the brothel – Alexander's in Kellett Street – to Yasmine as a backpackers hostel. Kate McClymont, writing in the *Sydney Morning Herald* of 12 July 2003, said 'Now that he's out of the clink, 48-year-old Roberts, who's changed his surname to Mainwaring, has recently opened a male brothel in Kings Cross.'

The Coroner's Court in October 2006 would be told of alleged conversations between Brian and Leonie shortly after Yasmine's death. The court heard Leonie said, 'It's all your fault, you killed her. You killed Ludwig, now look what you have done.' Brian allegedly replied, 'Don't you think I know what I've done?' and the conversation was allegedly overheard by Leonie's mother.

HIV had reduced the number of witnesses still alive from the original investigation, but Detective Charles Fountain and his team found ample evidence to prepare a fresh brief to persuade the Coroner to re-open the inquest into the death of Roger-Claude Teyssedre and Ludwig Gertsch.

A cold-case investigation is a different beast to the investigation of a fresh crime. Veteran homicide investigators quip, 'You don't turn on the blue light to get to a murder,' and even more so when the case is over a decade old. These investigations are often part of a detective's caseload rather than the focus. One of the early tasks for Detective Fountain and his team was to gather all the evidence, including statements and forensic finds, from the earlier investigation. They pulled together what Fountain described as a 'mishmash of documents', and 'hound[ed] the hell' out of a former crime-scene detective for the forensic material from the Winmalee site where Ludwig's body was found, and the Paddington house. With crime-scene material, being able to prove the continuity of the exhibit – when and where found, how stored, if removed by whom and so on – is essential, and proved a challenge, as was finding material. Time is the greatest challenge in these cases, with evidence, including memories, becoming blurred, disappearing, suffering damage and, in this case, documentary evidence being destroyed as part of record-keeping requirements.

In April 2004, the investigators examined the crime scene at Vince's former home unit at 2/131 Frederick Street, Ashfield using Luminol to check for bloodstains undetectable to the human eye. Fountain commented, 'The place had never been scrutinised let alone attended by any prior investigation.' Ludwig had been strangled, but competent investigation is about eliminating the possibilities rather than making assumptions. Assumptions not only risk missing vital clues, but leave you open to criticism in the cold, analytical atmosphere of a courtroom where your actions are microscopically examined. A lawyer's favourite question is,

If not, why not? When blood was found, the forensic experts took samples for comparison with DNA samples taken from a member of Gertsch's family. It was a technique available to the modern-day investigators but not back in 1990. They tracked down and interviewed key witnesses, including the two sex workers who'd seen Vince and a male person with a ruby ear stud moving what they thought was a roll of carpet. Detective Fountain told the *Sydney Morning Herald* on 25 August 2004 they were searching for the man with the earring who, in a moment of police speak, could provide 'information in relation to particular people's movements at the time in question'. Fountain also commented that the investigation had been 'monumental' but 'we are closer [to solving the crime] than the initial inquiry, and there has been significant inroads made.'

A few weeks after the inspection with Luminol, the police were back, this time with a roll of carpet and a sixty-five-kilogram dummy inside to re-enact and video the alleged removal of Ludwig's body. It was a useful exercise to see if the witnesses were correct. It was thorough investigation work, and Fountain said, 'My primary memory of the exercises was such that it was almost impossible for someone on their own (even Esposito's size) to remove a roll of carpet down the stairwell with such a weight inside it.'

He was also troubled by a private investigator's early arrival on the scene, and said, 'Why an independent non-sworn individual was inserted into the inquiry to do the work of a NSW Police detective, I'll never know.' With the investigation at a compelling stage, the police presented their brief to the Coroner, who decided another inquest was appropriate in light of the fresh evidence.

News of the second inquest rocked Vince Esposito, and it was delivered by way of a summons to give evidence in late September 2006. He'd spent over a decade trying to rebuild his life, and those lurid years of the early nineties were about to be splashed over the front pages again. They had caused rifts among his siblings, who had successfully managed to keep the stories from their parents – their poor grasp of English, insular social habits and lack of interest in current affairs helped. Vince made a sensible decision and instead of being guided by the likes of Brian Roberts or Dawn O'Donnell – then seriously ill with cancer that would kill her in June the following year – he contacted an old friend, solicitor Alex Maroulis, who recommended Vince engage the solicitor, now District Court Judge, Clive Jeffreys to act for him. I interviewed both Vince and Alex, and Alex, with Vince's consent, provided me with some of his files including notes of their initial conversations.

A few days after the first conversation Vince and Alex – as a friend and not solicitor – began to wade through the box of documents provided by the police with interviews and statements from key players including Vince and Brian Roberts and the first Coroner's inquest reports.

Maroulis, knowing Vince's lack of education, made sure his friend was clear on what the witnesses were saying in their statements, and the impact of the missing carpet and the doona Ludwig had been wrapped in when the body was found; these were key points in the case police were building against him. Maroulis recalled that Vince didn't respond at first, and then alleged that he still feared for his safety and that of his children if he told the truth.

On 28 September 2006, Vince met Alex again prior to them heading to the Coroner's Court. Vince told him, 'I am too scared to tell anyone what happened to him [Ludwig] and they will kill me.' Vince didn't specify who the 'they' might be.

After Vince's revelation, Maroulis told me he got some legal advice himself.

A few days later the men met again, and Vince reiterated, 'I'm still fearful I will be killed.' Vince went on, alleging: 'About two weeks before the [nineteenth of] October, Brian called me and we met for coffee in Leichhardt. Brian said he wanted me to do a favour for him, and he wanted me to get Ludwig to come to my house and that he'd do everything else.' Vince recalled Brian had a 'situation to fix up' and there was nothing for Vince to worry about. The *Australian* of 23 October 2006, reported Vince told the later inquest that he 'enticed Gertsch to his Ashfield flat that night [19 October 1990] at Robert's behest, and said "He [Roberts] said he could make my life a living hell if I didn't proceed with this little favour."'

Vince was still in the dark about why he had to be out of the unit but told me that after a few heated discussions with Roberts he finally capitulated. He said, 'I didn't want to have anything to do with these people, and thought that if I went along with it I could get on with my life.'

Vince admitted to Maroulis that he had tried to talk to the authorities but didn't have any luck. It was 1993, and Vince found that he had been locked out of the Newtown Gym he thought he'd owned through his inheritance from Ludwig, and that Brian and Dawn had taken over. Dawn's involvement saddened him because, he said, 'she'd been very kind and understanding in the mess that followed Ludwig's murder. I thought she was genuine, but maybe she fooled me.'

Vince, then without any money and his cash flow from the gym cut off, went to the Law Society of New South Wales to try to get some advice. Vince said, 'I wanted to tell someone what had happened, but the person I spoke to said I would have to go through the normal way to get that assistance and they couldn't assist further.'

He told Maroulis, 'I've been waiting to tell my story from the start, but I am fearful of my life and my kids. I never believed I could go to the police and tell my story.' Preying on his mind were the phone calls to Denise Coussens in which the caller alleged police involvement in Ludwig's murder.

On 10 October 2006, Vince was in the witness box at the Glebe Coroner's Court giving evidence to Coroner Dorelle Pinch, where he summed up his story neatly, telling her, 'I was confused, I was scared, I was lost. I was a young man, I was in a situation. I don't know why I said what I said . . . Brian reassured me I would get protection because he could arrange it. I was a simple idiot doing what I had to do to protect my kids.' Of the missing carpet that was about to play a major role in the inquest, he said, 'When I saw the carpet was gone, I said, "What the fuck's happened?" I knew something not good had happened. That's when he threatened me that night: "You open your motherfucking mouth and I'll make your fucking life not worth living!"'

Two key witnesses, known as Ms A and Ms B, followed, telling the Coroner they were both heroin users and sex workers who lived in the flat under Vince in Frederick Street. They hadn't been called to the 1994 inquest because the police had some doubts about their credibility – based on their profession and self-confessed drug use. Both told Pinch they'd heard Vince's angry voice that night – a change from his normal quietly spoken and polite demeanour – and they'd heard arguing and bumping noises. Shortly after, they'd seen Vince and the man with the ruby stud earring carry a big roll of carpet out of the building and place it in a beige-coloured truck parked outside, and then the two men drove off.

Brian Roberts had sat in court throughout Vince's evidence. Unlike his former friend, the years hadn't treated him well. He arrived in a wheelchair every morning, looking haggard and not the fashion plate he'd been as a well-paid solicitor. In the box, he aggressively denied all of Vince's allegations.

Coroner Pinch adjourned the inquest, and before doing so she made a public appeal for the man who had phoned Denise Coussens alleging police involvement in the murder to come forward. He didn't, but on 25 October, Detective Fountain interviewed another man who had come forward – Vince's brother-in-law John Revelos. In cross examination of the witnesses from downstairs by Alex Maroulis – now Vince's lawyer – their testimony, while well intentioned and to the best of their recollection around fifteen years later, hit a hurdle, and that was timing. They'd seen a man with a ruby earring with Vince and they'd seen something that looked like a roll of carpet, but it wasn't on that fateful weekend in October.

Revelos told the police he had a ruby stud earring around the time and a little truck, and he had helped Vince move out of the Ashfield apartment on a Saturday; he recalled that Saturdays were the only time he could get away from work. John couldn't remember exactly which month but he had a vague recollection of moving a roll of carpet, though it wasn't a big one. James Arcuri, John's other brother-in-law, also helped the men. Revelos recalled that 'we were basically taking everything out of the flat, he [Vince] was moving and we helped him on numerous occasions', and 'we made enough noise coming up and down the stairs'. Though Revelos couldn't recall the specific month for the move he thought it was either October or November 1990. Police questioned him closely but Revelos didn't waver – his honest evidence and good recall had fatally wounded the case they'd been building against Vince.

On 8 February 2007, Pinch handed down her findings. She noted that Vince's evidence 'differed markedly from his earlier versions', and that the evidence of Leonie Roberts that she felt she was being 'tutored' by Vince and Brian on the night of the murder, 'supports at least that part of Esposito's version given at this inquest'. She didn't canvass Revelos' interview with police and simply found: 'Whether or not Esposito assisted in removing the carpet, I am satisfied that the carpet was removed because it had been damaged by bodily fluids excreted by Ludwig Gertsch when he died. Esposito himself now acknowledges that Gertsch must have died in his unit on 19 October 1990.'

She left the killer punch until last: 'I am satisfied that the evidence is sufficient to meet the tests set out in Section 19 (1)(b) Coroners Act [1980], I may forward the papers to the Director of Public Prosecutions (DPP) to consider whether criminal proceedings should be instituted.' What she was referring to was part of the Coroner's Act that gives her power to recommend the DPP consider a prosecution against a person.

The inquest had also prompted Pinch to re-open the inquiry into Roger-Claude Teyssedre's death. After reviewing the files from the first inquest, she noted that some of the drugs he had been taking for thrush and a skin problem – two of the numerous horrors the AIDS virus inflected on sufferers – if taken in combination may have caused heart problems, and that friends had thought Ludwig had also been overdosing him on other drugs causing him to appear 'dazed and drugged'.

However, in spite of Roberts' shenanigans with Ludwig's will, she found the signature of Roger's will to be genuine, and noted: 'The passage to the two estates is perhaps best symbolised in the movement of furniture and jewellery. Items that had been located at Teyssedre's residence at 7 Sutherland Street, Paddington in April 1990 had been taken to Roberts' residence at Haberfield by Christmas that year.' She added: 'The matter in which the will was executed together with the facts that the contents were not what people expected and that Roberts ultimately benefited financially by forging Gertsch's will have raised the prospect that the contents of the Teyssedre will may not have been what he intended at the time he signed it. Any unauthorised alteration of the terms of the will would obviously have provided a powerful motivation to ensure Teyssedre's demise before he could discover it.'

She couldn't rule out overdose or asphyxiation – the method that killed Ludwig – but was 'satisfied that he died an unnatural death in suspicious circumstances'.

The excellent work by police and the strong finding by the Coroner unfortunately wasn't enough to sway the Director of Public Prosecutions (DPP). In response to a request on the status of the case the DPP said, 'As of 2016, there are no proceedings on foot for any person named in the Coronial inquiry into Mr Gertsch's murder. The state of the available evidence some twenty-six years after Mr Gertsch's death was not sufficient to charge.' When talking about crime, outlaw bikers say 'fire fucks forensics', and in the murder of Ludwig Gertsch, time has had the same effect.

The chance of a resolution to the case that finally stirred NSW Police to take a hard look at the murders of gay men was now zero. But one case that wasn't going away was the death of Scott Johnson. His brother Steve, now financially capable of supporting his quest for the truth, was ratcheting up the pressure on the police.

CHAPTER 25

WHEN A BEAT ISN'T A BEAT

Steve Johnson isn't close to his brother Scott's partner, so Steve was surprised when the man rang him. The partner had been keeping up with Australian news and read of the results of Operation Taradale and Coroner Jacqueline Milledge's findings. Steve said that when he read Leonie Lamont's article in the *Sydney Morning Herald*, 'I was thunderstruck. My world was turned upside down, and for most of that day I cried.'

He continued: 'Over fifteen years passed until we learned in 2005 that Scott had died at what's known as a gay beat – a public but secluded meeting area, where sex typically occurs between gay men – in an era when youth gangs had committed hundreds of attacks on gay men in the Sydney area. We also learned of other gay men who had died by being pushed or thrown off cliffs in Sydney during the exact same period as when Scott died. This was a bombshell.'

In the years since Scott's body was found on the rocks at North Head, Steve's circumstances had changed dramatically. The kid who'd grown up poor in Los Angeles, married young and started a family, then spent their meagre savings on trying to get justice for his dead brother, had added a doctorate from Harvard in 1990 to a Harvard Master's degree. It was the start of a career that coincided with the beginning of the Internet age, and Steve, along with his business partner Chris Grace, was responsible for the algorithm that means we can send pictures, video and sound files by email. Their company Johnson-Grace was bought by America On Line (AOL) in 1996 and Steve became Vice President of AOL's Software and Technology Development division. In 2000, he founded media buying company Choicestream. Steve was now very successful and had the funds and the drive to try to find the truth that had been eluding him since 1988.

He contacted the Manly police and wrote to the Coroner on the premise that Scott's death was similar to that of the men in Operation Taradale – and like Kay Warren, he didn't get a response. However, he also wrote to Stephen Page, telling him of the similarities between Scott's death and the Bondi cases Page had investigated – and also what finding the truth meant to him. In his letters Steve said, 'Scott's death, for the longest time, stopped my life. Scott was my closest friend; it's easy to say that Scott helped define me, and was one of my primary sources of joy and purpose. He and I shared and worked together on our most important dreams. When Scott died, I was shattered.' In Page, he found a skilled detective who gave a damn.

In 2006 he flew to Sydney to meet with Stephen Page, who'd left the police force and was now working in the private sector. The two went to Manly Police Station, where they spoke to detectives who said they couldn't find the file on Scott's death. If they thought this was a cunning ploy to get rid of the persistent

American, they were wrong. Steve said, 'I never, never believed Scott killed himself. I've spent more than twenty years at a complete loss to understand what happened to my brother. In all that time, no more than a handful of days ever go by without my longing for Scott and wondering what happened to him.'

The police version of events was a little different. They reported that Detective Senior Constable Richard Doherty had reviewed the 1989 Coroner's brief and transcript and 'no new lines of inquiry were identified'.

The following year Steve Johnson hired *Newsweek* journalist Dan Glick to dig into the case. Glick had covered the JonBenet Ramsey murder and Columbine High School massacre cases, and was not afraid to dig. Page told both men the investigation should focus on whether there was a gay beat active in Manly at the time of Scott's death, and reports of any anti-gay violence on Sydney's northern beaches.

Glick flew to Sydney and got a crash course in Sydney gay-hate crimes of the late 1980s, finding gangs of youths terrorising gay men around the inner city through to the northern beaches, and those gangs included Vojko Spadina and his mates from North Narrabeen who'd been arrested and convicted. He quickly found that the area where Scott died was a gay beat, and one well known to both police and locals. Glick spoke to Les Wicks who'd worked at the sewage treatment works near Blue Fish Point in the late eighties, who told him that gay men were there 'all the time', adding: 'They'd clear off little areas and make love nests.' Glick commented, 'If this place was a gay beat known to a straight sewerage plant worker, surely police should have uncovered that fact during their investigation.' Ulo Klemmer, who worked for the

AIDS Council of New South Wales, confirmed the place was a well-known beat. One of the great mysteries of Scott's death was Doreen Cruickshank's determined assertion it wasn't.

A little bit of detective work, done without the assistance of the vast NSW Police treasury of crime reports and intelligence files, came up with a 1986 incident at the same cliff from which Scott fell. Sadie – his nickname – was a local gay man, and when Glick met him he was sixty-three years old. He told Glick that in 1986 he'd gone up to North Head near Blue Fish Point, slipped out of his clothes and 'worked the beat', waiting in the scrub for a kindred spirit, but Sadie got an experience he hadn't planned on. He found a partner, and they had sex, after which the man plunged a 'bowie' type knife into Sadie's back and left him bleeding near the cliff. It was pure luck the knife didn't damage his spine, slice through an artery or pierce a vital organ. Manly Hospital is only a short walk away and Sadie made it there and survived. His attacker was arrested. At the end of the interview, Sadie pulled up his shirt and showed Glick the scar. In a relatively quiet area like Manly, a naked man on a cliff being stabbed with a bowie knife and surviving is something that should have lingered in the corporate memory of the NSW Police.

Glick also spoke to former Police Rescue Squad officer Wayne Plant, who told him Scott's death did 'not fit with the type of suicide we normally found around North Head. You would have to have known that place or have been led there by someone with local knowledge.'

On Sunday, 3 June 2007 Glick started the media component of his investigation when the *Sun Herald* published a piece by their police reporter John Kidman headlined 'Maths Genius Thrown Off Cliff By Gay-Hate Gang', which talked of the possibility of

Scott being murdered in a similar fashion to the men at Bondi. Kidman wrote that Blue Fish Point, rather than not being a beat, was 'one of five well-known beats in the Manly area'. The story quoted Dan Glick, who said, 'What was happening at Bondi at this stage has been pretty well established. We know that. But you'd have to say the hypothesis that this was also a place not immune from gay bashings, violence and even murder is a reasonable one.' Glick offered an alternate theory to the police view of suicide and said, 'I'm putting a fall after some kind of struggle gone wrong perhaps, at the top of the list. Homicide would be the second and of course, suicide way down the bottom of the list because if that's the scenario, nothing quite adds up.' A visit to the local library, where he browsed through issues of the *Manly Daily*, revealed around a dozen articles near to the time of Scott's death, detailing assaults of gay men in toilet blocks and places such as Reef Beach.

Glick sent a report of his findings to the Unsolved Homicide Squad and Coroner Milledge, who later met with him. Glick recalled of his conversation with Milledge: 'The new evidence sounded familiar to the Bondi revelations. She said it might be possible to reclassify the case from "suicide" to "open finding". Somebody would be in touch with us. Despite repeated emails and telephone calls, nothing happened.'

The case cooled again over the next few years, with Dan Glick and Steve Johnson monitoring media developments and working social-media links including a Facebook page. On 29 January 2011, Glick received an email from someone purporting to be a thirteen-year-old Sydney boy hoping to draw their attention to a 'confession' on another website about the murder of Scott. Glick alerted Steve Johnson and sent the information to the NSW Coroner and the NSW Police. Glick returned to

Sydney in early May 2011 and, along with Stephen Page, had a meeting with Detective Inspector Luke Arthurs at Manly Police Station. The police hadn't any success in finding the source of the confession or the emailer, and Glick and Page conceded that while it might have a been a hoax, they'd found plenty of fresh evidence to cast doubt on the original suicide finding. Arthurs told them the case had been reviewed in 2007 and declined to do anything further. Steve Johnson hired an expert and tracked down the emailer, but the lead didn't bring them any closer to the Facebook poster.

Glick and Page lobbied the Coroner for a new investigation, citing the information uncovered and supporting it with expert advice from Page and Sue Thompson, who believed Scott's death was likely to be yet another gay-hate crime played out on a cliff top. Included in the new information was evidence of at least five youth gangs that operated in the northern beaches at the time of Scott's death.

The team of Glick and Page was persuasive, and in late May the Coroner decided to re-open the inquest and directed police to investigate the evidence the men had uncovered. Steve Johnson wrote to Glick saying, 'I do not imagine it will be a relief to learn that my brother was the victim of a murder rather than a suicide, but understanding the true circumstances surrounding his death would be very important to me and Scott's family.'

The police, however, weren't pleased by the Coroner's decision. Steve Johnson received a call from a detective at Manly in late 2011. He said, 'It was the first phone call from an Aussie I'd had since talking to Troy Hardie [the officer who'd been responsible for the initial inquiries into Scott's death] just after Scott died. The detective told me I was "barking up the wrong tree" with my push to have Scott's death re-investigated and asked me to "desist for my own good".' The advice fell on deaf ears; as Steve recently said, 'There's no point in going into all the insults and rudeness that have been aimed at our family by the NSW Police. Suffice it to say they don't like victim's families questioning their conclusions. We just want Scott's death investigated properly.'

With his experiences of the NSW Police, Steve wasn't holding his breath. In June 2012, a second inquest into Scott's death began. The compelling evidence uncovered by the Johnson team – including the common knowledge that the area was a known gay beat, the attack on Sadie, and similar attacks uncovered by Operation Taradale – was presented to the Coroner. Manly Detective Tim Wilson, who had been tasked by the police to review the case, told the Coroner that the only scenario of Scott's death that he could dispel from the list of possibilities was suicide. It was a strikingly different result to the earlier review.

Deputy State Coroner Carmel Forbes gave her decision on 27 June, and said: 'The possibilities that Mr Johnson was the victim of a "gay hate" crime similar to those that occurred in Bondi or that he fell are also available explanations to the circumstances that surrounded his death.

'Accordingly, I find that the evidence adduced in Mr Johnson's death does not enable me to make a finding as to how he fell off the cliff and I make an open finding and refer his file to "cold cases" for further investigation.' The finding was greeted by tears and hugs for Steve Johnson, his family and supporters. They had finally taken a major step forward, and he told the media outside the court, 'We're incredibly happy with the outcome. For twenty-three years we've had a question mark hanging over why he died. Hopefully, now we can get some answers.'

His optimism, however, didn't factor in the stubborn nature of some factions of the NSW Police. Steve said, 'Shortly after Scott's case was referred to the NSW Unsolved Homicide Unit, the police informed us that Scott's case would still not receive a proper investigation. The unit chief told us he determined the case was virtually unsolvable after consulting with the original 1988 investigator. Incredibly, the police were still maintaining that Blue Fish Point had never been a gay beat, that there were no new facts and that there was no point in opening an investigation.'

Recalcitrance by the police didn't deter the Johnsons and they headed back to the media to provide some stimulus. Police senior management are exceptionally sensitive to publicity for a mix of reasons that include the good of the service and avoidance of politicians getting annoyed with them – a potential career killer – and so getting the right coverage is an imperative and avoiding poor coverage equally so. When police heard of the ABC's *Australian Story* going to air on 11 February 2013 with a story on Steve's journey to find the truth about his brother's death, they swung into action. Steve recalled, 'In the hours leading up to its airing, NSW Police officials contacted our family to see if they could join in a press conference we planned for the day after *Australian Story* aired to announce a $100 000 reward. They also promised to finally investigate Scott's death.'

The show included interviews with Steve Johnson, Dan Glick, the sister of Scott's partner, Stephen Page and John Lehmann from the NSW Police. Page told *Australian Story*: 'Scott Johnson, gay man, fits straight into the victimology of someone who would be assaulted for a hate crime at a beat.' He also expressed surprise at a police report rebutting much of the work the Johnson team had done, and said, 'The amount of critical information that has been omitted I just can't explain.' Page had a clear view on Scott's death, and said, 'I don't think the death of Scott Johnson was suicide. Playing the percentages, more likely than not I think it was murder.' On the magnitude of the Coroner's opening finding he said, 'It was a big day when we got the finding of suicide overturned, and we got an open finding. It's not often the courts will admit they made a mistake.'

John Lehmann didn't make any admissions but said, 'We've read all the material. I can tell this matter has been investigated and looked at several times. This is a very, very difficult case and it's very, very challenging and we don't have any direct evidence or direct links to determine how Scott's death was caused.' His comments didn't come with any acknowledgement of the calibre of the police work on the day Scott's body was found. He moved to police boilerplate and said that because the Coroner had referred the case to the Unsolved Homicide Squad he wouldn't 'comment what stage the investigation is at'. He added: 'We certainly haven't closed the books on this case, it's an open case.'

CHAPTER 26

DON'T GET MAD, GET EVEN

Lehmann's classic close-down line didn't work. *Australian Story* struck a chord with the public and media and they wanted to know more about a dark period. The gay community had become mainstream; the Mardi Gras was no longer a political event but a social one that now had police walking in the parade; Oxford Street was on its last legs; Grindr (a popular app for gay men to meet on) had brought casual and discreet hook-ups to your smartphone rather than loitering around a toilet block; and marriage equality was on the national agenda. The past declined to be buried and few accepted the police story because their track record in this area was at best chequered.

Two weeks after *Australian Story*, Paul Sheehan opened fire in the *Sydney Morning Herald* in a major piece titled, 'Gay Hate: The Shameful Crime Wave'. Sheehan was one of the paper's leading comment writers and one noted for his conservative views, but in his piece published on 4 March 2013 he grabbed his audience's attention by opening with: 'Piece by piece, month by month, the map of Sydney's greatest unsolved and unacknowledged crime wave has taken shape. What that map belatedly reveals is that thousands of men were stalked, savagely assaulted and, in at least fifty cases, murdered.' He wrote that of these fifty reported cases, at least twenty were written off as suicide, unsolved or misadventure – but were in fact gay-hate murders – by police oblivious to the thousands of crimes committed against the gay community and a police force that in 2013 remained 'oblivious to the scale of what they missed'.

In another part of Fairfax, journalist Rick Feneley was digging into a story that was even more startling than Sheehan's exposé of fifty cases. Feneley was ready to go by July 2013 with a series of articles spaced out over a few days for maximum impact. On 27 July the headline was 'Murderous Rampage of Gay Hate Crimes' and featured two dramatic angles. First was the then unknown story of Bondi chef David McMahon and the vicious attack on him as he jogged along the Bondi coast in the summer of 1989, close to the time and location of John Russell's death after being thrown from the cliff at Marks Park. McMahon told Feneley he refused to live in terror and hoped that one of his assailants, or the mob that cheered them on, would finally have the guts to come forward and tell police what had happened. He said, 'Maybe we can solve one of these crimes,' but guts remain in short supply.

Feneley then introduced the findings of Sue Thompson and Professor Stephen Tomsen. Thompson, a lawyer and former staffer at the NSW Ombudsman's office, had spent twelve years as NSW Police Gay/Lesbian Client Consultant and in that role had collated police intelligence data on gay-hate crimes. She later worked with Tomsen, whose research was based on Coroners' records of alleged gay-hate murders between 1985 and 1995. Feneley wrote, 'These statistics, as sensational as they were, never made big headlines. And they didn't go close to accounting for the full scale of the gay-hate murder rampage.' However, Thompson and Tomsen had revised their work and included cases of disappearances including Ross Warren and Gilles Mattaini, and cases with a finding of suicide such as Scott Johnson, and those cases written off as 'misadventure'. There was a dramatic change in the figures, and Feneley reported a 'tally of close to eighty cases which spans from the late seventies to [the] nineties'.

Feneley wrote that Stephen Page believed that 'society would not have accepted so many unexplained killings of women, children, teachers or doctors'. He said of policing: 'We dropped the ball.' And he joined McMahon in the hope the bashers and their supporters might, as they reached middle age, want to relieve themselves of the guilty burden they'd carried for decades and 'give these poor families some answers'. The police declined to be interviewed for the article and instead provided a statement which said, 'A number of the deaths were investigated by Stephen Page in Operation Taradale, the Johnson case is being reviewed and anyone with information should contact Crime Stoppers.'

Feneley's next article was on 1 August, with the headline 'Sydney's Shame – up to 80 gay men murdered 30 cases unsolved' and started with some of the chilling recordings of young bashers at the Minda Juvenile Justice Centre back in the early nineties as they awaited sentences for convictions of manslaughter and murder, then moved into the Scott Johnson story. Of the gay-hate crimes around the time of Scott's death, Sue Thompson said: 'It was never just a wave. It is much more accurate to describe it as an epidemic.' Feneley then commented that it was one peculiar to

Sydney, with Melbourne's gay community and police not reporting anything of a similar scale.

Steve Johnson's attitude to the case was also changing, and not in a direction sympathetic to police. He told Feneley: 'At first, I was focused only on Scott's death. Then we started hearing from other families and other men who had survived vicious assaults around the time Scott died . . . there were hundreds, possibly thousands, of assaults against gay men during this era. There was a culture of gay-hate bashings. It didn't stop at the Harbour Bridge. We've heard stories of the equivalent of the Alexandria Eight or the Bondi Boys who regularly gay-bashed along the northern beaches.'

The articles didn't prompt a rush of people keen to unburden decades of guilt. But they did prompt two men with stories to tell.

Twenty-four years after the vicious assault on him in Surry Hills, Alan Rosendale was browsing the *Sydney Morning Herald* when an article caught his eye. It was Saturday, 10 August 2013 and the article was about a man who'd seen another man assaulted in South Dowling Street, Surry Hills in 1989. Alan thought, '1989?' and remembered that while he was being assaulted he had seen car headlights turned on and hoped it meant that 'someone was doing something about it'. After all these years he wondered if someone had seen what happened to him. He said, 'I remembered that car and thought later, whoever did that probably saved my life.' Alan contacted Rick Feneley and told his story.

The possible witness was Paul Simes and his story had a couple of major surprises for Alan. *Sydney Morning Herald* journalist Rick Feneley's stories on hate crimes of the late eighties and early nineties, including Scott Johnson, Ross Warren and John Russell, prompted Simes to wonder what happened to a man he'd seen being viciously beaten near the Moore Park beat in 1989 – was it a beating or murder? He contacted the paper.

Paul was working a couple of jobs back in May 1989 and recalled one had been at JJ's Home Kitchen in King Street, Newtown and he was living at Bondi. One Friday evening around May 1989, though he can't recall the specific date, he was driving home from his shift at JJ's and decided to make a stop at the Moore Park beat. It was on his route home and usually busy. He told police in a statement of 16 August 2013 that 'it was a very cool morning and it was still dark'. While he was parking his car on the Surry Hills side [western] of South Dowling Street and planning to walk across to the beat he saw 'a car heading south stop suddenly adjacent to the beat'. He remembered the car was a large four-door sedan but not the make or model. He saw all four doors open and 'a number of men' – he can't recall how many, but at least four – exit the vehicle 'rapidly'. Paul saw one of the men take what he thought might have been planks of wood out of the car and hand them to the other men.

Paul saw the men climb up the ledge to get into the park, and stopped his car to watch. He had an unobstructed view, and about a minute later he saw a 'group of people running out of the park toward South Dowling Street'; as they passed behind their car he realised they were the same group he'd just seen go into the park, and they were chasing a man who ran across South Dowling Street. The man cleared the median strip but tripped and fell in the gutter about ten metres in front of Paul's car. The men caught up to the fallen man, surrounded him and 'started to beat him with the planks of wood. I couldn't see exactly where they were hitting him due to him being surrounded; however, by the actions of the men I knew he was being beaten.' He said, 'It felt like a scene out of *A Clockwork Orange,* watching it unfold.'

Paul's choices were limited. He was outnumbered by a group of obviously violent men, so his only option was to start his car and turn on the headlights. He pulled away from the kerb and drove slowly past them, hoping the presence of a witness would stop the attack. It didn't, and Paul said, 'They didn't stop, so I conducted a U-turn on the grass median strip and pulled up behind the car on the other side of the road. I wrote the registration details of that vehicle on a piece of paper.' In spite of his presence, he said, 'They continued to beat the man.' Paul then drove off quickly to find a phone box to call the police emergency line 000, and was lucky to find one that worked only a few minutes away. He got back to the scene about fifteen minutes later, but everyone had gone. He saw a car parked in roughly the same spot he'd been parked earlier and spoke to the driver, who, he thought, was in his twenties or thirties and probably from a Greek background. The man told him he'd also seen the assault and had driven off to contact 000 as well. Paul drove home but the incident nagged at him and a few days later he contacted the Gay Anti-Violence Project and gave them details of what he'd seen and the registration details of the assailants' car. What happened next was unusual.

Given the ferocity of the attack and the clear evidence of who was responsible, you would hope for quick action, but it was weeks later that Paul received a call from someone at the project. They told him the registration number he'd recorded belonged to a police car and asked if he'd come to a meeting at Police Headquarters in College Street, Sydney.

Paul recalled he was taken up to a 'very high floor and into a very large office with big views of the city, the north side and harbour'. The room was fitted with bookcases, cabinetry, conference table, double lounges and a coffee table, along with the usual big desk and chairs. In the room was Fred Miller, Gay Liaison Coordinator for the Police Community Relations Bureau who was the former Labor Member of Parliament for the state seat of Bligh, which covered Darlinghurst and Surry Hills; also present was a senior police officer in uniform who was the occupant of the office and the dominant figure at the meeting, along with a younger uniformed officer, and a female police officer. Paul can't recall their names. It was a very friendly meeting, with refreshments served – police joke that if you don't get offered tea or coffee then you're in strife – and when the discussion got to the actual assault, the police officers stopped him and asked if he could visualise what happened. 'At that moment,' he said, 'I could see in my mind's eye that one of the weapons was a silvery/black coloured metal pole. One of the officers showed me a baton, which I believed was a police baton, and asked if it looked like that. I told them the object I saw did look like that.'

When the meeting ended, Paul went home. Miller later contacted him and said the officers who'd been in the car that night belonged to a 'unit who were unassigned and were troubleshooters'. Miller told him they'd been chasing a suspect from an alleged stabbing and hadn't arrested anyone. Paul recalled that Miller also said, 'Because no-one had come forward as a victim, no further action could be taken against the officers; however, he did say that that unit was disbanded and those officers had been from Darlinghurst Police Station and were reassigned to other duties. He also indicated that particular unit had a previous history of trouble.'

Paul Simes was pleased that his complaint had been taken seriously and police had done their work. Paul, with no experience of what police should have done and no guidance from Miller or the police at the meeting, wasn't aware of the correct procedures that should have been followed. Instead of doing their job, the police gave Paul a nice massage and sent him home happy, which was a politically expedient result for them. The report of a gay man bashed and left in a gutter by police would have caused a media hullabaloo likely to cross state and national borders, and the police were mindful of the image they were trying to build after years of violence and corruption. They also hadn't come to grips with their new Police Minister, Ted Pickering, so were keen to avoid trouble early in that relationship. The other possible issue was who the police assailants were, such as someone with strong family connections in the upper echelons.

This is what should have happened. Paul would be asked to make a statement, in writing: the first requisite legal step to start a complaint. The ensuing investigation would have quickly found the culprits, who were probably a 'hoodlum patrol', which were general-duties police dressed in casual clothes who toured the trouble spots of the police patrol on weekends. Their task was to respond to brawls, or to chat to, and break up if needed, groups of potential troublemakers at transport hubs, snooker and pinball parlours, pubs around closing time and the like. Given the reports of violence against gay men at beats at the time, they may have been tasked to keep gangs of thugs away, rather than be a gang themselves. With the seriousness of Alan's injuries, the men should have been charged with criminal offences, not assigned to other duties. The actions of the police who met with Paul bring with them a whiff of criminality as well.

Irrespective of the motivations, it was a cover-up. A few hours of detective work might have found a victim – there was one lying at home recovering from bruises, abrasions and carefully eating soft food – but it's a reasonable bet they spent more time working on ensuring a successful cover-up than an objective investigation.

Feneley then wrote in the *Sydney Morning Herald* of 19 January 2015: 'Chillingly, the details were identical to his own assault, so Rosendale was horrified to discover that police may have been the culprits.'

Following Rosendale's call to Feneley, Paul Simes said he was 'more relieved than anything else' to hear that the possible victim that night was alive. However, what happened next didn't give either man any comfort. With the case gaining media prominence, the police assigned detectives from Surry Hills to investigate. They acted quickly at first, taking a statement from Rosendale on 13 August 2013 and Simes three days later. Rosendale said his meeting didn't get off to a good start. He arrived on time, only to find the detective he'd been told to see wasn't available, so another detective took the interview. He later met with a Detective Hancock, who told him that the two cases were 'not necessarily linked', which he found astounding given the similarity of the circumstances, and he was amazed when she told him that skinheads had allegedly been responsible for his assault. He said, 'It was the first time in twenty-five years I'd heard there was a report and that it blamed skinheads.'

The police also looked into their records, but the only thing they could find was Senior Constable Boyd's 'Crime Information Report' submitted on the day of the assault. Police didn't take either man to the crime scene for an inspection. They also interviewed the local milkman, who said he'd been delivering in the area since 1971 and didn't remember the incident, and given his probable age and profession it was unlikely he was the youngish, Greek-looking man in a car. The police also interviewed Boyd, who had left the force by that time, but he couldn't shed any light on the matter; however, his statement and/or interview wasn't made available to Simes or Rosendale after their Freedom of Information request. Fred Miller died in 1992.

The police investigation found that there was no evidence to suggest that Simes and Rosendale were talking about the same crime – an interesting result given the commonality of circumstances and the lack of evidence to suggest that bashing men in the gutter outside the Langton Clinic was a regular event. When Feneley followed up, the police issued a media statement saying the purpose of their investigation was to find 'whether the assaults are one and the same' and to 'ultimately, track down and arrest the men responsible for Mr Rosendale's assault'. They also commented, 'Over the course of the last thirteen months, detectives from Surry Hills have invested significant time and effort into this investigation. The investigation into Mr Rosendale's assault remains open and detectives encourage anyone who believes they have evidence relating to the matter to contact Crime Stoppers.'

Alan Rosendale found the statement bleakly funny, and said that by November 2013 the investigation was over, with the detective calling him and saying she couldn't find any evidence to link the two cases. 'She called me Paul,' he said. 'I said, "I'm Alan, not Paul."' He added, 'I won't hold my breath. I wasn't aware there ever was an "investigation" that could now be kept open. All they've done is take a statement from me that they didn't bother to get in 1989; and they've finally recorded a statement from Paul Simes, which they didn't bother to do at the time; and, oh yes, they've tracked down a milkman and a policeman who remember nothing. Is that what they call an investigation? It now seems likely that a gang of policemen beat me up, and that some of their superiors knew about it but covered it up. Doesn't that warrant a genuine investigation?'

The other issue they encountered was a lack of police records. Long gone, courtesy of government record-keeping requirements, were police radio (VKG) records, Surry Hills Police Station documents including rosters, note books, occurrence pads and car diaries that would have aided the modern investigators in their task. In writing this book, I confirmed the charge books for the Surry Hills Police Station were still in government archives. The books contain the details of everyone charged at the station in chronological order and also have the details of the arresting police. My purpose was to see if the team of alleged police assailants might have arrested someone on their shift, thus disclosing their own details on the arrest record so they could be identified. However, charge books have a hundred-year privacy embargo. A brick wall to me, but possibly available to the police reviewing Rosendale's case. I passed the information on to police, and also to Alan and his lawyers.

No records, if any ever existed, of Simes' contact with the Anti-Violence Project and subsequent meeting with Miller and police at College Street could be found – a situation that didn't surprise me. It isn't smart to keep records of a meeting like this.

Frustrated about the investigation, Alan Rosendale sought help from Alex Greenwich MP, the Member for Sydney whose constituency covered Darlinghurst and Surry Hills. Greenwich contacted the NSW Ombudsman, who has the power to review complaints about police. In a thirteen-page letter dated 24 June 2015, the then Ombudsman Bruce Barbour went into great detail to say very little.

The Ombudsman, rather than questioning the veracity of the original investigation or lack of it, or the calibre of the recent investigation, quoted the NSW Police Minister of 26 November 2014: 'The Surry Hills Local Area Command has conducted a thorough investigation into particular allegations made in 1989. No evidence was found to implicate involvement of police in an assault.'

The Ombudsman then made eight points to 'suggest the initial premise is incorrect', which, to paraphrase Paul Keating, flicked the switch for vaudeville.

Rosendale, accurately, 'was unable to provide any description of his assailants' and 'in those circumstances there was no information available to the police that would have helped them identify the assailants' and thus 'no basis for any further police investigation of the assault and it follows no basis for police to create any further documents in relation to that assault'. Following the Ombudsman's logic, a murder victim would have to rise up and speak, or hope someone was a witness in order to get an investigation going. It might have also been helpful if police had followed up with Rosendale.

The Ombudsman went on to point out that Paul Simes couldn't specify the date he had witnessed the assault and that Miller had told Simes 'police had not been able to identify the victim of the assault because no one has come forward'. Police keep excellent records of crime, so it wouldn't have been a major task to see who had been assaulted in a specific location and identify the victim.

Instead, the police took a different route and moved to massage Simes out of a complaint, rather than investigate.

As a sop to the allegation of a cover-up back in 1989, the Ombudsman pointed out that contemporary police hadn't been able to find any records and Simes hadn't been able to identify anyone other than Fred Miller at the headquarters meeting, so it was all over. Given the nature of the meeting, it would have been very surprising if there had been a record created. When you're actively burying allegations of a serious and politically volatile crime you'd be very silly to make records that could later be used against you. Barbour concluded by writing, 'I appreciate that Mr Rosendale may be disappointed with the outcome of my assessment of the matter. However, I do trust this letter will assist Mr Rosendale in understanding the reasons for that outcome.' Alan Rosendale didn't.

According to the NSW Ombudsman, 'We work with police to make sure the complaints system appropriately identifies criminal and serious misconduct and is accessible, credible, flexible and responsive.' Back in 1989 it would have been appropriate and legally compellable for police to mention Simes' complaint to the Ombudsman but they didn't, because they managed to persuade Simes out of making one. Alan Rosendale is disappointed by the failure of both the NSW Police and the Ombudsman, and said the response by both 'tried to fob me off and that's made me angrier and angrier'. He added, 'I'm an angry old poof living in the suburbs,' and one that isn't going to let the matter fade away.

CHAPTER 27

THE EMPIRE STRIKES BACK

Doreen Cruickshank was the first detective to investigate Scott Johnson's death. By 2015 she was a superintendent and the state's longest-serving policewoman. Leading Taskforce Macnamir, which was the official title of the new investigation into the death, was Detective Chief Inspector Pamela Young. Young was eighteen and fresh out of high school when she joined the police, attracted by a 'challenging physical job combined with an emphasis on people and behaviour', as she told Martine Harte for the blog (undated) *Engaging Women.* Young is a highly experienced homicide investigator and told Harte: 'Some still think policing is about brawn not brain. I have always found it an intellectual pursuit, above anything else. It has fully engaged me and developed me intellectually.' In the Johnson case she was about to get the challenge of her career, and it would be either make or break.

On 20 March 2013, Young conducted an interview with Steve Johnson that ran for five hours. She noted he was accompanied by

Dan Glick, whom she described as an 'employee'. Nine days later she interviewed Scott's partner, and what the two separate interviews showed clearly was that the relationship between him and Steve remained a deeply unhappy one.

The results of the investigation led by Young were collated in a statement that formed the basis of the evidence presented to the hearing at the NSW Coroner's Court starting on 12 April 2015. A statement dated 17 March 2015 was 439 pages and 2978 numbered paragraphs. It is a curious document for someone who has been around investigations – a mix of information from earlier police work, reviews and some investigation. What was striking was that none of the officers involved in the original investigations into Scott Johnson's death was interviewed. Troy Hardie, the officer in charge of the case on the day Scott's body was found, had been re-interviewed for the 2011 review; and Philip Flogel, the scientific officer at the scene, had returned with Macnamir detectives to North Head. There is nothing in Young's statement to indicate that Doreen Cruickshank had been interviewed since she had given her statement for the first Coroner's inquest.

Questions that might have been asked include the instructions given by Cruickshank's superiors, her line of reporting, who her workmate was – detectives of that time usually worked in pairs to aid in corroboration of evidence and for their own safety – what inquiries led her to assert that the location wasn't a gay beat, what inquiries were done with the local intelligence officer who collated all information from patrolling police – reports that included things like what car was seen where and when, people spoken to by police and so on, which was all information police may have recorded as they patrolled areas used as beats, her later reflections on what could have been done better, potential for a different outcome, consideration of alternatives to suicide, inquiries to see if any attacks against gay men or men who could be perceived as gay had occurred in the lead-up to Scott's death, and so on.

Young stated that the Unsolved Homicide Squad has 'protocols to manage and prioritise over 700 cases of murders, suspicious deaths or suspicious disappearances referred by a Coroner or identified since the 1970s. The protocols exist to balance the equity of all deceased persons and likely solvability of the case.' Then came the first public shot in the escalating tensions between the police and the Johnson family, when Young stated, 'When applied to the death of Scott, the re-investigation was deferred in preference to other cases. The Johnson family were dissatisfied with that decision.' Young would build on the theme of dissatisfaction on national television.

Young's team of investigators interviewed numerous men who had been members of gangs who carried out assaults on gay men back in the eighties and nineties, some of whom were brought to their attention by the work of the Johnson family and their team. Though the interviews were thorough, no new information on Scott's death came to light. What they did show was an odious culture among clusters of young men who revelled in attacking gay men. It was no surprise most came from the same areas and many had gone to school together. Like most who joined gangs, they'd felt disenfranchised and found comfort with kindred spirits in a mix of testosterone, brutality, cowardice and, I suspect for some, an internal battle with their own sexuality that resulted in violence rather than acceptance. Sue Thompson said of the period that 'targeted attacks were an everyday reality'.

There were some strange moments in the statement. One tip-off suggested that investigators should talk to two brothers who allegedly worked at City Tattersalls Club; the call had come via Crime Stoppers and didn't have any further detail. Rather than head to the club and ask the human-resources staff or any long-term employees if they knew of two brothers who'd worked there, Young stated, 'No further information was provided and the information was not investigated.'

In contrast, there was information that Scott had gone ice-skating at the Macquarie Centre Ice Rink, not far from the university where he was working on his PhD. This rated a visit by the investigators who found that no-one remembered Scott.

The unusual nature of the document deepened as I waded into it. There were references to the case of Stephen Dempsey, a gay man who, Young said, disappeared from Cremorne and was murdered at Deep Creek Reserve at Elanora Heights. The killing was on 4 August 1994 and, according to Young, occurred when the murderer Richard Leonard propositioned Dempsey and then shot him with a bow and arrow. Young stated, 'NP 128 [from the redacted statement], told police that after Mr Stephen Dempsey died at the reserve, he dismembered the body and kept it in his freezer until December and then threw it in a waterway near Palm Beach.' Peter Rolfe, Dempsey's business partner who now helps victim's families and friends through his organisation 'Support After Murder Inc' wrote to Young, pointing out that her statement had a few inaccuracies, including that Stephen's body had never been recovered when in fact his torso had.

It's interesting to note that though the murderer's name was redacted in Young's statement, it was public knowledge thanks to extensive media coverage of the police investigation and conviction of the murderer.

At paragraph 1676, Young turned her attention to Operation Taradale, stating, 'Its purported connection to the death of Scott Johnson has fuelled many sensational headlines and media stories. Some inaccuracies, misrepresentation and uninformed criticism has resulted [in] increased community fear.' What that fear was more than two decades after the spate of gay violence wasn't clear. However, it reminded me of the age-old cultural problem with the NSW Police – it's an organisation that doesn't take criticism well. Poke it and it bites. Young went on: 'It is for these reason[s] that it is relevant to look more fully into the aspects of Taradale.'

Pamela Young opened by quoting Coroner Milledge's 2005 comment that Marks Park was a 'known area for brutal attacks on gay males', but then commented: 'Presuming that this refers to the time of Mr Warren's disappearance and Mr Russell's death in 1989, the actual evidence is that by November 1989 when the body of Mr Warren was recovered the only violent offence identified was the assault upon [victim's name redacted].' Mr Warren's body was never recovered, so it's likely Young meant John Russell, not Ross Warren. She also reckoned that attack wasn't recorded as a gay-hate crime, and said, 'If there are no indicators of a gay-hate motive, then how are police at the time to know that Marks Park is a place of attacks on homosexual males?' A conversation with the retired Sergeant Adrian Ingelby, who'd recalled of the area back at the time of the deaths that 'I already knew from previous local knowledge that the area was frequented by the homosexual element', might have been a good start, or even to read the statement he provided to Taradale. By this point in Young's statement

I was getting the distinct impression it was more of a defence of policing failures than an objective review. Some basic detective work was notably absent.

She pressed on, critical of some of Taradale's methodology, and noting, 'I have been unable to identify a forensic purpose for testing the memories of witnesses to events that occurred and were recorded up to ten years previously. The whole effect is to unreasonably lower the confidence as a whole.' She ended that segment with the comment, 'Taradale forms the view that Mr Warren was known to attend gay beats for sexual liaisons and it relies in part on Mr Warren's conviction for an act of gross indecency in 1985. The statement concludes, "The relevance of this conviction information to this investigation is Warren attended gay beats for sexual liaison as opposed to suicidal motives." This is a flawed conclusion as it generalises single purpose usage of gay beat areas, which is not reliable or factual. The conclusion is not relied upon by the current investigation.' I'd put money on Ross heading to Marks Park, where he'd met his host for the weekend a few years before, for a sexual liaison.

Young then moved on to the police view of the 'characteristics' of gay beats. It was a detailed summary, but based on police records it didn't include matters such as gay men not always doing local beats but travelling – like the men I'd spoken to who motored through the 'Stations of the Cross'. Other popular beats were in the Sutherland shire and the wooded areas of the park on the Botany Bay foreshore. These were places where men from the inner city would try to fulfil a fantasy of hooking up with locals – tradies, married men, rugby league players, surfers and so on – but all too often bumped into men they knew who'd travelled to the suburbs with a similar intention. Bashers, like Vojko

Spadina and his colleagues back in the mid eighties, also knew where the beats were, and they too travelled.

Former NSW Homicide detective John McNamara was interviewed. He'd been hired by the Johnson family to 'assist Mr Glick in 2006 and 2007' and told Young's investigators he believed that 'The Johnson family has one agenda, and the agenda was that Scott had been murdered.' McNamara said that he wasn't 'convinced of a link between Scott's death and the gay-hate crimes in the eastern suburbs in that period'. He thought the *Australian Story* program was 'overwhelmingly one-sided' and 'wished he'd been contacted because he would have given a different point of view to what was presented'. McNamara told the investigators he'd been responsible for finding media articles about possible gay-hate crimes and following up one of the witnesses who found Scott's body. He had also had a chat with Troy Hardie who, according to McNamara, 'did not have any concerns about how the matter was investigated or the outcome of the inquest'.

Given the depth of McNamara's investigations, Young's statement finished the McNamara segment by saying that during his career in Homicide, he hadn't come across any investigators with a poor attitude to gay people or who 'lacked a commitment to a gay-related investigation', and his investigations for the Johnsons 'did not identify police inaction or corruption'. Young seemed to be preparing a defence case for the dismal performance of her policing predecessors rather than going on the front foot with a fresh, detailed and vigorous investigation of the case

The statement then moved on to the work of Sue Thompson and Stephen Tomsen, and at paragraph 2473, Young spoke of their mention of a possible gay-hate murder in Wollongong as 'the death of Mr I in Wollongong in 1986'. She said, 'There are no Coronial records of a death of a person of this name. The source details of Ms Thompson's spreadsheet [of the possible eighty-eight gay-hate crimes that had stirred the media into action] indicate the information is from academic Mr Stephen Tomsen. (Mr Tomsen is also a Johnson family consultant referred to later in this statement.) It is unable to be verified.'

A bit of detective work could have identified the case – the spelling of the victim's surname was incorrect and should have been Rooney. It took me a few hours to track down the actual name as Rooney, then contact the Coroner's media people to request the file, find police who'd been involved and Mr Rooney's partner, and get some background on the terrifying story of Mark Scerri. (At the time of writing, I had passed this on to police after they announced Operation Parrabell in late May 2016 – another investigation into the alleged gay-hate crimes.)

On 12 April 2015, Scott Johnson's death was back at the Coroner's Court in Glebe. John Agius SC for the family told the Coroner Michael Barnes that their investigations had uncovered fifty 'people of interest' and five gangs of bashers operating on the northern beaches. Police didn't oppose the family's request for a new inquest. Coroner Barnes said of the potential new witnesses: 'Some purport to have evidence that could well lead to a different finding were it accepted.

Further, there are other legitimate considerations such as the right of the family and the public to have the new evidence tested in open court. That may allay suspicions and concerns that are held by the family and perhaps some members of the community. It may lead to a different finding as to how Mr Johnson died.'

Outside the court, Pamela Young told the media she was pleased with Barnes' decision and said: 'I believe there are some new pieces of information and potentially some evidence that the Coroner could be interested in. But nonetheless, none of it directly relates to Scott being murdered. We very much look forward to the public of New South Wales getting to scrutinise the facts of the matter.'

Steve Johnson had flown in from the United States for the hearing, and told the media after the decision, 'I came into this same building twenty-six years ago, in 1989, when the police had rushed to judgement, as they've done in so many other deaths of gay men in Sydney in that time. [The police] decided Scott had committed suicide with no evidence, without talking to the family and with no investigation whatsoever. The Coroner at that time simply accepted the police judgement out of hand. The second inquest in 2012 considered the family's investigative work. No police investigation had been done at that time. So, we really see this as the first inquest.' Though both police and the Johnsons were pleased with the outcome, the moment of accord didn't last long.

CHAPTER 28

LATELINE

Emma Alberici, the presenter of ABC television's late-night current affairs show *Lateline*, led with the Scott Johnson inquest story on 13 April 2015. She recapped the history of the case and said that for the past eight years Steve Johnson 'has employed a team of investigators to prove that Scott met with foul play', then cut to Steve at North Head. Johnson said as he walked around the location from which Scott fell, 'The breeze always makes me remember how peaceful and serene a young man he was. Then I think about what his last moments might've been like, the last moments, possibly of terror, looking into the eyes of his attackers, if that's what happened, and, you know, it's horrible to think about.'

She reported Scott's partner's comment, 'You can go to a gay beat seeking sex with somebody and be so full of remorse afterwards or disgust that you can then suicide,' then followed with Steve Johnson's rebuttal, 'It's a possible explanation. It's very doubtful,' and his comments on Scott's likely state of mind just after he'd got the news about his PhD. Alberici followed up with the curious observation that just before his death Scott had become 'fascinated' by Alan Turing and had read the biography of a 'brilliant gay man who took his own life at forty-one'. It was a piece of alleged information that left the Johnson family scratching their heads and wondering if Alberici were hunting round for a parallel. Then she introduced her studio guest, Detective Chief Inspector Pamela Young.

It's part of the role of senior police to give press conferences, issue media statements and the like, but it's unusual for them to appear on television in a question-and-answer interview format. Police like to be in control, and interviews in this format can go astray – as this one did. Then Alberici introduced her interview – recorded earlier that evening – with the provocative comment that Young 'rejects any suggestion that police did anything but a thorough review of the case'. Alberici also promised that in this 'exclusive' interview, 'DCI Young accuses Steve Johnson of using his status as a powerful and connected businessman to influence the investigation into his brother's death.'

Young rejected the suggestion that the 1988 investigation was flawed, and commented, 'It was the standard of the day' – which it certainly wasn't. If she had tracked down the Rooney case in Wollongong and looked at the fine work that led to the capture of Mark Scerri, and the work of Steve McCann and his team in the gay murders that were solved, she might have been less dismissive. Young appeared to be on a mission from the outset of the interview, and it was unlikely to be one that her superiors had anticipated or welcomed.

After talking about methodology and defining hate crimes, she turned her focus to Scott Johnson and the Golden Gate

Bridge – reprising her support of Doreen Cruickshank's original investigation, which presumably was also 'standard of the day'. Young said, 'I think it's very important to mention the Golden Gate Bridge and compare it to North Head in that people can choose many varied ways of suicide. Scott, some years before 1988, chose to at least speak about him thinking of suiciding from a height over water; it happened to be the Golden Gate Bridge. Lo and behold, in 1988, his body is found at a height of sixty metres from a cliff over water.'

Then Alberici asked about Steve Johnson's allegation of 'open hostility' toward him, and lack of motivation to 'move beyond a suicide finding', to which Young responded as mentioned at the opening of this book, by accusing Steve of trying to influence the outcome of the investigation. She also said, 'I felt he had that thought: if I wasn't with him, then I was against him, and that was never the case.'

She warmed to the theme of Johnson family influence, telling Alberici, 'I have the responsibility of hundreds of families who expect thorough reviews and expect successful re-investigations. They have lost loved ones too. And they come from all walks of life. Some are not as well off as others. And my role and the role of the commander of the Homicide Squad is to treat them equally. It is about their loss of a family member. It's not about who they are, who they influence, their status or a network that they have. And I found it very unsettling and I haven't seen that before. And when our Deputy Commissioner became aware of that meeting, he was shocked that it had happened. It was something that's not protocol and not – not routine.'

Moving on to *Australian Story*, Alberici asked Young about the meeting between herself, Police Minister Mike Gallacher and

Steve Johnson the day after the show went to air. Young said, 'To be frank, there was some panic over the *Australian Story* that came out the night before. We had word that the Johnson family were being profiled by *Australian Story* – which is fine. I'm actually – I very much like that show. I like the format. It's a nice profile piece. But unlike myself, others were very concerned that it would be overly critical of the police. So, one of those people apparently was the Minister, who rang my commander of the Homicide Squad and also rang the Johnson family and arranged the meeting and gave them their strike force, their priority over everyone else's death.' Alberici asked, 'And you think that was improper?' to which Young said, 'Absolutely improper. Wrong on every level in relation to homicide investigations. Victims are equal. It was very wrong.' The interview was over on that ringing allegation that the former Police Minister had behaved improperly by kowtowing to an affluent American. Young had just dropped a hand grenade on national television.

Around that time, Mike Gallacher was under investigation for allegations around election-campaign funding and had resigned his Ministerial portfolios; however, he was later exonerated. Emerging around this turbulent time was the story that Gallacher was a right-wing conservative Catholic, which is a good yarn but wrong. During his long police career Gallacher was one of the first Gay Liaison officers, which isn't something for which a right-wing Catholic would volunteer. Gallacher also wasn't a wimp, and the night after Young's appearance, he went on *Lateline*.

He told Emma Alberici he had met the Johnsons 'two or three times', and when Alberici questioned whether it was 'unusual' for a Police Minister to meet the families of victims he replied, 'No, if people request to come and see me. I've done it as Shadow Minister and I've done it as Minister. It's always been my objective to make sure that the wellbeing of family members and people who have been victims of crime are looked after. And that's exactly what I've afforded them: no different than I've afforded anyone else who's requested it.'

She asked Gallacher about his alleged direction to set up a taskforce to investigate the Johnson case that would take preference over hundreds of other unsolved homicides. Gallacher, an experienced copper who'd spent his share of time in the witness box being attacked by defence counsel, was direct and said, 'That allegation is totally incorrect. I saw that it was aired yesterday. It's misconceived.' After taking a few potshots at Gallacher allegedly 'not being very victim friendly', which he refuted at length and in detail, Alberici changed tacks and asked, 'Were you persuaded by representations [of] the Kennedy family in the US? Steve Johnson is, of course, a multi-millionaire Internet-pioneer businessman. Were you persuaded by the fact that he has connections to the Kennedy family?' Gallacher said, 'I don't know anyone in the Kennedy family,' and added that he didn't know of any representation they had made to the government. Alberici's question may have been intended to lend substance to Young's line of affluent Americans getting preferential treatment, but the fact was Edward Kennedy had asked a question back shortly after Scott died – when Steve Johnson was still a poor student studying at Harvard. She finished her interview by asking if the Johnson family had donated money to the Liberal Party, which Gallacher said he didn't think they had, and 'most certainly haven't donated to me'. He said, 'We haven't even had a cup of coffee.'

Pamela Young's interview caused an uproar, with John Agius SC for the Johnson family demanding the Commissioner remove her from the inquiry, and that she retract some of her comments and formally apologise. As a public-relations ploy by the police it was a disaster. Coroner Barnes described Young's comments as 'unprecedented' and asked that she be removed from the investigation. Senior Crown Solicitor Naomi Malhotra wrote to Clair Hodge, the general counsel for the police, and said, 'When the officer in charge of the investigation speculated on national television about the weight to be given to key evidence she knew would come before the inquest and in effect queried whether the investigation she had undertaken was even appropriate, she engaged in a departure from the usual standards of conduct in such matters that is unprecedented in the State Coroner's experience. It clearly has the potential to undermine public confidence in the impartiality of DCI Young's investigation and her commitment to it.' Young was removed from the case, and it was handed over to Detective Sergeant Penelope Brown.

When I interviewed Michael Gallacher in late 2015 he said the meeting that caused the hullabaloo was initiated after the Johnsons had contacted Police Media. He recalled preliminary discussions with Deputy Commissioner Catherine Burn and members of the Unsolved Homicide Squad, and said, 'I told them it was an ideal opportunity to heal the rift that still exists between older gay men and the police,' and to finally deal with the murders and assaults from the 1980s; however, the police resisted. Gallacher said he was disappointed they didn't seize 'the opportunity to address the demon' and look at the bigger picture of the public and particularly the gay community's perceptions, and 'to take a look at a problem that still exists among some of the older generation of police'. He reiterated that he hadn't, and would never, direct the police to 'drop everything to pursue the Johnson case', and suggested that it would be worth considering getting a 'fresh set of eyes' by asking the NSW Crime Commission to review Young's investigation. One other reason that prompted his suggestion was the fact that Young's work was based on data from the Coroner, so it didn't include information the Crime Commission might hold on serious assaults and robberies.

The difference between assault and murder is often slender – good luck or bad. Gallacher said of the spate of gay attacks of the eighties: 'When someone dies and family or friends believed something was wrong then we owe it to them to act and to fail them is inexcusable.' He added, 'The wrongs against the gay community either by police indifference or direct involvement must be looked into. It's not too late.'

Relationships between the police and the Johnson family didn't improve after *Lateline.* The NSW Police as an entity – and the following isn't directed at individual police, who usually show great compassion and understanding as they work in an extraordinarily tough and thankless job far outside the experiences of their critics – doesn't have a culture that encourages apologies, acceptance of errors or diplomacy. It still maintains vestiges of the insularity I found during my service over three decades ago.

Steve Johnson, while welcoming the third inquest, made his view of Pamela Young's inquiry clear: 'After what was claimed to be a two-year investigation, Detective Chief Inspector Pamela Young went on national television to say that police had learned nothing new about Scott's death, except one additional tidbit supporting the suicide theory. The police did produce a 400-page report which can only be characterised as a veiled "We told you it was suicide" tome. Without details, how lame and unsupported by evidence the suicide theory is, I will just say the family still does not feel that the NSW Police have conducted a professional, unbiased and thorough investigation into Scott's death.'

Johnson then took aim at Young's *Lateline* comments: '[She] responded to the Coroner's action [ordering the third inquest] by publicly expressing her indignation over being forced to expend police resources investigating Scott's case when she's been certain all along that nothing more can be learned. This is despite the fact that a police detective reviewed the police evidence of suicide in 2011 [and] said that suicide should be ruled out, and the fact that Deputy Coroner Forbes in 2012 ruled that there was insufficient evidence to support a finding of suicide.' He then turned to Young's on-air comments about the influence the Johnson family might have had on 'politicians' and about the former Police Minister Michael Gallacher 'kowtowing'. 'More sadly,' he said, 'she managed to pit victims' families against each other by claiming that cold-case investigative resources are a zero-sum game. If she is forced to investigate Scott's death, she claims, that means that other families will be deprived of answers.'

Steve Johnson continued, 'No, Scott's life is not more important than anyone else's. It is, however, equally important – and he deserves the investigation he never received.' He added, 'Young's statements confirm for us that the NSW Police have somehow doubled-down on claiming that no mistakes were ever made in the investigations of gay-hate-related violence. This, however, has failed to bury Scott's case. Scott has now become symbolic of the dozens of gay men who died suspiciously during the 1980s and 1990s but received inadequate or no police investigations.' He concluded by saying, 'The question is thus whether the

NSW Police will come to its senses and acknowledge that mistakes were made in the past, not only with respect to Scott's case but others as well. It is only with such an acknowledgement that honest investigations can be conducted and answers be discovered to many unexplained deaths.'

CHAPTER 29

BACK TO BASICS

A year later, the Johnsons and the NSW Police were back in the Coroner's Court, with Coroner Michael Barnes on the Bench. It was Monday, 4 April 2016, and the hearing followed Barnes' all-day sitting on the Lindt Cafe siege. John Agius SC for the Johnsons told Barnes that in an 'ideal world' NSW Police should have nothing to do with the investigation, because they 'had demonstrated their position to be one of such bias that it could only unfairly infect the Coronial process' – but he conceded that the ideal world was unlikely. The case was adjourned until Thursday. At that hearing three days later, Barnes said the inquest would begin on 1 July 2016, and that the investigation would be under the 'close supervision' of the court in order to address concerns of police bias. He also gave the NSW Police five weeks to re-examine their 4000-page brief of evidence, and noted that after opening addresses the inquest would adjourn so police could follow up with more investigation. Agius promised a fiery opening address to the inquest. However, the inquest didn't open on 1 July 2016, and at the time of writing, the inquest is expected to be at the end of 2016. The Johnson family took the adjournment stoically and await the next chapter in a story that started nearly thirty years ago.

On 22 May 2016 the NSW Police went public with their next step, reviewing the eighty-eight possible gay-hate-related crimes, thirty of which are unsolved and include alleged suicides and brutal beatings.

The *Sun Herald* noted of the investigation: 'A team of eight detectives attached to Operation Parrabell are meticulously reviewing every archived document in these cases in a bid to decide whether gay hatred motivated the victim's death.' The report said the investigators 'will use ten bias-indicators from the FBI over the next few months to assess whether the eighty-eight cases are gay-hate crimes. The process will focus on the motive of an offender and whether he or she is driven by a hatred for homosexuality rather than robbery or other reasons.' The report also noted, 'It is understood in at least one case – based on anecdotal information given to researchers – detectives haven't been able to find a death certificate or Coronial file.' That case was the death of William Rooney, and I contacted the police and later sent them a copy of the Coroner's report I had obtained through a media request to the court.

One contentious issue in the saga has been the definition of a gay-hate crime, and the police use of FBI indicators. Sue Thompson wrote in her May 2016 paper 'Gay Violence Epidemic of 80s & 90s' that she and Professor Stephen Tomsen determined in a 'conservative review of the homicide lists' that in the twenty-three years from 1976 to 1999, there 'were at least twenty-one unsolved gay killings,' of which 'the NSW police accept only eight of those unsolved cases as satisfying the criteria of gay-hate homicide'.

She argued: 'It makes no sense for police to now retrospectively apply a strict FBI code, designed for uniform crime reporting and not for operational police investigations of possible hate crimes, to old possible anti-gay murders. To now look for FBI-type "sufficient objective facts" with a "prudent person" test to a time twenty [to] forty years ago when police themselves were often incapable of recording truly objective facts about the deaths of gay men, is nonsensical. Furthermore the cases from 1989–99 have already been tested and verified by the preeminent Australian Institute of Criminology. It is far too late to rewrite history.'

Ultimately the story is about crimes, as Thompson wrote, in which 'the victim may have been gay or perceived to be gay and the offender's actions motivated to some significant degree by prejudice or homophobia'. She also noted, 'All relevant cases should be recorded and gathered together in order to understand patterns, prevent further cases and solve the unsolved cases.'

Superintendent Tony Crandell, who is heading up Operation Parrabell, gave a glimpse of the investigation that is now running. He said, 'The true beauty of Parrabell is it is an open and honest and transparent investigation and we are here to make sure that happens. Whether the outcomes are good or bad for the police I am not concerned about that. We will report the truth.'

ACKNOWLEDGEMENTS

To the usual suspects – a gang of old coppers who've always given a damn and that hasn't dimmed with the passing years – who've helped my on many projects with their experiences, gossip, insight and reminders of what we should expect from our police. And to the people I've interviewed for this book who told their stories and offered their help – they also give a damn and have no intention of giving up.

ABOUT THE AUTHOR

Duncan McNab is a former police detective, private investigator, investigative journalist and media adviser to government and the private sector. He is the author of nine books, including the phenomenally bestselling *The Dodger – Inside the World of Roger Rogerson* and *Dead Man Running.*